NORTH STAR
TO
SOUTHERN CROSS —

By Steam and Sail to ARGENTINA

By the same author

TERSCHELLING SANDS

IN GRANMA'S WAKE: *Girl Stella*'s *Voyage to Cuba*

RUSTLER ON THE BEACH

SCHOONER INTEGRITY

SINGLE-HANDED CRUISING AND SAILING

SWEET ADELINE (with Patricia Slack)

DEAR DOLPHIN

NORTH STAR
TO
SOUTHERN CROSS

By Steam and Sail to ARGENTINA

Frank Mulville

Ashford, Buchan & Enright
Leatherhead

First published in 1993 by Ashford, Buchan & Enright
31, Bridge Street, Leatherhead, Surrey KT22 8BN

British Library Cataloguing in Publication Data

ISBN 1 85253 291 2

Parts of this book have been published in *Practical Boat Owner*
magazine. The author would like to thank the Editor for his
permission to reprint.

Information about the Battle of the Atlantic comes from
John Sladen's excellent account, *The Red Duster at War*, published
by William Kimber.

A catalogue record for this book is available from the British
Library

Cover illustration by Vernon Wildgoose
Line drawings by Walter Kemsley
Maps by Tony Garrett

Typeset by Priory Publications, Haywards Heath
Printed in Great Britain by FotoDirect Ltd, Brighton

Contents

To Patrick –
wherever he may rest

To come, after months at sea, at rosy dawn,
Into the placid blue of some great bay,
Treading the quiet waters like a fawn,
Ere yet the morning haze has blown away.
A rose flushed figure, putting by the grey
And anchoring there before the city smoke
Rose, or the church bells rang, or men awoke.

And then in the first light to see grow clear,
The long expected haven, filled with strangers -
Alive with men and women; see and hear
Its clattering market and its money changers;
And hear the surf beat and be free from dangers,
And watch the crinkled ocean blue with calm
Drowsing beneath the Trade, beneath the palm.

John Masefield, from *Dauber*

Part One

Steam

S.S. Celtic Star (1935)
original photo courtesy of Blue Star Line

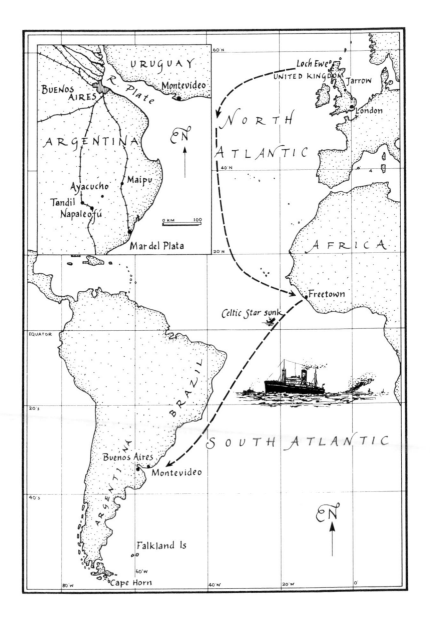

URUGUAY

Buenos Aires

R. Plate

Montevideo

ARGENTINA

N

Maipu

Ayacucho

Tandil

Napaleofú

0 KM 100

Mar del Plata

60°N

Loch Ewe

UNITED KINGDOM   Jarrow

London

NORTH

ATLANTIC

40°N

AFRICA

20°N

Freetown

Celtic Star sunk

EQUATOR

BRAZIL

20°S

SOUTH ATLANTIC

Buenos Aires

Montevideo

40°S

N

A R G E N T I N A

Falkland Is

60°W

80°W   Cape Horn   40°W   20°W   0°

2

I

First Voyage

My first trip to sea was in a tramp steamer called the *Marcella*. I was nine years old, it was in 1933. The *Marcella* was a coal burner; I used to watch the stokers bring up the ashes, once in every watch. They were hauled up the ventilator shaft from the stokehold to the boat deck in iron buckets. The stoker would lick his finger and hold it to the wind, then carry the bucket to the lee side of the deck and empty the ashes down a chute into the sea. Sometimes he would take the bucket to the wrong side, or sometimes a rogue draught of air would catch the ashes and send them back all over the deck. Then there would be an unholy row. The mate would come out on deck and call for the engineer on watch, pointing to his new paint. The Chief Engineer would emerge from his cabin at the after end of the starboard alleyway, alleging that the man at the wheel had been off course, causing the wind to come round to the wrong side of the ship. Sometimes Captain Downie would lumber down the bridge ladder, gold braid cap and pyjama trousers. The row would rumble on for a few minutes and then simmer down, the protagonists retreating to their lairs growling under their breaths.

My father spent the voyage in the Chief's cabin, yarning over bottles of whisky. The volume they consumed must have been prodigious. I sometimes saw the empties flying out through the Chief's scuttle although I never dared go into the cabin to see what happened inside. The Chief was an old Scot who had spent his life at sea. He knew all the places my father had worked in – Argentina, South Africa, Mexico, Egypt, Turkey and a dozen more, where he and my uncle Billy had worked together in the contracting business, constructing railways and dams and roads and bridges; the infrastructure of an expanding world. The two brothers would work together on a job and then, being Irish, they would quarrel and part for ever, sharing the spoils and going their separate ways. Then another job would come along and they would be together again because they were each indispensable to the other. Billy was the business brain, Charlie the man who did the job. Together they were successful, apart they never prospered.

Charles Blood Mulville, or CB as he was known, had married my mother in Tucuman, way up in the central plain of Argentina, when he was building the Central Argentine Railway. She bore him seven children, dragging them about the world after him, or sometimes staying at home in England, or France or Ireland or wherever home happened to be. Sometimes the children were left in the care of a nurse or servant. I was the seventh and last – clearly a mistake, six years behind my next elder sister. After me, my mother had a hysterectomy so that there were no more.

My father's fortunes ebbed and flowed as he and Billy were together or apart; my mother was accustomed to riches, closely followed by poverty. There must have been half-a-dozen fortunes made and lost during their lives together. I can remember, as a small child, living in a beautiful house, number 8 Stafford Terrace on London's smart Camden Hill; before that there was another in York Terrace, bordering Regent's Park. There were six storeys, parquet flooring, Persian carpets and a service lift between the kitchen and the dining room above. It was possible to squeeze into the lift for a hair-raising descent, arriving in the kitchen with a house-shaking bang that sent Cook into a paroxysm of fury. Sometimes there was no money for a cook, or a housemaid and then my mother did the work herself. Being rich, I soon realised, was a sham. There was money for pretentious houses with parquet floors but none for pocket-money or toys or a cricket bat. There were Hornby trains belonging to my brothers, in an attic playroom but they were sold before I was able to get my hands on them.

After Stafford Terrace, a decline to a pleasant maisonette in Lexham Gardens, in Kensington. There was a wind-up

4

gramophone with Gilbert and Sullivan records which I played over and over again, a piano I was able to pick out tunes on but never money for music lessons. My mother was tone deaf and no one else in the family had an ear for music except my brother Dan. By that time I had managed to extract a second-hand fairy cycle which I used to ride all over London, on the pavement until I got clear of home and then on the road. I knew every inch of Kensington Gardens; the Round Pond was my special province. I used to watch the well-off children with their nannies sailing boats. Sometimes the boats were left in the middle of the pond when the park keeper came round shouting 'All out – All out'. The children were led home in tears. I was up at six the next morning and round the gardens on my fairy cycle. I knew where there was a loose railing along Palace Avenue and I would go straight to the leeward side of the pond to collect any boats which I considered worth saving.

CB and I boarded the *Marcella* after a plunge into real poverty – he lost every penny in the Stock Market crash of 1932. This time it was for real. The family moved from comfortable Lexham Gardens to a two-room flat on the fourth floor over a fish shop at number 80 Marchmont Street, London WC1. As far as I remember the rent was fifteen shillings a week. My mother went out to work as a cook, the rest of the family were by then off about their business. My youngest sister went to work in a hat shop – she qualified as an architect during the war. Only I was left. There was no money for school and there was no one to look after me at home. It would have been unacceptable for either my mother or my father to have sent me to the council school. The fairy cycle joined the Hornby trains at the auction mart.

By the time I had taken the gas geyser to pieces and had been seen climbing out of the window and crawling along a narrow ledge to the next window, it was decided that something had to be done with me. CB had come together with Billy again on a project to build the new Shell-Mex building in Buenos Aires and it was decided that I should go with him to Argentina. There, my mother thought, were kind aunts, on her side of the family, to look after me. CB and I set out for Argentina on board the *Marcella.*

Unlike CB, Billy was a wise man when it came to matters of money. Whereas Charlie would squander his share of the profits from the contracting jobs, on investments that invariably ended disastrously, Billy, by careful husbandry, accumulated a fortune. From humble beginnings — my grandfather was a policeman in Auckland, New Zealand, where they were born — they were rich men by the time they were in their twenties. Billy became progressively richer and Charlie veered between boom and slump. Billy settled in Argentina and bought himself an *estancia*, a farm, a couple of hundred miles south of Buenos Aires, called El Choiqué. His instinctive feeling for the value of things was astonishing in one whose origins were so lowly. He became a considerable art expert, furnishing the *estancia* house with impeccable taste. He would buy things for next to nothing which turned out to be priceless; a Waterford glass chandelier now hangs in the British Museum which Billy found in a thousand pieces in the loft of an old church in Ireland. He gave the priest five pounds for it. He drove around Europe in splendid cars, Rolls-Royces and a Hispano-Suiza. He had an old La Salle on the *estancia*, with big wheels, a long bonnet, running-boards and a dickey seat.

CB was a big man, over six feet tall, with massive shoulders. Billy was smaller, one or two years older. In some ways they were remarkably alike; their way of walking was identical, a kind of march with arms swinging and head erect. Rather than take a bus, CB would walk for miles at a cracking pace, me hurrying along behind. I don't believe either of them had been athletic; they didn't know what it was to take part in any sport. They were both indifferent horsemen. CB was undoubtedly the better looking. There is an old photograph of him sitting at the controls of a primitive aeroplane, all wires and struts, from his days in the Royal Flying Corps at the beginning of the 1914 war. He looks like a film star. They

CB was a big man – over six feet tall

stopped him from flying because he drank too much. He had fine wavy hair which he never lost, a rather square face with a wide forehead and high cheek bones. Billy was altogether less spectacular. He had piercing eyes that took in everything and the same memory for detail as CB. Billy's character was more subtle, more discerning and more erratic. He was subject to bouts of furious temper. Both of them were in the habit of making on-the-spot decisions, sometimes involving thousands of pounds. Billy's were invariably right, CB's invariably wrong.

The *Marcella* steamed through the tropics and down the Brazilian coast at a steady 8 knots. I found myself transported into a wonderful world that seemed like Heaven. There was no one to tell me what to do; I hardly ever saw CB, he seemed to spend the whole voyage in the Chief's cabin. There were no other passengers. I spent hours in the engine room with my friend the Third Engineer, watching the huge con-rods of the triple expansion steam engine as they turned the shaft. When no one was looking one of the greasers would let me drop oil into the bearings, moving the big can up and down with the rhythm of the engine and shooting in the oil on the down stroke.

The Marcella steamed through the tropics at a steady 8 knots

I was allowed to crawl down the stern tube to the *lignum vitae* stern-gland as the great silver shaft revolved smoothly on its bearings, within half a foot of my body. I watched in the stokehold as the furnace doors were flung open, letting out a blast of heat and a light like the sun, watched the stokers, the sweat pouring from their tattooed bodies as they shovelled coal into the very back of the furnace. I would stand for hours on the top engine room grating, or sit with my feet dangling over the great cylinders, looking down at the maze of lagged pipes. The engineer with an old cap on the back of his head and the greaser, sweat-rag round his temples, walked slowly, methodically round the monster, observing, checking, adjusting. The noise it made was slow, low, soothing; the smell was of steam and oil. When the ship came into harbour — Santos, Pernambuco, Rio de Janeiro — I would stand on the bottom grating, by the bridge telegraph, listening for its urgent ring as the pilot's orders were conveyed to this heaving mass of hissing, snorting engine.

At night I would join the lookout on the fo'c'sle-head, listen to his yarns about home. In those days every ship carried a lookout. He would report any light he saw, shouting through his cupped hands, 'Two points starboard bow Sir – white over red'. The answering cry 'Aye, aye' would float down from the wing of the bridge. The lookout would make the bells at the turn of the watch. On the bridge, under the tropic stars, the Third Mate would point out the constellations for me and check that I remembered them the next night. He showed me how to find latitude from the Pole Star. I would stand on the wing of the bridge, watching the phosphorescent bow-wave as the old ship ploughed the ocean, watching the dolphins weave their patterns in the sea. A boy from the highlands of Scotland served in the galley as 'spud barber', peeling potatoes for the ship's company. He was a lunatic, affected by the full moon. He would run round the ship's bulwarks in the night, balancing on top of the rail until he was forcibly restrained by the stand-by man.

It was the aftermath of the great shipping slump when there was no work for seamen. Every officer on the *Marcella* had a master's ticket and four of the seamen sailing in the fo'c'sle had mate's tickets. One night I picked up a flying fish that had strayed into the well deck as the ship rolled. The bo'sun preserved it for me, stuffed it and put it on a varnished board, its delicate wings spread out, its mouth open, its body gleaming. It was stolen from me when I went to school in Buenos Aires. One of the sailors made me a belt from blue and white twine, decorated in an intricate pattern, with a buckle fashioned from an old wooden block, all polished and varnished. I wanted to stay in the *Marcella* forever and I sobbed when the old ship reached Buenos Aires. I ran down the gangplank after CB as he strode off the ship and I made a vow that the moment I grew up I would go to sea – a resolve that never left me.

In March 1943, the old *Marcella* was torpedoed by the German submarine U.107 in the Atlantic 600 miles to the west of Lisbon. She was lost with all hands.

My honeymoon with the ocean was rudely shattered when CB sent me as a boarder to the Scots' School in Calle Constitution, Buenos Aires. It was Scottish in name but in nothing else; it was an Argentine school where the boys spoke Spanish and behaved, naturally enough, as Argentine children behave. CB was going to have nothing to do with my aunts and uncles on my mother's side of the family. Possibly he knew they disapproved of him, not without reason. He was a big drinker and a considerable philanderer, which was probably well known in the gossip-ridden Anglo-Argentine community of Buenos Aires. In his turn he considered them strait-laced and boring – their greatest sin in his eyes. One of these uncles was a Christian Scientist who was prone to converting the young, enough to condemn him and anyone connected with him in CB's eyes. In fact, he despised these relations, and made quite sure that none of them came near me even had they wished to do so.

There was one boy at the school who was my first cousin on my mother's side and we immediately became arch enemies. I imagine CB sent me to the Scots' School because it was an easy way to dispose of me while he attended to the serious and urgent business of retrieving his broken finances. For me, the school was total disaster. I spoke no Spanish and was set upon and bullied by the other children. I sat in the classrooms oblivious to what was going on, made my way mechanically from one part of the school to another when the bell rang, accompanied by jeers and torments.

I have a vivid memory of a long, L-shaped dormitory with the lavatories at the opposite end to my bed. I started wetting my bed because I was terrified to walk the distance to the lavatory in the night. The matron ruled with iron discipline. She would come to me each morning, strip back the bed and expose my shame for all to see. Then she would cane me with an instrument known as the rubber ruler. It was a metre long, made of a stiff, hard, brick-coloured rubber, riveted to a strip of steel with the inches marked on it. I doubt whether the chastisement hurt much – I never cried as a matter of principle – but the humiliation was complete.

All the boys in the school were Catholic. Most of them spoke some English, although they never used it. I was a Protestant in as far as I had any religion. I lied and said I was a Catholic because I wanted to be the same as the others but this was detected the first time I attended church and I was taunted with charges of heresy, giving me a deep sense of guilt. I remember the school as a tall concrete building, with a courtyard in the middle surrounded on all four sides by tall walls with row upon row of windows. One day I fought with my cousin in the centre of this well, surrounded by a tight ring of jeering children, chanting with a mixture of mockery and encouragement. I can't remember who won – probably he did. I was never a physically strong child.

There were two Sunday visits per term. On the first Sunday no one came, confirming to me that I was abandoned forever. On the second, CB came with a lady I had never seen or heard of, called Auntie Eva. She was a big, blowsy woman, probably very attractive. She brought sweets and CB gave me a letter from my mother, whom I had almost forgotten. Auntie Eva must have observed the state I was in because at the end of the term I was taken away from the Scots' School.

My apprenticeship with schools was always unfortunate. After Auntie Eva's intervention on my behalf I was sent to another school, Oates College, named after the Antarctic explorer who died with Scott. This was marginally better but not better enough to cure me of bed wetting. It was in a suburb of Buenos Aires called Hurlingham and had extensive and lovely grounds with tall eucalyptus trees and wild areas where tarantulas lived in holes in the ground. They could be extracted by pouring water down the holes, captured in a glass jar and put in a scraped out earth pit, where they would fight to the death. Small boys are not very nice.

One of CB's rich friends came with him and Auntie Eva one day. 'What would you like, my boy, if you had a wish?' he asked. 'A bicycle with a three-speed,' I replied without hesitation. The bicycle was delivered to the school a few days later; I saw it when it came off the delivery van, it had my name on it. But I wasn't allowed to have it until I stopped wetting the bed, which, predictably, caused the bed wetting to increase. After another intervention by Auntie Eva I was given the bicycle a few days before the end of term. It was a splendid bicycle but it had no 3-speed. By this time it must have occurred to the

11

people who ruled my life, whoever they were, that school was having no desired effect. I had steadfastly refused to learn Spanish, I was pale and thin, withdrawn and silent. Presumably Auntie Eva exerted her undoubted influence because I was sent to El Choiqué.

I remained at El Choiqué for most of my stay in Argentina which was, in total, a little over two years. On the *estancia* I could conveniently be forgotten. The Shell-Mex building was coming on apace; I had spent my time in it during the school holidays, when I would be left there all day. My friend there was the *capataz*, the foreman, who allowed me to clamber over the framework of the building, to explore the foundations and discover the works office that CB had caused to be constructed at the very top of the structural steelwork. The Shell-Mex building was bigger than anything else for miles around and from this tiny office at the top one could look out over the whole city, out over the River Plate and to the countryside beyond. Down below was the criss-cross framework of the building, the miles of reinforcing bars and hundreds of men working away with wheelbarrows and concrete-mixers and wooden cladding and pulleys and lifts and pile-drivers – a small boy's Nirvana. I began to learn Spanish, stopped the bed wetting. A tiny lift connected CB's office to the whole scenario, which he could overlook from his vantage position.

With all his failings as a husband and a father and all his lack of business acumen, CB was a brilliant engineer. I always loved him in spite of his failings – love seldom discriminates. CB never bothered to learn very much Spanish, yet his workmen trusted him and respected him; my friend the *capataz*, I believe, worshipped him. He was known as 'Inginiero Mulville'. He knew everything about every detail of the work. He carried figures in his head; levels, quantities, gradients, heights. He would make notes on the backs of envelopes in a tiny, immaculate hand and these were the only written records of the construction of his buildings. He was always there, all day while the men were working and often at night he could be found prowling about, taking note of every tiny detail in the

12

huge work. He had no staff, no secretary, he never wrote a letter. There was no management team or structure, he did the whole thing himself. The jobs were always finished on time or before time and were invariably well within the contract price, so that the profits were enormous.

Billy took no part in the day-to-day running of the jobs. His role was separate and distinct, more subtle perhaps but nonetheless essential to the success of the partnership. When the jobs were over, the entente always fell apart and their quarrels were bitter and protracted. My mother once had to separate them when they went for each other, one with a knife, the other with a gun. They were, I suppose, among the last of a line of commercial adventurers who built the financial empires of the 1920s and 1930s.

CB was arrogant when it came to officialdom which he despised. Leaving Mexico on one occasion he chased the ocean liner in a rowing boat, with my mother and two or three children, having knocked down a customs officer who tried to stop him. They all climbed aboard up a rope ladder. He hated waiting about for trains or ships to leave so he would arrive at the station or on the dock at the last possible moment. Once, when he and I were catching the train out of Retiro station in Buenos Aires, we found the platform gates already closed a quarter of a minute before the train was due to leave. CB wrenched the gates open. When the ticket man tried to stop him he put him in his little sentry box and pushed it over, imprisoning the man inside. Then we ran after the already moving train, me holding on to his hand and bundled ourselves onto the end platform of the last carriage.

The train to Napaleofú, the nearest station to the *estancia*, was a delight. The railway network in Argentina was built with British capital in the early part of this century, although the first line was built much earlier, in 1864, when a section of the Central Argentine Railway was opened. CB and Billy constructed a considerable part of this railway; somewhere along the line there is said to be a station called Mulville (it is pronounced 'Mul-vi-je', with the double L spoken as a J.) The railway was not only built but to a great extent was administered by the British so that you can still see the same kind of booking office, the same tickets that used to be used in England.

I first went to the *estancia* with Uncle Billy. He was a bachelor for most of his life, he must have been in his late 50s before he married an aristocratic lady who lived somewhere near Virginia Water in Berkshire. I went there once, soon after the war. It was the only time I ever met her but I remember her as being gracious and charming. The *estancia*, when I first stayed there was a male establishment except for Dolores, the cook, who was fat and the housemaid, Andrea, who was beautiful. But Uncle Billy was a great lover of the ladies and as a highly eligible bachelor, attracted them from all quarters. Certainly, ladies were much in demand among the young, mostly European, men who worked in the 'camp', as the countryside is called in Argentina. Major-domos (managers), *segundos* and the odd remittance man working in the camp were often English. When my much older sister Eva came to stay in El Choiqué she caused havoc, the whole population of unmarried males falling in love with her.

It is strange that I still have a vivid recollection of everything that happened to me in Argentina although other periods of my life, much later periods, are a blank. We took a sleeper on the night train; a large compartment, with one ample bunk above the other, panelled with dark mahogany, a wash-basin and mirror in one corner. In the early morning the train arrived in Napaleofú. Our carriage was shunted onto a siding while the rest of the train went on its way, so that we should not have the inconvenience of being woken too early. We were brought *café con leche* by the sleeping-car attendant, with bread to dunk in it. I don't remember whether there were any other passengers for Napaleofú, probably not. Being in a siding we had to climb down to the ground with the aid of a special ladder and then walk across the line and up to the station platform, which was only a few yards long. Most of the train stopped on the open line, the platform was only for important people in the middle carriages. The canopy over the platform had a wooden skirt round the edge, decorated with cut-out stars and a fancy fringe, the booking hall was like an English one. Ramón was waiting outside the station with Uncle Billy's old La Salle to take us to El Choiqué.

II

El Choiqué

When I was young, my life alternated between periods of bliss and periods of misery – there wasn't much ground in between. I always hated being young, wanted only to grow up and be rid of the tyranny imposed by adults. I hated all schools since I attended kindergarten in Penywern Road, when we lived in Lexham Gardens. The teacher was a tall, straight lady with a long dress, her hair in a tight bun. She wore a black ribbon tight round her neck, I think it was called a choker. There was a pretty little girl called Rosie with whom I struck a friendship. One day I slid my hand up her skirts, in a friendly way, for no reason other than a desire to find out what was at the top. I was expelled immediately.

There were periods of bliss when, as a child, we went for holidays in Brightlingsea and learned about sailing boats, bliss when I stayed in a country farmhouse with an old friend of my mother's, bliss on the Marcella. School was misery all the time. In a mistaken concern for my future, after my mother divorced CB she spent the £500 he gave her on my education at St Paul's School; a high price to pay for a toffee-nosed accent, particularly as the accent can readily be acquired without spending £500. I was bullied brutally by the prefects in the boarding-house, who exercised a fascist discipline. I was beaten with army corps swagger-sticks until the weals on my bottom squeezed blood. Most of these young men were killed in the Army fighting for king and country. The 'fags' in this establishment were known as 'offals'. Part of their duties was to empty the prefects' pee pots every morning, to carry the prefects' books over to the school, to clean out the lavatories, sweep the prep room every evening. The Housemaster, Mr Young, ran the house with a minimum of domestic staff, so as to make what he considered a reasonable profit. I did my best to learn nothing at school; any education I have must have slipped in when I wasn't looking. The happiest day of my life was when I left and went to sea as an apprentice in the Blue Star Line, having lied a year on to my age.

The alternating patterns of misery and bliss have gone on all my life, taking me through happy and unhappy marriages, poverty and affluence, mental peace and black disquiet. All this has had the effect of blunting my sensibilities so that I have always been able to withstand shocks and traumas such as death or sudden financial disaster. My time at El Choiqué was a period of bliss; my stay on the *estancia* was an unique experience. It gave me an insight into a way of life that disappeared quite suddenly very soon after I left. In the political and economic turmoil that overtook Argentina in the 1940s with the advent of Peronismo, the gaucho's way of life disappeared.

Napaleofú was like a Wild West town in an old cowboy film. The hub of the place, on a corner where the road takes a sharp turn towards El Choiqué, was the *boliche*, the store, where everything was sold. There was a baker as far as I remember, a blacksmith and the post office which was part of the railway station. The *boliche* was by far the biggest and most important building in town. It was on one storey, there were no two storey buildings in the town, but it had a high facade on both sides of the corner, all decorated round the edges, which suggested a larger and more important building than actually existed. There was a wooden rail outside where the gauchos' horses were tethered, their girths loosened, their heads hung low, one back hoof tipped up in repose. There were no cars, no tractors. The houses were clustered about the *boliche* in rough squares, the roads between disappearing into the *pampa*. They were built of mud and straw adobe, baked in the sun, some were whitewashed; they had no windows, only square holes in the walls, the doorways hung with skins. The roofs were flat corrugated iron covered with earth which supported a meagre growth of grass. A few of the better houses had tiled roofs and glazed windows. There were no made-up roads or pavements, a few thin dogs loped about the village.

Ramón greeted us as we emerged from the station. He was a short, dark man with a neat black moustache, a black scarf tied round his neck, a black hat, the brim turned up all round. He wore *bombachas* and *alpargatas*. *Bombachas* are like voluminous trousers, drawn together round the ankles with a button and strap; the gauchos wore them with short, black boots. They are comfortable and cool. *Alpargatas* are rope soled shoes, the uppers of strong cotton duck. We squeezed into the front of the La Salle, our luggage, such as it was, piled into the open dickey. Uncle Billy introduced me. 'Este es el niño Ponky – mi sobrino' – this is the boy Ponky , my nephew. The nickname was a cross I had to bear throughout my childhood. It was given me, I believe, by my sister the day I was born; she found it hard to reconcile herself to no longer being the youngest child. It means 'smelly'. My parents and elders allowed this monstrosity to continue into my teens, when my brother Dan stopped it. But it stood me in good stead in El Choiqué. I was known as 'el niño Ponky' all over the *estancia*. Incredibly, it was still remembered when I went back fifty years later.

The car drove out of the *pueblito* and across the plain along a straight, dusty road; slowly, because the road was pitted with ruts left by the carts that carried grain to the railhead after the harvest. A wire fence skirted the road on either side for as far as the eye could reach, converging into the distance in front of us. There was no traffic, an occasional horseman on his gaucho pony gave us a grave salute. After five or six kilometres we came to another, smaller, road off to the left. 'This is where the *estancia* begins,' Uncle Billy said. El Choiqué has a little hill at its southern end, immediately distinguishing it from the other *estancias* around. It also has a profusion of trees, mostly poplars and eucalyptus planted, presumably, by Mr Wesley, from whom Uncle Billy bought El Choiqué.

The trees were grouped in *montes*, small woods, to give shade for the cattle and to supply firewood. I never saw another *estancia* with as many *montes* as El Choiqué. In five more kilometres we came to a big white gate. I jumped out, pushed it open and held it for the car to pass. It let out a plaintive, high-pitched squeak. The *estancia* house was in front of us, about one kilometre away at the end of a newly planted avenue of trees. The young eucalyptus were about four feet high. We passed through another gate into the garden, the drive sweeping round and up to the front door. Dolores, Antonio, Andrea and Guillermo stood in a group round the door to greet us. When Uncle Billy got out of the car he shook hands with each of them in turn. These were the people I was to be with for the next year and a half of my life. I was ten, it was 1934.

Andrea was beautiful; I suppose she was about seventeen. She had classic Spanish features, dark hair, brown eyes, a rather prominent, rather Roman nose, faultless white skin, red, slightly sensual lips, a slim body, a smile that lit the sky. She was the housemaid. Dolores, her mother, was fat, round, with skirts like a bell-tent, good natured, complaining. Antonio was the gardener, a bent man as I remember, with a sarcastic edge to his tongue and an eye that observed every movement of man or beast or plant in his garden. Guillermo was a lad of about

Dolores, Antonio, Andrea and Guillermo stood in a group round the door

twelve, two years older than I. He was taller, dark, with curly hair and brown eyes full of humour. He wore a small, round black beret. I believe he was a waif whom Uncle Billy had taken in and who had been brought up by Antonio and Dolores. I must have presented them with a strange figure of a boy; fair against the universal dusky skins of the camp, weedy, with very imperfect Spanish and wearing short trousers too small for me and a blue and white striped school blazer which CB had been forced to buy for me when I went to the school in Hurlingham.

The *estancia* was very grand. There was a long room with a billiard table, an oil painting of Captain Charles Blood, a seventeenth century adventurer, allegedly my ancestor, who stole the crown jewels from the Tower of London in an attempt to raise money for King Charles II. He was caught, but instead of being executed he was given lands in Ireland. CB's second name was Blood. A last throw of snobbery must have persuaded him to christen me Blood, a conceit that caused me as much distress in early life as the nickname Ponky. There was a dining room, a veranda giving on to the garden and Dolores's domain, kitchen, pantry, scullery and laundry. My bedroom was upstairs at the end of a passage. At the other end of the passage was the guest room, Uncle Billy's room and various other rooms that meandered about off the upstairs landing. It wasn't like an Argentine *estancia* house, rather it might have been some prosperous businessman's residence in one of the pleasanter London suburbs with its red roof, sash windows and pebble-dashed exterior. I always thought of it as a friendly, happy house. Uncle Billy stayed for a few days and then left for Buenos Aires, leaving me in my new home, a great improvement on the other places I had been dumped in since coming to Argentina.

I had the run of the place. It was a friendly instead of a hostile environment. I became fluent in Spanish very quickly. Andrea was kind, even loving. She looked after me, did her best to patch up my ridiculous town clothes, even procured me a pair of *bombachas* and some *alpargatas*. I was never given leather boots like the gauchos wore although my soul craved them. Guillermo found me a horse called Chico which became mine. There were about twenty horses belonging to the house, they lived in the home paddock, a wire fenced field on the *pampa* about a mile square. Each morning they were rounded up into a corral and those that were to be used were separated out, haltered and tied to a long rail. There was a *palenque*, a kind of stockade with a tiled roof to give shade, where the horses for the house were tethered. Some of the horses were wild, only half broken. Separating them in the corral was a sight worth watching.

One horse was always kept tied up all night, the *nochero* to be used to round up the others in the morning. I was given an Argentine saddle called a *recado*. It consists of leather and felt undercovers and then the *bastos* – like rolling pins made from thick leather, fastened together with leather thongs. The *bastos* are placed across the horse's back to make a flat seat. Then the whole affair is covered with sheepskins. The gauchos used the *recado* as a bed at night, covering themselves with their long ponchos. The *recado* is a seat rather than a saddle. You sit on top of the horse with knees well up, feet in big round stirrups, made of wood covered in leather, balanced on the horse rather than gripping it. It is a distinct technique of riding and the horses behave differently. The *recado* and the big round stirrups probably grew out of the gaucho's need to protect his legs from being crushed when he was among cattle. The criollo horse is a small fellow, not much bigger than a large pony. He is stocky and tough with a short head. He doesn't trot like an English horse but breaks into a slow canter, a kind of lope which he can keep up for hours. In the 1920s an English writer called Schiffeley rode two gaucho horses from Buenos Aires to Washington, a distance of some 5,000 miles.

The gauchos are a lost breed of men. They were fathered, originally, by descendants of the Spanish immigrants who drifted into the *camp* in pursuit of livestock first brought to America by the Conquistadors. The cattle and the horses proliferated at an astonishing rate on the grass of the open *pampa*. The horses were descended from seventy stallions and mares turned loose on the land by Pedro de Mendoza's disastrous expedition to the River Plate in 1536. By 1780, according to the Spanish historian Azara, there were at least 42,000 wild horses roaming the *pampa*. Cattle were introduced from Bolivia in 1580 when Juan de Garay founded the city of Buenos Aires. They too, multiplied rapidly, creating the enormous wealth that Argentina supported for more than a hundred years from the 1780s.

The gauchos' mothers were Indians, mostly of the fiercely independent Guaraní and Pampa tribes. Because the ships from Spain only brought men, there was an immediate mixing of races with Indian blood. The Spanish invasion of the River Plate was resisted with bitterness and determination by the Indians. Perhaps there is something in the vast, rolling plain that makes for a spirit of freedom and adventure, the same spirit that drove the Conquistadors. At all events the mixture of the two races produced, in the gaucho, a man with a savage love of liberty. It was the gaucho armies of Argentina's liberator, San Martin, who were responsible for defeating the Spaniards in the wars of liberation.

The gaucho lived on horseback, on the open *pampa*; his *recado* a pillow, his poncho a blanket. He carried his wealth with him, his silver belt worked with intricate designs, silver spurs, silver studs on his horse's bridle, beautiful leatherwork on his *recado*, a silver handle to the long double-edged knife, the *façon*, he carried in his belt and a silver-topped whip called a *rebenque*. He was a romantic, a fighter, a generous man always hospitable, often cruel like his Moorish and Indian ancestors. Montenegro, who worked on and around the *estancia* when I was a child, was a real gaucho, among the last of the breed.

Montenegro was a splendid sight on a horse. He seemed to be a part of it, moving with its rhythm, feeling with it, communicating with it by imperceptible sways and pressures and sounds so that the reins hardly moved in his hand. I saw him in action at branding time, when the cattle would be rounded into the corner of a paddock, hundreds at a time, the young steers and calves lassoed or brought down with *boleadoras* then dragged behind the horse to the fire where the iron was heating. His horse would spurt like a shot from a gun after a young steer, the lasso would swing once or twice round his head, snake through the air, the noose falling unerringly over the animal's head. Then the horse would stop dead in a cloud of dust, the young steer spinning to the ground when the lasso came taut.

Boleadoras were used by the Indians to hunt the ostriches which then inhabited the pampa. They used them against the Spaniards with devastating effect, bringing their horses down so that the Indians could attack with spears. The gauchos took the idea from the Indians, using *boleadoras* to bring down the wild horses and cattle. They consist of three heavy balls, made of stone or lead, covered with leather and joined together by plaited leather thongs. Thrown with great accuracy they can bring down a steer at twenty yards from a galloping horse. Montenegro had black, piercing eyes, a few days' stubble on his chin, a hooked nose like Andrea's. His bearing on horseback was dignified, upright, even arrogant but on the ground he was short, bow-legged and slightly stooping. He taught me to play *tabas* with the knuckle bones of steers.

The branding operation would shift from paddock to paddock and then the half a dozen-odd gauchos would move on to another estancia. At night they slept rough, some of them lived miles distant. There would be an *asado* when the work on the *estancia* was done. A young steer or a sheep was killed, its throat cut with a *façon*. It was skinned then and there and a long iron spike driven through its back and into the ground so that the carcase hung at an angle, the fire on the ground under it. All the people from the *estancia* would come, Montenegro would bring his guitar, sometimes there was an accordion and everyone would sing the old camp songs. I still remember some of them. Wood was collected from a *monte* near at hand. The gauchos would drink *caña*, a kind of white rum, while the meat was cooking. The sauce was prepared with red wine, onions and garlic. There was dancing, sometimes a horse race.

His horse would spurt like a shot from a gun

I remember taking part in a race from way over on the other side of the paddock to where the *asado* was. I remember too the thrill of it – the drumming hooves, the horses' necks stretched out, their long tails streaming, the extraordinary exhilaration of a horse at full gallop, the gauchos swinging their *rebenques*, shouting. Chico usually came in somewhere near the back, but not last; he was a good little horse and I was a light rider. I felt proud and happy to get back without a fall. Then the *asado* would be ready and everyone would cut pieces of meat with their *façon* and eat it, with no such conceit as plate or fork. There would be hunks of hard, white camp bread, never a vegetable; the wine bottle would be passed from hand to hand. The gauchos were big meat-eaters; if they were not eating *asado* or steak it was *puchero*, a kind of stew with meat and sweet potatoes and sweetcorn. They were, for the most part, coarse men, particularly sexually coarse. They made coarse remarks and jokes, coarse gestures with their hands. They were quick to fight and often cruel, quick to forgive.

I was soon given jobs to do around the *estancia*. Guillermo and I had to go into Napaleofú twice a week to collect the mail and to do what shopping could be done in the *pueblito*. El Choiqué was virtually self sufficient and in any case, there wasn't much to buy; we would ride there and back in the morning. We became great friends. Guillermo was highly intelligent as I remember and he had a great sense of humour. He taught me songs, some with coarse words which I didn't quite understand. Sometimes we would go and visit another *estancia* on the other side of Napaleofú, I think it was called 'La Suiza'. The mayordomo was an Englishman called Miller, or Millie. We would drink *mate* for an hour and then ride back. On one fine morning we were passing a simple adobe house on the edge of the *pueblito*, on the way to visit Millie. A young girl was walking towards us along the dirt track. Egged on by Guillermo I called out a coarse suggestion to her. We thought we were great men but on our way back we passed the house again and this time a large, angry woman came running out with a *rebenque* in her hand. She caught Chico's bridle and began to lash out. Fortunately for me, Chico reared up on his hind legs and bolted, with me clinging on for my life and Guillermo bringing up the rear, a happy grin from ear to ear.

In the autumn the grain *carretas* trundled along the dirt roads to the station loaded with sacks of corn. If it had been raining the road would be a sea of mud with huge *pantanos*, or lakes, making it impassable for Uncle Billy's car. Then, if he came down from Buenos Aires, Guillermo and I would harness the *sulky*, a small trap, and drive to the station to fetch him. The *carretas* were very large wagons, the sacks of grain piled high up over the sides. Extra wooden sides were put on to increase their capacity at harvest time. The *carreteros* were paid by the size of their load. The wagons had enormous back wheels, perhaps ten feet in diameter, with smaller wheels in the front; some of them were balanced on a single axle. The sacks of grain would be piled up to make a pyramid, cunningly packed so that the load didn't topple. Argentina was still the granary of the world at that time and huge areas of the *pampa* were given over to wheat cultivation. Wheat was exported to England and Europe in vast quantities. The wagons were drawn by teams of horses, perhaps twenty to each wagon and the *carreteros* slept in hammocks slung between the axles.

One day when Guillermo and I were collecting mail from the station in Napaleofú a *carrete* with a full load of sacks was drawn up in front of the *boliche*, waiting to unload at the station across the road. An argument developed between the *carretero* and a local gaucho – they had been drinking *caña*. The argument degenerated into a fight, the two men faced each other in the road outside the *boliche*, the gaucho with his *façon* and the *carretero* with a *calador*, the long, hollowed-out steel spike used to take samples of grain out of the sacks. It is an ugly weapon in the right hands. The two men, each with his poncho over his right arm as a shield, were circling round each other, one or the other making sudden, vicious thrusts. They were silent, intent, watching each other's movements through narrowed eyes. The *carretero* was a short man wearing a black beret, an open shirt, *bombachas* and *alpargatas*. The gaucho was taller, stooping, his long knife and his silver belt glinting in the sun, a gaucho hat, his *bombachas* tucked into short boots. A group of men stood round, silent, like the boys in the school where I had fought with my cousin.

Guillermo and I were outside the ring, looking down from our horses. The *carretero* already had a wound on his hand which bled steadily. Suddenly he made a lunge with his spike, at the same time side-stepping so that the gaucho's knife flashed past his face an inch away. Then he brought the spike down in a devastating sweep, the sharp point tearing away the gaucho's shirt and cutting a deep weal across his chest. The gaucho went down – it looked horrific, I thought I was to witness a man killed for the first time in my life. The *carretero* stood over the gaucho, his foot on his belly, the spike raised over his head. The men stood round in silence. Then the *pueblito*'s policeman shouldered his way through the crowd, revolver in hand. Guillermo pulled Chico's bridle and we galloped off at top speed.

My special friends were the *tamberos* and their families who lived round the estancia. I can't remember how many *tambos* there were – possibly five or six. They were simple dwellings with adobe walls, the roofs covered with bamboo, sods of earth acting as some form of insulation against the sun. Sometimes they had red tiled roofs but few had windows, only window-shaped holes in the walls with sheepskins hung over them. The *tambero* looked after the cattle on his patch of the *estancia* doing the milking, tending the cattle and keeping an eye on the fences and gates.

Some of the gates were made of wood but many of them were wire gates, no more than breaks in the fence. Chico knew how to come up to the side of the opening so that I could lift off the strop that held the post in position. He would pass through while I held it, cleverly turning round so that I could put the post back in its wire socket at the bottom and slip on the strop without dismounting. He liked the soft job of carrying me round the *estancia*. Unlike most of the horses, which had to be caught with a halter in the corral Chico would

He liked the soft job of carrying me round the estancia

come up to me and offer his nose most obligingly, knowing that he would be spoilt with a lump of sugar.

There was a cheese factory on the *estancia* which the *tambos* supplied with milk. The churns were brought in each morning on carts pulled by two or four horses. In the rainy season the tracks across the camp were so churned up and muddy that it took four horses to pull the carts through. I was sometimes sent out to one or other of the *tambos* with a message for the *tambero* and then I would sit with the gaucho and his wife for half an hour. Everyone in the camp drank *mate* — it is made from a green herb, *hierba mate*, grown in northern Argentina, mostly in the province of Misiones. It is pronounced, 'ma-te'. Everyone drank it except perhaps Uncle Billy's friends from England and Buenos Aires who regarded the habit as degenerate and unsanitary.

The *hierba* is put into a gourd and this is filled with boiling water from a kettle heated in the ashes.

The *mate* is drawn up through a *bombilla*, a silver tube some six inches long with a bulbous, perforated end. The patrón, or host, draws the first drink into his mouth and spits it out, usually on the floor or sometimes outside the door. Then the *mate* is good for the guests and it is passed round from one to the next, being returned to the padron after each draught for refilling. *Mate amargo*, without sugar, is the gauchos' drink although people from Buenos Aires, regarded scornfully by the gauchos, might like it *dulce*, with sugar. The *mate* would go round and round from one person to the next; it was always a natural aid to conversation. If you didn't want any more you would say *gracias* when you passed the gourd back and you would be missed out on the next round. The gauchos have been drinking *mate* round their camp fires for 200 years, they learnt it from the *guaraní*. I used to tell them stories about the sea, loosely based on my experiences in the Marcella and largely fictional, I imagine. None of them had any idea what the sea was like.

I didn't see much of Uncle Billy and even less of CB. They would come down occasionally and spend a few days, usually with friends, but I was left much to my own devices. I was happy enough with Andrea, who cared for me, and with my friend Guillermo. I roamed about the camp on Chico in a state of bliss, un-brought-up and uneducated. There was a big water tank in the garden, fed by a wind driven water mill, where I could swim. I never received letters from my mother as far as I remember although I am sure she wrote to me. Sometimes I would be taken to Buenos Aires for a few days, where I spent my time at the Shell-Mex building and occasionally I was taken out to tea by CB and the mysterious Auntie Eva. CB would take us to the Boston Bar in Calle Florida where the bill was 'all in' so that I could consume as many potted-meat sandwiches and cakes as I could eat at no extra cost to him, thus effecting a considerable saving.

My sister Eva, some fifteen years older than I, came from England to stay for a few months. Eva was an actress and a very remote person to me. She thought she ought to take a hand in my upbringing, which didn't endear her to me but otherwise she brought many diversions to the settled life of the *estancia*. She clearly failed to persuade anyone to buy me anything to wear other than Andrea's *bombachas* and *alpargatas*. Apart from a couple of shirts I only had the blue and white striped blazer. Probably both CB and Uncle Billy considered it the other's responsibility. People who never came in the normal run of life flocked to the house when Eva was there. She was young, vivacious and very good-looking. She organised theatricals, treasure hunts on horseback and all manner of unheard of things. All the young men and women from the *estancias* round about came on horseback, some in cars and there was an *asado* in the garden. For me, it was tame stuff compared with those wonderful, impromptu fiestas of branding time. Millie, my friend from La Suiza, fell so deeply in love with Eva that he remained single for the rest of his life; I met him fifty years later when he was an old man and Eva was dead. He still talked about her.

Sometimes Guillermo and I would ride to La Esperanza, which was much further away, on some errand or other. This involved swimming Chico across a river which I think he enjoyed, with me hanging on to his mane as he scrambled out on the other side. He was remarkably sure-footed. He had a habit of shying suddenly if some odd thing caught his eye. As well as owls, which sometimes frightened Chico, the *pampa* is inhabited by the *hornero* — the oven bird. He builds a little house for himself out of mud, often perching it on top of a fence post, with a small hole at the bottom for entry. It is round and domed like an oven, about eight inches high. One day I was riding along in the kind of dream that children who are alone a lot fall into, talking to the horse and

Sometimes Guillermo and I would ride to La Esparanza

gauging his responses by the movement of his ears, a game I often played. Suddenly an *hornero* flew out of his oven and across our path. Chico shied and I came flying off, landing on the hard ground, my fall slightly broken by a clump of thistles. There was no one about for miles in any direction. I was lucky to be able to recapture Chico and ride him home to the sympathy of Andrea with no more than a bruised shoulder.

Uncle Billy had a streak of adventurous spirit in him. He taught me to drive the La Salle, with a big cushion behind my back so that I could reach the pedals. While Eva was at the *estancia* he devised a 100-mile horse ride to Mar del Plata for the three of us. Ramón came to drive a four-wheeled covered cart with Uncle Billy's and Eva's luggage and a red and white striped tent for us to camp in for two nights. Dolores packed sandwiches and *tortilla*, omelette, and there were bottles of wine and cold salad. A small folding table from the conservatory at El Choiqué was packed in, canvas chairs, knives and forks. Uncle Billy did nothing by halves. We set off at a brisk pace, leaving Ramón to bring up the rear with the cart, which also contained camping equipment, blankets and two air beds for Uncle Billy and Eva; I slept on the ground between them, perhaps out of propriety, to lend some notion of respectability to the escapade. We passed through Napaleofú without causing comment – the *pueblito* was fast asleep.

We stopped for lunch at another tiny *pueblo* where there was a *boliche* identical to the one in Napaleofú, and waited for Ramón to catch up with the cart and the provisions. We had lunch under the astonished gaze of the locals, who stood round in a silent, intense circle observing our every movement. The folding chairs were set up by the side of the road, the table was set, the *tortilla* was cut open, Ramón waved his scarf about in a vain effort to keep off the buzzing horse-flies. Uncle Billy produced a folding corkscrew out of his pocket and opened a bottle of wine. The population looked on in solemn amazement.

Then we moved on a few miles until we came to an *estancia* whose owners were known to Uncle Billy. The *estanciero* was not at home but his majordomo gave us a paddock to camp in and to graze the horses for the night, which, he said, would be a suitable place for us. The tent was set up. It was quite a large, square tent coming to a peak with a little red flag fluttering from the top, like a Crusader's tent. It took Ramón and me some time to get the whole affair rigged with its pegs and ropes and to get the beds and blankets and the furniture moved in. Uncle Billy and Eva sat and sipped a glass of wine, passing occasional titbits of advice until it was all in position. The horses were turned loose, we had a meal from the stores in the cart and then we went to sleep, we three in the red and white striped tent and Ramón on the floor of the cart.

I slept the night through without stirring, until Eva woke me early when it was still dark. She had been disturbed by the hooting of owls and a lowing, rustling, rumbling noise which she thought might be bulls. Uncle Billy woke up and we all listened. It sounded to me like a growling, groaning, chewing noise. When we looked out of the tent at daylight our encampment was surrounded by a tight circle of cattle, several

... there was a concerted move forward
and an increased rumble

bulls pawing at the ground and regarding the red and white tent with suspicion; it was a large herd, its ears pricked up in a state of animated interest. As soon as we appeared at the flap of the tent, as if they had been waiting for us, there was a concerted move forward and an increased rumble of conversation as the ring tightened round us. I was hurriedly despatched to wake Ramón and together, with some difficulty as I remember it, we succeeded in dispersing the cattle, Ramón waving his scarf and me uttering loud cries of '*vaca, vaca*'. We saddled our tethered horses, broke camp and set off for new pastures.

Our next night's lodging was vastly different. We stopped at a very grand *estancia* some thirty miles on with stone gateposts and an avenue of eucalyptus leading to a fine *estancia* house in the old Spanish style; a U-shaped single storey building with a red tiled roof, a flowering creeper along one side of the house and trees all around. Each room led from one to the next, there was a well in the patio, horses tethered to a *palenque*. The *estanciero* was at first highly suspicious when we asked if we could camp in his paddock but when Uncle Billy explained in his 'gringo' Spanish who we were and what we were doing he insisted that we stay the night in the house as his guests. We had a grand dinner party with wine and *bife de lomo*, steak, from the *estancia* and sweet coffee with *dulce de membrillo*, a kind of solidified jelly made from guavas.

It was a stiff gathering that sat at the long table, the *estanciero* at one end and his señora at the other with a selection of children, mothers-in-law, the majordomo and his wife and various *pegotes*, hangers on, seated between. Uncle Billy's Spanish was hardly up to enlightened conversation and Eva's was non-existent, so I had to answer questions and attempt in some way to justify our journey to Mar del Plata in this odd manner, particularly odd when it became clear that we could have made the journey by car. As I seemed to be shouldering the burden of keeping the conversation going I resorted to stories about my experiences in the *Marcella*. I was beginning to dine out on these stories, which they must have thought even odder. We all went to bed in the greatest comfort, Uncle Billy and Eva at separate ends of the house, me in the middle in a room with the *estanciero*'s two young sons, Ramón with the servants. Eva at least was relieved to have a real bed to sleep in. She wasn't used to riding long distances and was stiff and sore.

The next day we rode the last twenty-five miles to Mar del Plata. Our cavalcade progressed through the centre of the city to the hotel, with the populace staring at us in astonishment. The horses had never been in a city, had never seen a car other than the old La Salle and had never been taken on paved roads. They were nervous and frisky. We stopped outside the front entrance, Uncle Billy and Eva and I dismounted leaving the horses with Ramón and walked into the vestibule. At first the porter refused us entry, protesting that with our boots, that is to say Eva's and Uncle Billy's boots, my *alpargatas*, our dirty breeches, the aroma of sweat and horse that enveloped us, we had come to the wrong place. The manager was called, he recognised Uncle Billy as an eccentric English Milord and showed us to our rooms with due deference. Perhaps my blue and white striped school blazer, now two sizes too small and still my only coat, swung the balance in our favour. More likely it was Eva's youthful beauty, her white shirt, flowing golden hair, bright blue eyes and vivacious manner.

The next day I was allowed a quick swim in the sea and an ice cream. I was then despatched back to El Choiqué with Ramón and the cart, the red and white tent and all the horses. As far as I remember we made the journey in a day and part of the next night. Andrea was pleased to see me home. A couple of days later Ramón fetched Eva and Uncle Billy back in the La Salle. Our ride to Mar del Plata is still talked about around El Choiqué.

Uncle Billy was kind to me – I think he must have had some affection for me because I was told, much later, that I stood to inherit the *estancia*. He was an extraordinary mixture of generosity and meanness; I recognise some of the genes in myself. He would take us to stay at a first class hotel and when

Andrea was pleased to see me home

it came to leaving, calculate the bill to the nearest penny. He would give the money to my sister, leaving nothing for a tip and send her to pay the bill while he waited in the car outside.

He hated waste, another gene that seems to have found its way into my metabolism. He once saw me loading my toothbrush with a full length of toothpaste, instead of a tiny spot at the end. He let out a kind of roar, seized the tube in a passion and squeezed it in his fist with all his strength so that a ribbon of toothpaste shot over the whole bathroom. Then he stalked off down the passage leaving me cowering and terrified in the corner of the bathroom. Equally, he gave me £200 when this was a lot of money, to start my first business. He was a wonderful judge of antiques of all kinds, having an instinctively accurate feeling for values, but a poor judge of people. For some six months he left me on the *estancia* with a mayordomo who was homosexual. He was a tall man with a superb carriage on a horse; it was he who taught me to swim, by throwing me into the pool by one arm and one leg, not a

36

method to be recommended. I soon discovered that he was a homosexual, which may have taught me something about how to avoid things you don't like.

Uncle Billy had planted the avenue of eucalyptus between the *estancia* house and the road. It was a generous avenue with a triple row of trees on each side of the road. The trees were young, about four or five feet high when I was there. It was our task, Guillermo and me, to water the trees once every week through the dry season. We would catch a docile old mare called Mama from the corral in the morning and harness her to the water cart, a two-wheeled vehicle with a cylindrical tank placed over the axle, holding perhaps 200 gallons. We would lead Mama to the water-mill to fill the tank and start our work at the house end of the avenue, otherwise Mama would trot home whenever we stopped at a tree and we would have to run after her and lead her back. We extracted the water from the tank by siphoning it through an old hose that blackened our mouths so that we looked like circus clowns. First Guillermo led Mama from one tree to the next while I watered the roots, then we reversed roles and I led the horse while he watered. It took the whole day to water one side of the avenue and the whole of the next day for the other. It was hot, there was no shade, the avenue stretched to the horizon. Guillermo would sing a sad song about unrequited love.

By lunchtime we had watered half of one side. We would mount the cart, sitting on a baulk of timber across the shafts as Mama trotted home for a rest and a nosebag in the shade. In the afternoon, after siesta, we finished the first side and the task was repeated the next day. I remember those scorching days as if they were from last week.

III

Ocean Graveyard

Either Uncle Billy or CB or perhaps both of them got tired of having me at El Choiqué, or perhaps my mother wanted me back in England, or perhaps it occurred to someone that I was receiving no formal education; at all events it was decided that I should go home and I was despatched forthwith. Uncle Billy came down to the *estancia* one Friday and announced that we were both going to England in the *Avila Star* on Monday. Andrea wept, Guillermo shook me by the hand, Dolores and Antonio patted me on the back, Montenegro gave me a present of a *rebenque* with fancy leatherwork fashioned by himself. My daughter Chantek has it now. Chico laid back his ears, assuming, rightly I imagine, that his soft number was at an end. I went round the *estancia* for a last time to drink *mate* with the

Montenegro gave me a present . . .

tamberos, rode up to the top of the hill from where I could see the whole camp, establishing the picture in my mind for the rest of my life. I patted Chico on the neck and gave him a last lump of sugar. I probably shed a discreet tear. On Monday Ramón drove us to Napaleofú in the La Salle and on Tuesday the *Avila Star* steamed out of the port of Buenos Aires with a cargo of chilled meat in her hold and some 80 passengers in the first class, of which Billy and I were two.

The *Avila Star* wasn't a patch on the *Marcella*. I regarded the passengers as a boring lot. I was made to play games of deck quoits, there were a few children on board dressed in fancy clothes whom I despised, a feeling that was returned by them to me. I still wore the *bombachas* that Andrea had bought me and my *alpargatas* and a few shirts that were remarkably too small. I believe the blue and white striped blazer had been abandoned by this time. There was no fraternising with the lookout man, let alone the Third Mate, no climbing about the engine room, no lunatic running round the ship's rail at night. If I strayed out of the passenger accommodation I would be led politely back by a steward. The best that happened was that Uncle Billy got off the ship in Rio de Janeiro for some reason, leaving me to continue the voyage to England by myself. He left enough money for my rail fare from Southampton to London with the Chief Steward, who had instructions to see that I caught the train. I was told to take a taxi from Waterloo Station to a new address I had never heard of, in Priory Road, Hampstead. This was something of a disappointment. I had been looking forward to Marchmont Street, which I had rather liked. It was my first inkling that life was about to take a turn out of bliss and into misery.

The *Avila Star* was torpedoed and sunk in July 1942, 500 miles to the west of Lisbon by the German submarine U201. Sixty-two souls were lost.

The human brain is a curious instrument. It can store up pictures and details of the distant past, coating them with some preserving substance which defies corrosion so that they are as fresh when picked out and turned to the light as if they only came from yesterday. Other events which one would believe were of equal merit it will have nothing to do with, throwing them away into the mental dustbin. It seems to pick the fragments of experience it wishes to preserve at random so that trivialities from long ago which appear to have no relevance to anything are lodged in the memory forever. Some of us have crystal recollections of events, others remember them differently or not at all. The business of remembering the past is subjective and may bear little relation to what actually happened. It is the effect events have on our minds that is important, not the events themselves. In my case I was able to confirm many of my recollections of Argentina fifty years later.

My mother was shocked when she saw the state of my wardrobe. She bought me some replacements, this time much too big. Her fortunes had taken a turn for the better during the two years I had been in Argentina, not through good luck but through her own hard work. Instead of a cook in a private house she was now in charge of the catering at Islington Polytechnic. In fact, over the years, she went from strength to strength in the profession she had picked for herself from necessity. During the war she was in charge of all the catering at the Canadian Forces' Beaver Club, in Trafalgar Square, and later she became Catering Manager for Cable & Wireless on the Embankment. She had a talent for being liked by everyone who came into contact with her. Her staff always worshipped her. I met Canadian sailors and soldiers during the war, in all parts of the world, who knew her and thought her wonderful. She was wonderful, although by the time I came back from Argentina, after bringing up seven children, her emotional reserves were exhausted. It was not until she was much older that she and I developed a really close relationship. At that time, on balance, I would have preferred Andrea.

I was sent straight to school when I arrived back in England, as a weekly boarder to Colet Court, the preparatory school for St. Paul's, which is a part of that unique and archaic institution, the English public school. I can't remember much about it except that I and another boy developed a good system for robbing the tuck shop. The headmaster was a musician. He split the school into three huge choirs, positioning them on the three galleries that surrounded the main hall. On Speech Day, when all the parents were present, we performed a part song – something about a Swazi warrior. The effect was electric. It was the only cultural experience of my education that I have any recollection of.

By standing up on the washstand in the cubicle I inhabited I could look down through a broken window on the buses and cars in Hammersmith Road and yearn for my freedom. It came, briefly, at weekends. I went home by bicycle through Kensington, Notting Hill, Westbourne Park and Kilburn to the flat. I learnt how to hold on to the backs of lorries; they often had a convenient piece of chain that hung down from the tailboard and in those days they went at a civilised speed. I found that I could also get along quite nicely in the partial vacuum caused by the back of a bus, or, you could hold on to the bar that was fixed to the back step as long as the conductor wasn't looking.

After a year or so, CB came back from Argentina, loaded with money, the Shell-Mex building having been completed. He didn't stay in the flat, presumably he didn't want to (there wasn't room anyway), but at the Mount Royal Hotel at Marble Arch. Very grand, I thought. He didn't give much of the money to my mother I believe, or offer her a holiday, instead he took Eva and me to Switzerland for winter sports, to the Hotel Observatoire in San Cergue. I was kitted out with ski clothes at Simpson's in Piccadilly; trousers not unlike my *bombachas* and a smart peaked hat. We went by air, which was a great thrill. The skiing was fine. After ten days I was sent back by train across Europe while CB and Eva went to Monte Carlo.

When I arrived back in London and found my way to the flat in Priory Road there was a note pinned to the door. 'We have moved to 31 Priory Terrace, round the corner', I went there, a little perplexed, clutching my suitcase, to be confronted by my sister Peggy and my mother with the stark news that they had left CB for good and my mother was going to divorce him. I would have to choose whether I would stay with them or go back to Argentina with CB – if he would have me. After some reflection, it being near supper-time, I decided to stay. I never knew the ins and outs of the business and still do not, although I now know from my own experience that it must have caused both CB and my mother pain and unhappiness. It gave me a feeling of guilt which I never got over. The guilt was soothed to some extent, much later, when I was able, together with my brother Dan, to look after CB when he was old and ill, lonely and friendless.

The next time I went to Argentina was as junior apprentice on the SS *Celtic Star* in 1940, when I was sixteen. My sister Eva was by then married. I had the greatest respect for her husband George, perhaps because he owned a fine gaff cutter called *Talisman* in which he occasionally took me sailing. One of George's friends was the private secretary to Lord Vestey who owned, among other things, the Blue Star Line. Through his influence I was granted an interview with Captain Angus, the Marine Superintendent of the Blue Star Line in St Mary Axe, in the City of London. I remember a lot of men with bowler hats and rolled umbrellas, all in a hurry. I was signed on as a cadet although I was really a year too young. It was the beginning of the German submarine and air offensive against British merchant shipping. My engagement in the Blue Star Line was quite informal, no permission was asked of my mother or anyone else.

I was instructed to buy my uniform, go home and wait to be told when to join a ship. I bought my kit at Gardner's Corner in Whitechapel; uniform, bridge coat, all shiny brass buttons, shoes, sea boots, blue guernsey, dungarees, oilskins, peaked cap with a smart badge and a canvas kitbag to put it all in. It cost exactly £50, which was the last money I ever asked of my mother, except for occasional loans when I was on leave and broke. I looked very grand and slightly self-conscious, like a child at a fancy dress party. The air raids were on in London; I used to walk about the streets in my bridge coat watching the searchlights, listening to the gunfire and praying that the war wouldn't end before my letter of appointment came.

After an agonising wait, one day my letter fluttered through the door. I said goodbye to my mother when she went off to work, dressed myself in my uniform and caught the train to Jarrow-on-Tyne, clutching my rail warrant and my new kitbag. I was told I would find the ship in Palmer's Yard – I was to report to the Chief Officer. I felt that the *Celtic Star* belonged to me. She would be like the *Avila Star*, with long passenger decks and rows of lifeboats and a beautiful dining saloon all done out for troop carrying now, no doubt, her white painted bridge and upperworks in grey camouflage. I saw myself on watch, pacing the wing of the bridge under the tropic sun, a neat white cover, in the bottom of my kitbag at this very moment, over my smart peaked cap with the gold braided Merchant Navy badge. I was very proud. When we got to Newcastle I humped my kitbag on to the railway that runs along the banks of the Tyne. There were ships everywhere, some lying alongside the wharfs, some on the launching ways, some steaming down the river, others still skeletons ringing with steam-hammers and riveters – men working, tugs puffing about, launches, bustle, smoke, dirt, hurry – work. The train stopped at Jarrow-on-Tyne. There was an old man in a little hut at the gate of Palmer's Yard. 'Could you tell me where the *Celtic Star* is lying, please?' He glanced at me, took in the peaked cap, the brass buttons, 'Number 8, down there at the bottom, sonny', and then, with a smile, 'You'll be the new Chief Officer, I suppose'.

I found the *Celtic Star* was in no respect like the *Avila Star*. She was more like a run down, dirty, rusty, superannuated *Marcella*. I couldn't believe it was her until I made out her name across the stern in faded white lettering through the grime and the smoke and the glare of welding-torches – *Celtic Star*, Liverpool. I climbed a rickety gangway. There was no one at the top. I made my way to the well-deck.

The hatches were off, there were men working in the hold. A young chap a year or so older than I, with brown curly hair supporting a hat which at one time must have been like my hat,

43

was heaving a basket up out of the hold. The hat had been through some metamorphosis of coal dust and oil and sea water and general filth so that its bright gold badge had been fossilised in grime. 'Hallo', he called out, 'here's the Admiral come to see us'. I said, 'Could you tell me where I can find the Chief Officer?' The Mate was standing on the other side of the hatch. He was a man in his forties, stooping, with very blue eyes with a replica of Curly's hat over balding, greying hair, a pair of blue serge trousers and a stained and worn uniform jacket, two of the brass buttons missing. He had a kind, tired voice. 'Jesus', he said. Then he shouted across the hatch, 'Curly – show 'im – look sharp, he can start right here', and he pointed down the hold.

Curly took me to the cabin I would share with him for a year. I had the top bunk, one drawer, one locker that didn't lock, two blankets with 'Blue Star Line' written on them. The heads were across the alleyway. The cabin was right inside the ship, with no porthole, a single, flickering bulb giving a yellow light. It was the beginning of a rapid, often painful, sometimes cruel adjustment from the values and precepts instilled into me by St Paul's School to life in the real world. To live with and eventually to be accepted as an equal by Curly and the crew of the *Celtic Star* I had to put into reverse everything I had been taught. The values I had assimilated were only a hindrance to me. I had to put aside the idea that I was in some way above the general run, learn how to accept people for what they are, not for where they come from and how they talk. It was a painful journey but one I have never regretted making.

The *Celtic Star* finished her refit in two weeks and we sailed in convoy for London to load general cargo. She was an old ship the Blue Star Line had bought from the Greeks, originally a coal-burner like the *Marcella*, recently converted to oil. They put a new and bigger funnel outside the old one to make it look a bit grand, made her into a frozen-meat ship for the run between Liverpool and the *frigorífico* in Buenos Aires. I learnt how to shovel muck and coal out of an empty hold, how to clean lavatories, how to check lifeboat gear, how to polish brass, how to get enough to eat, how to keep out of the Mate's way. I was sent to the Naval Gunnery School in Newcastle to learn how to use a Hotchkiss gun and a Lewis gun (there was one on either side of the bridge). I was paid thirty shillings a month and later, after the intervention of the Fourth Mate, I was paid the war bonus of eight pounds per month. At first Curly treated me with some contempt but as I dismounted from my high horse he began to soften. We left London bound for Buenos Aires, sailing in convoy up the east coast of England and round the north of Scotland to Loch Ewe, where we joined an ocean convoy that took us far out into the Atlantic.

It was October 1940. Sixty-three British ships were sunk in that month. Our convoy was attacked by U boats. One night I stood in the wing of the bridge and trembled as six ships were torpedoed and sunk, one of them the next in line astern. It was blowing a gale, freezing cold. There could have been no survivors. The convoy broke up in mid ocean and we sailed without escort to Freetown, on the west coast of Africa, for fuel. Then we sailed across the Atlantic and down the Brazilian coast to Buenos Aires. We had been at sea for six weeks without going ashore.

Buenos Aires was very different from the place I had left seven years earlier, or perhaps I saw it through different eyes. English influence was already on the wane in 1940. Although, through British influence, the Nazi party had been officially dissolved in 1939, it still existed with a large following. It was supported by Argentina's acting President (and later dictator) Ramón Castilla. It was soon after the Battle of the River Plate when the German pocket battleship, *Graf Spee*, was scuttled after a running fight with three British cruisers. The *Graf Spee* lay on the bottom in the shallows just off the port of Montevideo, her upperworks, her gun turrets, her bridge and control tower all plainly visible to every ship entering and leaving the port of Buenos Aires. She became a kind of monument to British power, the fact of her bones sticking up out of the shallow river for all to see was a potent factor in keeping Argentina neutral in the war. Hundreds of German sailors from the *Graf Spee* found their way to Buenos Aires, many of them settled in Argentina. They roamed around the bars under the Arches of the Paseo Colon in groups, drinking and sometimes fighting with sailors from British ships.

With my new-found allegiance to my new companions of the *Celtic Star* I was at first reluctant to take up my family connections in Buenos Aires. Instead I would spend my free time and my new wealth from the war bonus, round the bars of the Arches. Liverpool firemen, Glaswegian greasers, Welsh seamen, sometimes sailors from the Hebrides, singing their strange, sad Gaelic songs, were all let loose when a British ship docked in Buenos Aires. They sped to the bars along the Arches like greyhounds from a trap. All were drunk by midnight. Many were rolled, staggering back to the ship penniless in the early hours. Many fought and were rounded up by the police, staying in the jug until the ship sailed unless the Captain chose to bail them out; some were knifed. The Arches along the Paseo Colon were notorious. By evening they would be packed with swaying, singing, fighting sailors from British ships, some in their best shore duds, some in sweat-shirts and dungarees. There were always half-a-dozen British ships in the port. The prostitutes of the Boca made a killing.

Prostitution was big business in Argentina. Buenos Aires was a centre of international ill repute as the white slave traffic was exploited by a ruthless mafia. In the years up to the outbreak of the war, girls from Poland, Germany, France and Italy were persuaded that marriage to an expatriate in Buenos Aires was an easy option and they came in hundreds. The lucky ones were given a flat in the city and became the mistresses of English businessmen. The rest gravitated to the Arches.

In the Liverpool Bar, Rosa, or Rosie as she was called, would dance the Fireman's Dance. It was a cavern of a place – marble floor, tables and chairs, a long bar down one side, the bottles under it, out of reach. There was a shorter bar across the end where the girls sat. You could buy them a drink and they would talk to you in broken English, put a hand on your leg, show their cleavage. They were burdened with cheap scent and utterly desirable after two months at sea – a short time cost the whole of your advance.

Rosie danced on a balcony across one end of the bar, there were two guitarists, a man with an accordion. Her voice was coarse and loud and full of frenzy. She herself was a large lady with a wide scarlet mouth, scarlet flamenco dress with full skirt, black hair in Spanish ringlets, dangling earrings. She had a certain unrefined beauty about her. She would start low key with a few sad songs from the mountains of Galicia, then she would move on to 'Roll out the Barrel', translated in some way to the Spanish language, to which the sailors, those of them who were sober enough, would bawl the chorus. She would start a flirtation with some great tattooed fellow in the hall, picking roses out of a vase on one side of the balcony, kissing them and throwing them down. During the Fireman's Dance she would hurl herself back and forth across the front of the balcony with great leaps in the air, singing a wild song, half Spanish, half Liverpudlian, whose words could not be distinguished. Her castanets clattered like machine guns, her audience roared.

Rosie had the artiste's knack of creating tension, the whole seething mass of drunk and half-drunk sailors rose to her, cheering and shouting, the music swelled in a roll of sound. The moment came – the moment the dance was all about. The music stopped suddenly, the bar went quiet as if the police had arrived, the mob gazed up at Rosie, expecting something, not knowing what. Rosie slowly and deliberately lifted the red skirt high above her head, exposing the nothingness underneath it. The music rolled again. She picked out the last rose, passed it across her private parts and threw it lightly down into the bar. There was pandemonium.

Merchant Navy seamen wore no uniform; only the officers wore peaked caps and brass buttons. On shore, the seamen could only be distinguished from civilians by the small MN badge they wore in their lapel. In the early part of the war when losses were at their most gruesome, the seamen were largely unrecognised. They resented this casual disrespect for the work they were doing. They would turn the badge upside down so that it read NW – not wanted.

I made six voyages to Argentina in the *Celtic Star*, or, more accurately five and a half, each one more terrifying than the last but, as I grew up, each one more exciting. It took time, but I was able to throw off most of the rubbish instilled in me by St Paul's School – there was some sense as well – and equate with the people I shared my life with. We sailed through the centre of the submarine war against the Merchant Navy. On every voyage out of and back into the seas round England we passed through a nightmare none of us expected to survive. We all had the certain knowledge that sooner or later we would be torpedoed, the only uncertainty was whether it would be in winter or in summer, in cold or hot. If it was winter, we knew we would die. If it was warm we thought we might have a chance. The Merchant Navy suffered enormous losses during the war as a proportion of its total manpower, yet we were always regarded as a cut below the Royal Navy.

On one voyage the ship sailed past Buenos Aires and 190 miles up the river Paraná to Rosario where there was a meat *frigorífico*. The pilot stood on the bridge in his pyjamas, like Captain Downie of the old *Marcella*, conning the ship through ever-changing shallows, sometimes close to the forest, bright coloured birds darting through the rigging, sometimes in a brown sea, the banks far away, the trunks of great trees, slowly turning and twisting as they made their lugubrious way to the estuary of the River Plate and the open sea.

We sailed through the centre of the submarine war

At one stage, in 1941 and 1942 before Churchill negotiated the purchase of fifty ancient destroyers from the USA in return for military rights in the island of Bermuda, before those destroyers came into service in the North Atlantic, the convoys were unescorted. In those early days, some of the U boat commanders were compassionate men, concerned about killing defenceless Merchant Seamen. They would stop the ship first, allow the crew to take to the boats and then fire their torpedoes. Sometimes they even reported the position of lifeboats so that the men could be picked up. In February 1940, a U boat commander towed a string of lifeboats from a torpedoed ship towards the Irish coast so that the men could be picked up. He was spotted by a Coastal Command aircraft. A destroyer, just over the horizon, was alerted by radio and the U boat was sunk. After this incident Admiral Dönitz signalled his commanders: 'Do not rescue any men, do not take them along and do not take care of any boats from the ship. Weather conditions and the proximity of land are of no consequence. Concern yourself only with the safety of your own boat and with efforts to achieve additional success. We must be hard in this war.'

A few days out from the convoy assembly points in Loch Ewe in Scotland or the River Mersey, the two or three corvettes escorting us would leave to join another, homeward-bound convoy. Then the forty, sometimes fifty, ships lumbering across the ocean at 8 knots, would be at the mercy of the submarines. In the winter of 1942 the submarines hunted in wolf packs. Five or six of them in a group were controlled by radio from Admiral Dönitz's headquarters in Germany. When they found and attacked a convoy, moving in from all sides, the losses were horrific. On one dark night I stood on the wing of the bridge of the old *Celtic Star*, watching and listening as fourteen ships were blown up. A single submarine, U124, sank 47 ships in thirty months until she was destroyed in April 1943. We would hear the dull thud as the torpedoes struck, sometimes we would see an explosion, more often nothing. We all stood at action stations, the lifeboats swung out, our pathetic 4 in. gun on the stern loaded and ready, waiting for the bang, everyone tense and silent, each of us lost in his own thoughts. The convoy would take what evasive action it could, following the signals from the Commodore ship; sometimes we would be ordered to scatter and continue the voyage alone. This was worse.

One night I watched the phosphorescent wake of a torpedo speed across our bow to hit the ship immediately to port of us. Sometimes we steamed through what seemed like hundreds of men in the water, each with a little red light winking on his lifejacket, heard their cries as we passed through them, unable to help them in any way – it was certain death to stop the ship. In the morning we would count the cost – 22 ships left out of 50. By some extraordinary fluke of chance the *Celtic Star* came through eleven times.

In spite of her new funnel, the *Celtic Star* was really an old and rusty tramp steamer. Compared with a modern ship, even then, she was a relic, an archaic throw-back with her steam winches, her rod and chain steering, her magnetic compass, her old fashioned davits. Yet the old triple expansion steam engine that drove her, much the same as the one that drove the *Marcella*, was a remarkably reliable and smooth running piece of machinery. In the years I was in her I don't remember a single mechanical failure at sea – more than can be said for most modern ships. There was no vibration except perhaps at

... the ship immediately to port of us

maximum speed and the engines were virtually silent. Her Achilles' heel was in her boiler room.

She had two boilers, side by side, taking up the whole width of the ship except for a narrow space on the starboard side where an alley-way ran from the stokehold to the engine room. It might be a curt message through the engine room speaking tube to the bridge or it might be the Chief climbing the bridge ladder with a solemn face. 'There's a tube leaking – one boiler must be shut down – immediately'. There could be no delay. If the boiler wasn't shut down with a damaged tube it would explode. Steam pressure to the engine would drop, the ship's speed would drop, she would slip back astern of the convoy. One of the engineers would have to climb inside the boiler as soon as it was cool enough, crawl to the back, find the leaking tube and screw a blank flange on to a through stay to block the tube off. It would be four or five hours before steam could be raised again and the ship could put on her best speed to rejoin the convoy. It happened once at night, in a gale, when the convoy was under attack.

A ship had been torpedoed and sunk, the two corvettes comprising the escort were at the far side of the convoy, the muffled thump of depth charges shook the ship every few minutes. The *Celtic Star* soon lost speed. As we pulled out of line we saw the black shape of the next ship in line slip past – then another, then another, then nothing but the dark night. We couldn't send a message to the commodore ship or the escort because we couldn't break radio silence or show a light. We were on our own. It was a lonely ocean, charged with menace. We stood to action stations, waiting, watching. I don't believe there was a man on board who was not afraid. If we hadn't been seen and we were very lucky we might be able to catch the convoy up. If there was more than one submarine – a wolf pack – we were as good as finished. The boats would be difficult to launch in this weather.

The fourth was on watch in the engine room – it would be he who would crawl in through the furnace door as soon as enough heat had gone out of the boiler for him to stay alive.

If he was quick he might be in and out within twenty minutes. If anything happened to the ship while he was inside the boiler, he was dead. The minutes ticked themselves away like hours, the hours like weeks. Soon we lost sight of the convoy. We could still hear the depth charges, once an explosion. Even at six or seven miles, it shook the ship. The fourth was inside the boiler. The ship was rolling. Working inside the half-cooled boiler was a refinement of torture. The tension held itself taut as the ship staggered through the gale at little over half speed. There was an overwhelming silence, no word came from the engine room. The captain stood in silence by the engine room speaking tube – the rest of us strained our eyes into the night. The whistle shrilled after three hours and forty minutes. 'Job's done – we're making steam – quick as we can'.

Slowly, speed picked up, the ship began to shudder and shake, the Atlantic waves broke across the fore'ard well deck. At dawn we saw the convoy on the horizon, by afternoon we were back in the dubious safety of our station. Two more ships had been torpedoed in the night, one from beside us in the next line.

During the Battle of the Atlantic, 2,828 British merchant ships were sunk by U boats. Over fourteen and a half million tons of British shipping was lost; 32,000 British sailors were drowned, thousands injured for life. Losses in the Merchant Navy were far greater in proportion to total numbers than in any of the armed services.

We heard some harrowing tales from other seamen we met in the bars and in the Seamen's Mission; they were never told in the press. The *Auckland Star* was sunk by a German submarine ace, Otto Kretschmer, in July 1940. In September he sank the *Baron Blythswood*, carrying iron ore, a notoriously lethal cargo. Kretschmer was astonished to see her sink in forty seconds, taking all hands with her – all hands, that is, except one. He hauled himself up onto a piece of wreckage, erected a makeshift mast and tied his shirt to it in the traditional manner of a comic cartoon, leaving himself in his underpants. He was seen by the same Kretschmer sometime later, who went back and picked him up, gave him dry clothes, water, food, a shot of brandy, wrapped him in blankets. Kretschmer transferred him to a lifeboat with the survivors of the *Invershannon*, another of his victims. He gave the survivors food and water and gave the officer in charge of the boat a course to steer for Ireland. They were all picked up and saved. Kretschmer went on to sink many thousands of tons of shipping; U 99 was finally sunk and he was captured after an astonishing attack on a well defended convoy.

As the going got tougher more and more armament was added to the Lewis and Hotchkiss guns until the old ship resembled an armed cruiser. The 4 in, gun was manned by a naval rating, quite an elderly man, he seemed to us. He had been rejected for active service in the army. He used to cut our hair – we paid him with a tin of 50 Woodbines, which cost one shilling. We called him 'Guns'. He once told me he never wanted to go to sea, he had never learned to swim and was always frightened of water. When he went to join up they persuaded him to go into the navy because they wanted gunners for merchant ships and they thought an old fellow would be just right for the job.

The ship was fitted with a box kite which we flew from the top of the foremast. It was about six feet square, held by a wire passing through a sheave at the top of the mast. Flying it was a tremendous game, steam had to be fed to the winch on the foredeck, the kite hauled to the top of the mast and then slacked out as it caught the wind. Its purpose was to discourage dive bombers when we sailed up and down the east coast to and from London. One day it took a dive when we were hauling it down and neatly snatched the Captain's gold braided hat overboard. It was never used again. Instead, we were given a barrage balloon for the coast, a more docile animal which we handed back when we arrived at the convoy base. There were things called 'pig troughs', banks of 16 rockets on the boat deck which we were supposed to loose off at enemy aircraft, things called Fram projectiles which went off with a bang, trailing wires from a parachute. We would loose them off at anything that came in sight, regardless of whether it was ours or theirs, doing not the slightest damage but raising our morale remarkably.

During the early part of the war no one was told how disastrous were the losses of merchant ships and merchant seamen. We ourselves were told nothing, we only had the evidence of our own eyes and the experiences of our mates to go on. For weeks on end we got no news of the war, no news of the bombings of London, Liverpool, Glasgow, sea ports all over the country where most of our crew lived. We had to keep strict radio silence and were not allowed either to transmit or receive for fear of giving away our position. Although we made light of it, sailing in merchant ships was a deadly serious business. Losses were so heavy in 1940 and 1941 that the war could have been lost for that reason alone. On March 18th 1941 Churchill, in a broadcast to the nation, said 'We must regard the Battle of the Atlantic as the most momentous ever fought'. This remained true for at least two years. By a huge margin the losses of ships exceeded their rate of replacement until 1943. It was touch and go. In the month of October 1940, the month I went to sea, a homeward bound convoy lost 15 out of 31 ships in one, black night – October 19th. The next day another massacre took 13 ships out of another convoy. In 1941 there were more U boats; at one time 113 submarines were cruising the shipping routes across the Atlantic to within 500 miles of the USA, at least 300 ships were always at risk. By the end of 1941 the submarines, the new magnetic mines and enemy aircraft together had sunk or damaged a thousand merchant ships. Churchill wrote to President Roosevelt, 'Unless we can establish our ability to feed this island, we may fall by the way'. The Blue Star Line alone lost seven ships in the first seven months of 1941, 92,253 tons of shipping.

In all my voyages to Argentina during the early part of the war, I went to El Choiqué once, when I managed to get a few days off from the ship. Strangely, I remember nothing about it, only that I went there. But Buenos Aires became my stamping ground. I used to spend all my money there so that when I got back to England my war bonus had melted into the advances I took in Buenos Aires and I was broke. I had a wonderful, unattainable girl friend, ate huge steaks and lived the high life. I used to see Uncle Billy, but CB had disappeared. He was thought to be in America but no one knew. The Shell Mex building stood solid and proud in Calle Diagonal Norte, CB's office at the top now buried and lost among the lifts and corridors and office suites. He had quarrelled with Billy and gone off, this time, as it turned out, irrevocably.

On one voyage Billy asked me to bring him two new suits from his tailor in London. 'Just go in and tell them you want two suits for Captain Mulville', he said. 'They'll make them in a week and you can bring them out on your next trip'. I went to Poole's in Saville Row as soon as I got home. Miraculously, they had escaped the bombing and the two old men were still there. They made the suits, just as Uncle Billy said they would, entirely on my word, without even a note from him and with no thought of payment. I collected them before I left and took them to Buenos Aires, smuggling them through the Customs by wearing them. Uncle Billy was delighted.

On another voyage the *Celtic Star* shipped four thoroughbred racehorses on board for Buenos Aires. The Mate called me in, 'You know about horses, Mulville – you can look after them.' The Mate was new to the ship, the kindly, blue eyed, soft-spoken man who was Mate when I joined had been promoted. On his first voyage as Captain of another ship he was blown up and drowned. Curly, as well, was drowned. He went for his ticket, passed it with flying colours, shipped as Third Mate and was blown up a week out of Liverpool.

The horses were in loose boxes, two on either side of No. 4 hatch. They were brought from Newmarket by three short tweedy men in breeches and they were slung on board with a crane. Their fodder – hay and straw and their food – was all stowed in the square of the hatch and there was a substantial box of medicines and potions and powders. I was given instructions about feeding them and looking after their ailments and left to it. There was a strong hint that if the horses reached their destination in good order there would be something in it for me.

They were beautiful creatures, all stallions, each one of them worth many thousands of pounds. One of them, I remember, was called Sunlaw and had been a famous horse. The sailors were all frightened of them. They occupied the ship's deck between the rail and the hatch, two on either side, their stalls opening on to the hatch so that when the top half of the stable door was open, in the day time in fine weather, you had to pass right under their noses to get to the poopdeck and the accommodation aft. The sailors preferred to climb over the middle of the hatch when they passed by.

I soon got to love the horses, I was the only one who fed them. As soon as I appeared through the alleyway they would set up a loud whinnying and stamping. I had to clean them out every day and ration their food so that it would last the voyage. For six weeks the animals never left their stalls, except for one day when I left the bottom door of the box open and Sunlaw walked out on to the deck. I had a terrible job getting him back in. No one would lend a hand. At first they were seasick and had difficulty keeping their feet when the ship rolled. When the convoy was attacked the horses felt the fear and tension, stamping on the wooden floor of their boxes and neighing so that I was sent off the bridge to No. 4 hatch to calm them down.

They suffered dreadfully in the heat of the tropics. We lay in Freetown for a week where the horses could smell the shore. They began to get sick in the stifling heat; I didn't know how to keep them alive. It was desperately hard work and the Mate would give me no time off to look after them so that when the ship berthed in Buenos Aires I was in almost as bad shape as they were. I don't know whether the people that came to fetch them really knew what the animals had been through. At all events the horses all refused point blank to leave their stalls, splaying out their legs and sticking fast to the box however their new masters struggled to prise them out. In the end, I led them out, speaking quietly to them as I always did. They emerged from their six weeks' ordeal unsteadily. I got Sunlaw onto the deck first, a sling was put round his tummy and he was whisked away by the derrick. Once one had gone the others followed more easily.

Fortunately for me not one of the horses' new owners spoke English and I was called to the Mate's cabin to act as interpreter. Doubly fortunately, the Mate spoke not a word of Spanish. I was able to explain to them that I had done all the work and all the looking after, in addition to my work on the ship and the Mate was a son of a bitch anyway so the roll of 100 peso notes was slipped into my hand and not his. The Mate hated me from that moment until he died, which wasn't very long afterwards.

With this new wealth – I had never seen so much money in my life - I lived the life of Riley in Buenos Aires on that last voyage. I had long since moved up market from the bars under the Arches. Now, with the beautiful girl friend, we went to the races and out in rowing boats along the Tigre and to dinner and dancing in all the posh restaurants. It wasn't quite so easy-going in Buenos Aires as it had been. The place was crowded with Nazis and we had to be careful. One of our sailors was knifed in one of the bars, we left him in the British hospital when the ship sailed. By the time the old *Celtic Star* left the South Dock, loaded with another cargo of frozen meat, I was broke. There wasn't a high spot in the town I hadn't been to. In fact, I was always broke, it didn't make any difference how much money I had, as were all my friends on the ship. We knew that any voyage might be our last voyage and none of us wanted to leave any money behind. Perhaps it would have been better if the Mate had got the horse money after all, he had a wife and children who could have done with it.

When the war was over the House of Commons passed a unanimous resolution that, 'The thanks of this House be accorded to the officers and men of the Merchant Navy for their steadfastness and resolution, ... etc., etc.' It was a hollow collection of empty words.

The Merchant Navy has been systematically destroyed.

From the days of its glory, when it alone saved the nation from certain destruction, it has been allowed to shrink away until it is no more than a myth, remembered by a few survivors. The very politicians who rant about the glories of war, many of them having no experience of it themselves, are those who have achieved the systematic destruction of the Merchant Navy.

I didn't know when we sailed out of the port of Buenos Aires that I would not see Argentina again for forty-five years.

IV

Misfortune

CB got old and frail. He left Argentina for good during the war and went to the USA with a considerable fortune. I didn't see him or hear of him for years; I didn't know whether he was dead or alive until he turned up in London in the early 1950s. He lived with his sister, my Aunt Ellen, in her back-to-back house in a poor street in Kilburn, at that time a not very salubrious suburb of London. The house had been given to her years earlier by Uncle Billy, together with a tiny stipend. At first she was quite rich and drove about in an old Ford car; she used to take me for drives when I was small. She never managed anything faster than 20 mph in second gear. As time went on and inflation took its toll the car went and Aunt Ellen and the house became steadily poorer and dirtier. CB went to live with her because he had no money to live anywhere else. They had quarrelled all their lives and continued to do so until the end. They enjoyed quarrelling; it is an Irish trait that carries on into my generation of the family. Most of my brothers and sisters have it although I escaped it, perhaps the relevant genes came to me from my mother.

CB lost every penny of the fortune in some crackpot hotel deal in America; all that remained of any value, apart from a few pounds he eked out to keep himself in bus fares, was a life membership of the RAC Club in Pall Mall which he had bought for £25 before the First World War. He still had the grand manner. He would go to the club, sometimes he would meet old cronies and talk about railways and bridges and docks and the great enterprises he had once been engaged in. I gave him a job in my small business. He did the books, meticulously, in his tiny handwriting. I loved him and so did my brother Dan; love has its own set of ethics, takes no account of whether the recipient is good or nice or ugly or beautiful or kind or cruel.

Uncle Billy got married, much to everyone's astonishment, when he was in his mid-50s. I believe he had a few years of real happiness on the *estancia*; as far as I know he and his wife were devoted to one another. Freda loved the *estancia* and made great improvements, especially to the garden. She is remembered as a loving, caring person. Not only did Uncle Billy get married, which probably scotched any chance I had of inheriting El Choiqué, but soon afterwards, Freda gave birth to a fine, healthy boy. A couple of years later another boy was born and Clive and Julian now live on at El Choiqué. Then misfortune and tragedy overtook Uncle Billy. I remember him and Freda and the two boys when they were small, in England on a visit in the 1950s. It was when Uncle Billy helped me with my business. I spent a day with them just before they went back to Argentina and we talked about Guillermo and Andrea and old Dolores and Montenegro and the flamboyant life Uncle Billy had led with his Rolls-Royce cars and his dinner parties at Claridges. He gave me an old dinner jacket he had to spare, it is the only one I have ever possessed, from the same Poole's in Savile Row. A year later Freda died of cancer.

Misfortune followed the tragedy quickly. British influence in Argentina began seriously to wane under the pro-Nazi president Castillo. The big Argentine landlords and much of the army thought that Germany was going to win the war and that Argentina would be better off if it did. A form of fascist government could then be established, enabling democracy to be suppressed and the country made safe for the landlords and wealthy families and army officers. Pro-Nazi sympathy was skilfully fostered by a powerful German Embassy in Buenos Aires with a network of political agents throughout the country. At that time, fewer than 2,000 families owned a fifth of the land. In the province of Buenos Aires itself, the most fertile and prosperous part of the country, fewer than 250 families owned nearly half the land; average holdings were 50,000 acres per family. These people wanted no truck with democracy, which would at once offer a threat to their cosy way of life.

Castillo imposed a state of siege after the Japanese attack on Pearl Harbor in December 1941, making him, in effect, dictator. All pro-democratic meetings and rallies were ruthlessly suppressed, only pro-Axis propaganda was permitted, the press was censored, life became difficult for the English community. The country's government was firmly in the German camp and times were dangerous for the crews of British ships. There was never a voyage to Buenos Aires in 1940 and 1941 when we didn't lose two or three men. Sometimes we left them in prison on some charge or other, sometimes they simply disappeared.

It was the Germans themselves who caused the tables to be turned in favour of the Allies. For some reason Argentine ships were refused neutral status by Germany and three of them were attacked by German submarines. Two were sunk and one badly damaged, with some loss of life. In spite of the work their embassy in Buenos Aires was doing, the German government warned Argentina that her ships would be treated as enemies if they were caught by German submarines within the blockade zone around the United States.

This extraordinary short sightedness caused a tide of Argentine public opinion to rise up against Castillo, whose government did not in any case represent a majority of the people. The Argentine establishment, backed by the people, asserted their fundamental commitment to democracy by defying Castillo's censorship and his proscription of public meetings. By 1943, by which time America was in the war and the tide was beginning to turn, there was massive support for Roosevelt and his New Deal policies which held out hope for the oppressed lower middle classes in Argentina. Apart from political considerations, Britain was buying Argentine meat and Argentine grain in big quantities, which Germany could not do.

British influence did not take its final tumble until 1946 when Perón nationalised the British owned railways. By this time the rail network was run down and in need of repair and modernisation. It was bought, with an inconvertible sterling debt owed to Argentina by Britain, for the knock-down price of 150 million pounds, although the railways had been valued at nearly double that figure in 1940. It was the aftermath of war, Britain was weak and exhausted. Perón whipped up anti-British feeling; there was even some harassment of the British community. Nationalism was the cry and an impoverished colonial power was an easy target. There was a general exodus of English people from Buenos Aires and British influence waned rapidly. The Blue Star Line stopped trading to Buenos Aires, the Anglo Frigorífico was shut down, even the Royal Mail Line stopped sailing to Argentina and British investment virtually came to a halt. It was with this background that Uncle Billy fell foul of the law.

The firm of Mulville Brothers had modest but pleasant offices in Calle Reconquista, in the centre of Buenos Aires. The big bust-up between CB and Billy took place in the office, in front of Oliviera, the firm's accountant. He had been with them for years (I remember him from when I was a boy) and he was used to their periodic explosions. This one was to be the last; they never saw each other again after it. It may have been the influence of Freda, who had no time at all for CB. She considered him an unprincipled philanderer and wanted nothing to do with him. After the bust-up all traces of CB's influence were removed from the firm.

Oliviera, who had always been one of CB's men, was sacked by Billy. This turned out to be a damaging error of judgement on Billy's part. Oliviera went to the police and gave them explicit details of the firm's transactions, some of which may have been legally borderline, and particularly of Billy's dealings with the tax authorities, with details drawn from Oliviera's intimate knowledge of the firm's business. No doubt Billy paid as much tax as he had to and as little as he could get away with, like everyone else, but to be laid open to a minute scrutiny left him hopelessly vulnerable to an anti-British establishment. He was arrested in the office in Calle Reconquista and taken to the police station in handcuffs. It cost him a considerable sum to get himself out of it. It may also have cost him all Freda's jewellery, which has never been seen since she died.

Uncle Billy himself died soon afterwards, at the time CB was in London working in my office. His death had a profound effect on CB. He seemed to discount all their quarrels and disagreements and flare-ups of emotion, remembering only their lifelong community of interest and their partnership, which was the foundation of Billy's fortune. CB was deeply hurt that Billy never mentioned him in his will although he knew that CB was living in poverty.

In some strange way, by an unique mixture of loyalties, the British community in Buenos Aires has survived, retaining much of its original culture as well as adapting itself to the often hostile vagaries of succeeding political fashion. The community still retains its identity and of course, its language. If you go shopping in Martinez or San Isidro, both pleasant residential suburbs of Buenos Aires, you will hear almost as much English spoken as Spanish, all with that odd, not unattractive accent which is peculiar to Anglo-Argentines; the habit of saying 'No?' at the end of a sentence as an expression of the affirmative. The habit of throwing in the word '*che*' as a term not quite of endearment but of familiarity. The accent is not quite sing-song but has a lilt all of its own which can immediately be recognised whenever it is heard. Martinez and San Isidro are not unlike suburbs of London – Hampstead or St. John's Wood. They evoke in an English visitor a homely feeling, as if a No. 31 bus would come round the corner at any minute.

Only a handful of those bilinguals will ever have set foot in England or will ever hope or wish to do so. The British left a deep mark on Argentina, more enduring than that of any other nation in this most cosmopolitan of societies although the number of British immigrants was far exceeded by Italians, Portuguese and Spanish, let alone immigrants from Japan and Central Europe. The British stamp is the more remarkable because British influence lasted for a very short period of time. In a hundred years, from the 1830s, it grew until it dominated the country's economy and then died away as quickly as it came. Now there is effectively no British influence in Argentina; only the running sore of the Falkland's War remains.

The British stamped the country forever with their misuse of the Spanish language. The Rio de la Plata became the River Plate – *plata* means 'silver'. The Club de Extranjeros became the 'Strangers' Club' – an *extranjero* is a foreigner; *el campo*, the countryside, became the camp. By calling the country, 'the Argentine' they made a noun out of an adjective. The English in Argentina spoke Spanish with an appalling accent, sometimes, like CB, not bothering to learn the language properly or, like Billy, speaking it like a gringo. In the 1920s, when British investment and influence was at its height, it was actually a mark of distinction to speak Spanish with an English accent.

The British gave Argentina football, called '*futbol*' and tennis and polo, the railways, which transformed the country in a decade and public utilities – waterworks, a drainage system, a post office with red pillar-boxes. The Central Post Office in Buenos Aires might be a copy of the GPO in London. British investment was responsible for docks, trams, telephones. Retiro Station in Buenos Aires is like Victoria Station in London was until recently, the same ticket offices, even the same tickets. The trains are unmistakably English, they make the same noise as an English train. The first foreign loan to the new republic, in 1822, was made by British banks. It was used to build the harbour mole in the port of Buenos Aires and the first waterworks. In 1941 when I was in Argentina, the British community numbered 50,000. Now it is less than 10,000.

By 1943 it was clear that Britain was going to win the Battle of the Atlantic. There were more escort vessels and they were more efficient, the new Liberty ships were being built very quickly in American yards. The wolf packs were often beaten back, radar was having a significant effect on submarine detection. Even so, on the *Celtic Star*'s last voyage to Argentina

I was the only apprentice on board – it was becoming impossible to recruit boys to go to sea because of the terrible losses.

In convoy four days out of Liverpool, we watched from the bridge as a U boat was depth charged out of existence. It had been detected by the improved sonar carried by corvettes and destroyers and within minutes it was being hunted by one of Churchill's four-funnelled American destroyers and three corvettes. They made runs in a criss-cross about half a mile on our port side. The ship shook with every explosion of a depth-charge; the Second Engineer told me that in the engine room, they could see the plates of the old ship give every time there was an explosion. We saw the 100 foot plumes of water thrown into the air as the charges went off, then we saw the shattered bow and the conning-tower poke itself out of the sea for a second before it slid down. There was silence, followed by a round slick of oil like a guilty stain on the surface of the ocean. There were no survivors. It occurred to me, perhaps for the first time, that the one hundred odd men inside that submarine were real people, just like me, with girl friends or

We watched from the bridge as a U-boat was depth-charged out of existence

perhaps wives and children and mothers and lovers in some corner of Germany they would never see again. It made me feel sick. I must have been just beginning to ask myself questions about the reasons for and justifications of this misery.

The wolf packs were beaten only just in time. Although it was never admitted, we could see clearly that if ships continued to be sunk at such a rate, Britain would be starved of food and raw materials and forced to give in, which was what the Germans believed would happen. From our viewpoint, as we observed and trembled for night after night, it looked as if the war was lost, although we never allowed ourselves to believe it.

By the end of 1942 we could see that the convoys were better protected. We saw aircraft circling round the ships by day, some of them from the new carriers, some land-based from airfields in the north of Ireland. We saw the old Sunderland flying boats, those most majestic of aircraft, circling round the convoy from first light until sunset like gliding birds. Sometimes we saw the big 'Queens' the *Mary* and the *Elizabeth* – in their wartime camouflage, streaking across the horizon loaded with troops, a cruiser as escort. The convoys were better disciplined, practising zig-zag manoeuvres, Aldis signalling lamps winking across from ship

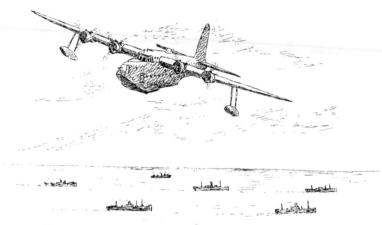

The old Sunderland flying boats circling round the convoy

to ship, flag signals fluttering as messages were passed from the Commodore and the escort ships. The submarines were forced to develop new tactics. Instead of wolf packs they began to hunt alone, much further afield, way out into the South Atlantic, looking for ships that had left the convoys and were routed unescorted to far off destinations such as Buenos Aires. These were long range U boats fuelled from bases in fascist Spain and North Africa and Brazil.

I had put in for a transfer from the *Celtic Star* and had been promised a change of ship after this last voyage to Argentina. I was soon due to sit for my Second Mate's ticket and wanted to make a voyage to Australia in one of the company's fast motor ships. I had nobbled Captain Angus when he was aboard the ship in Liverpool and he had promised to arrange it for me. I liked the *Celtic Star*, I was used to her and knew every inch of her. The Captain I regarded as a very special man. Captain Macay had been Master of one of the company's passenger ships before the war, then he had had command of a motor ship on the Australia run and now he was reduced to the old ex-tramp steamer *Celtic Star*. He must have committed some sin or indiscretion somewhere along the line, or have been involved in a mishap of some kind, or perhaps it was because he was an alcoholic.

Captain Macay had already been torpedoed in one of the company's ships at the beginning of the war, though he never talked about it. He had two daughters, both married to Merchant Navy officers. He used to sit in his cabin all by himself, dressed in his immaculate white uniform and his gold braided hat, and drink whisky; sometimes he would be paralytic when I went to his cabin to give him the ship's position. He taught me to navigate, lending me his sextant, insisting that I worked my position independently of the Second Mate and the other officers. I had to hand it to him, every day at noon, in a sealed envelope. In return for borrowing his sextant, I was instructed to make certain that I saved it if the ship was torpedoed. 'Had it all my life, boy', he said, 'can't lose it now.' He would open my envelope, look at the position and compare it with the official ship's position as calculated by the officers. Sometimes he would grunt, a kind of grudging approval and sometimes he would say 'Bloody nonsense – useless boy, do it again,' and I would have to go through my calculations and check my altitudes in my watch below until I got it right. He had me working star sights, even moon sights and taught me how to find the planet Venus, on the meridian in the afternoon. I use the method he taught me to this day, with a few minor variations.

The Mate made my life as much of a misery as he knew how to, he never forgave me for pocketing the money for the horses. The boys, as we were called, worked a sixty-six-hour week. By that time I was earning £3 per month as well as my war bonus. An AB, or able bodied seaman to give him his correct name, earned £8 per month. We were on watch for eight hours a day, every day and we worked an extra ten hours a week 'field days'. For any extra work, in addition to sixty-six hours, we were paid sixpence per hour. The boys worked around the deck, chipping rust and scraping and painting; they did most of the dirty jobs the ABs wouldn't do. I seemed to find myself with the dirtiest of them. As senior apprentice I had charge of the lifeboats and had to make sure all their gear was checked and in place and that the emergency rations were intact. It wasn't such a bad life, when skiving off was taken into account, or a little bit of thieving from the officers' pantry; thick buttered toast and fried egg cooked on the galley stove at two in the morning.

The Fourth Engineer was my particular friend. He came from Manchester – I believe he was a brilliant engineer, he was at the Tec. when war broke out. He used to tell me about his girlfriend, who was going to be a doctor. It was all fixed for them to be married when the ship came home. He was a good bit older than I, in his mid-twenties. It seemed to me a very wonderful thing to be able to contemplate endless nights beside the lovely creature with long hair and red lips and smooth legs in the photograph that graced the Fourth Engineer's bulkhead. I had spent my adolescence at sea. I knew nothing about sex although my senses made me aware of its existence. Apart from the beautiful but unattainable girls I knew in Buenos Aires, my sex experience was limited to a few encounters with the girls of the Arches and similar establishments in other sea ports. First at St Paul's School and then at sea, I inhabited an exclusively male world.

Life on board ship was a settled, in many ways a happy business. The routine, a little harsh perhaps since my contretemps with the Mate, was essentially satisfying and had a kind of timeless continuity. The Merchant Navy got us away from drab wartime Britain with its rationing and blackout and austerity and there was always the prospect of high adventure close round the corner. One day, or perhaps one dark night, I would turn the corner and find the adventure – if it had not happened, I believe I would have felt cheated. Being young, the notion of my own demise never bothered me. It is the old, with little to lose, who fear death.

It all came to a sudden end one starlit night when the *Celtic Star* was torpedoed.

V

Shipwreck

It happened in the middle watch, from midnight to 4 am, the graveyard watch it was known as. Soon after I came up to the wing of the bridge, wiping sleep out of my eyes, I saw a black shape on the surface of the sea, perhaps half a mile away to starboard. It could only be a submarine. Without waiting for confirmation, I ran into the wheelhouse, pulled over the switch that rang alarm bells all over the ship and gave the order, 'Hard to port' to the man at the wheel. The Second Mate came running out of the chart room behind the bridge where he had been making up the board with the ship's position marked for every hour of the watch. 'I saw a submarine,' I spluttered, 'close to starboard'.

... wiping the sleep out of my eyes, I saw a black shape...

By this time the ship had turned through 90 degrees. The Second Mate steadied her on a new course and we looked out astern with binoculars. Neither of us could see anything. The Captain came up, his breath smelling of whisky, which it usually did. But he was steady and calm. He was in a pair of red and white striped pyjamas and his gold braided hat. I told him what I had seen. He grunted. The watch below came up and stood by the lifeboats, the gunner and his crew manned and loaded the 4 inch gun on the poop, the Second Mate gave the man at the wheel a zig-zag course, carefully worked out to make it difficult for a submarine to get itself into position to fire a torpedo, the Captain whistled down to the Engine Room through the speaking-tube and gave the Chief Engineer instructions for maximum speed, the Mate went round the four lifeboats checking that everyone was in place, everything ready for lowering. The radio operator – 'Sparks' – reached through the hatch into the chart room for the position board, started the transmitter and sent 'SSSS – SSSS – *Celtic Star* – submarine sighted position 4 degrees 20 minutes north, 22 degrees 36 minutes west – taking evasive action.' Everyone wore life-jackets, everyone knew what to do. The old ship charged through the calm, empty sea, throbbing, quivering with the effort of her maximum 12 knots.

We stood by at action stations for an hour but no one saw anything. 'Are you certain?,' the Captain asked me, 'Why didn't you call the Second Mate?' 'He was in the chart room Sir – making up the boards – it was close.' He grunted and turned away. We waited and watched for another half an hour. The men were getting impatient – they were missing their sleep, 'It was only the boy saw it', I heard the Mate say to the Third Mate on the bridge. He said it so that I would hear. I began to doubt myself. I stood on the wing of the bridge wanting, wanting to see it again but there was nothing but the serene, starlit sea. It was clear nobody believed me. 'Stand the men down,' the Captain called to the Mate, 'put the ship back on course.' The men shuffled off back to their bunks, the ship slowed back to her normal speed. 'Bloody boy,' I heard someone say. The stars shone down just as bright, the sea was as calm; from the wing of the bridge I could see the phosphorescent plume of the ship's bow-wave as she pushed her way through the ocean towards Buenos Aires. Halfway through the watch I went to the galley to make tea for me and the Second Mate.

I was back on the wing of the bridge, drinking my tea when the torpedo struck. I saw it coming through the night, from the same starboard side, saw its luminous wake making a direct, purposeful streak through the sea towards the engine-room. There was no doubt this time. It exploded with a dull thud that shook the ship as she had never been shaken. It was as if she had been lifted bodily by some monster hand and dropped on a stone floor. It was all over for the *Celtic Star*.

I have been shipwrecked twice in my life, once in the *Celtic Star* and once, many years later, in the ketch *Girl Stella* on the island of Flores in the Azores. Although I didn't appreciate it at the time, both experiences made a profound impression on me. A ship, any ship, is a little world of its own. It has its routine, its laws, its own values, its own logic. Every person in a ship has his place, his part to play in its progression. Every person is important, if not vital, to its life, every person knows his role, is aware of how his effort fits in with the general weal. When a ship sinks and is wiped away for ever, perhaps like the *Celtic Star* in a few minutes of confusion, alarm, death even, it leaves a vacuum in the mind that can only be filled by recollection. Consequently, every detail of such an experience is etched indelibly on the mind. As in my case, the passage of time only serves to clarify the detail, to bring every shade, every aspect into closer focus. Recalling my experiences as a boy in Argentina, of which the *Celtic Star* is, in a sense, a part, brings back a flood of memories as if the film of life itself were turned slowly backwards. I have written about these events before, but have never before been able to summon up remembrance in such detail.

Events moved so fast in the next eight minutes that it takes longer to tell them than it did to live them. The ship began to settle by the stern very quickly but her engines continued to run and she did not lose her way. The Second Mate went to his station in the port lifeboat, the man at the wheel ran off to his lifeboat station, the Captain went down the ladder to his cabin, I was left alone on the bridge. What I must do had been drilled into me. The secret papers – radio codes, the convoy instructions, details of rendezvous positions with Naval escorts, secret convoy signals – were kept in the chart room in a big, perforated metal box, painted Admiralty grey. This box must be thrown overboard so that the codes would be destroyed, even if the ship didn't sink. I struggled to get the heavy box out through the chart room door but at some time, long after the box had been put there, the chart room had been protected against dive bombers by a cladding of concrete. No one had noticed that the concrete slabs had been put up round the doors in such a way that the metal box would no longer fit through. I got it hopelessly jammed so that I couldn't move it in or out – but I managed to open the lid. I climbed out of the chart room over the box, took a handful of books, ran to the starboard wing of the bridge and hurled them over – then went back for another load. I saw the Captain walk out of his cabin on the lower bridge towards the port lifeboat, setting his cap on his head and buttoning the jacket of his white uniform. The ship was beginning to list to port – her stern was going down, she was still rushing through the sea.

There seemed to be people running about and shouting all over the ship. The starboard lifeboat was half down but it was foul of the hull because of the ship's list and wouldn't shift any further. The lifeboat's crew left it and ran over to the port side. When I went with another load of books I saw the forward fall slip and the lifeboat plunge into the sea, smashing itself against the ship. Then it came free of the falls and crashed into the next lifeboat astern which, in turn, was carried away and smashed to matchwood with four men in it. Its crew, as well, left it and ran to the port side.

'Sparks' was in the radio cabin behind the chart room by now – we were the only two on the bridge. He was an Irishman.

He had been in the ship as long as I had. 'Bejasus,' he said, 'They've got the old girl at last.' I passed him the board and he began to send out 'SSSS – SSSS - *Celtic Star* torpedoed – position 4 degrees 5 minutes north, 22 degrees 38 minutes west – sinking'. As I took the last load of books, I remember it occurred to me, as an astonishing revelation of truth, that what I was doing was a futile waste of time. No one would ever be reading those books, regardless of my efforts. I ran through the wheelhouse and back into the chart room. 'Come on Sparks,' I shouted, 'you'll be left man – come on.' I ran towards the port lifeboat. It was swinging on the falls, full of men, almost in the sea. Two of the men were lowering away, more men were scrambling down a rope ladder into the already full lifeboat. There was a long painter from the bow of the lifeboat up to the ship's foredeck. Then I remembered the old man's sextant. 'Christ,' I thought, 'he'll kill me.'

I ran back to the chart room. Sparks had gone. It seemed to take an age to get in through the door – it was dark now, no lights. I knew where I had left the sextant, on the chart table – it wasn't there. Everything had slid over to the port side. I felt round in the darkness, my hand came upon a box, I grabbed it. I found the chart, the nautical almanac and a book of Burton's Tables in their place in the bookcase. I got out through the door onto the bridge with a sextant – I didn't know whose it was, but it was the right one. Now the boat-deck was deserted, the ship was listing about 20 degrees. I ran to the edge of the deck and looked over. The ladder snaked dizzily down. The boat was crammed with men. They were letting the falls go, she was being towed along by the painter, the ladder was hanging into the boat, a man was standing by the painter, ready to pull out a wooden pin and let the lifeboat free. I shouted down, saw the Captain look up and see me. 'Come on, boy – quick,' he shouted and then, to the man on the bow, 'Hold hard there – wait for the boy.' Then I was climbing down, the sextant in one hand, the chart and the books under my arm, half sliding, half falling down the wooden rungs of the ladder, the sea rushing past under me.

The officers' accommodation was under the bridge. As I went swinging and turning down the ladder my eyes suddenly focused on the Mate's scuttle. It was open. It was too small for a man to get through. The Mate was inside. The door of the cabin must have jammed shut, trapping him. No one had missed him, no one had heard his frantic shouting, his pounding on the door. He looked at me as I swung past. He seemed to be miles away, in some kind of reverie – he looked quite calm. As he saw me, a vague smile of recognition flickered round his mouth. I fell the last ten feet to the bottom, still clutching the sextant, the chart, the books, landed among a mass of cursing sailors. The bowman pulled out the wooden pin and the sinking ship sped past us in the starlight.

She looked like one of those cardboard ships in a fairground shooting gallery as she slipped past us. The sea was over the aft well-deck now, the engines had been stopped, the hatches where the horses had lived were awash, her bow was up at a crazy angle, the poop-deck with the 4 inch gun was just going under. The old gunner was still there. 'Jump,' we shouted, 'go on Guns – jump.' He looked at us, frightened, pathetic – he had cut my hair a few days earlier. He jumped as the after part of the poop-deck went under. He was washed back onto the deck like a bundle of clothes left on a beach. He picked himself up and jumped again. This time he was dragged down into a yawning hole in the ocean. We never saw him again. There was an explosion, followed quickly by another as the boilers blew up and the ship was gone, leaving a slick of oil, a few life-rafts and some flotsam.

The lifeboat had no engine. We shipped oars and rowed through the filth, dragging in men we found in the sea, some of them silent, others crying out for rescue. We saw the Fourth Engineer in the sea, held up by his lifejacket and hauled him into the boat. He had lost his glasses, his face, his eyes were covered in oil. He was retching piteously; he never spoke, his face was white and blank. I hardly recognised him for my friend. We put him in the stern of the boat – somehow a space was made for him. He died on our second day in the lifeboat.

We shipped oars and rowed through the filth,
dragging in men we found in the sea

I only knew he was dead because his warm body, pressed close to mine, turned cold. The Captain said a prayer, improvised out of his heart, 'Oh God' he said, 'Let this sailor go to Heaven. He never harmed a soul and he was well loved.' And then he said, 'Oh God, forgive those who sent this boy to his death.' I saw the tears roll down his old, weathered face. The crew mumbled 'Amen', and we pitched him overboard. The sharks took him.

There were forty-five of us in the lifeboat – ours had been the only boat to get away from the ship. It was the Second Mate's boat, he was a first-class seaman; the bo'sun and the lamp-trimmer, also fine seamen, had been in charge of the falls, lowering the boat carefully and calmly into the rushing sea. The men were all piled into the boat in a confusion of arms and legs and bodies, each one made more bulky by his bulging lifejacket. Some were covered in oil, others, like the Captain, had stepped into the lifeboat without dirtying their hands. There was hardly room to move.

Then we heard the noise of a diesel engine. I saw the Captain snatch off his hat and his gold-braided jacket and stuff them under a thwart. A powerful light stabbed through the night, sweeping its beam over the muck-strewn, oily sea. It found the lifeboat and paused, moving slowly over the boat from forward to aft so that we felt embarrassed, as if our humiliation was being made into an exhibit. We saw the long cigar shape move closer. Men were on the narrow deck, some in shorts, jumping up and down and swinging their arms around to ease their cramped limbs. An officer with a notebook stood by the conning-tower. A long boat-hook was thrust out, grabbing our boat over the gunwale and pulling it in so that the wooden planks dashed against the iron bulge below the submarine's waterline. 'What ship?' – no one answered. Then, 'Hey – what ship?' This time the voice had menace in it. A sailor standing beside the officer rattled the bolt of his machine-gun and moved the muzzle purposefully along the length of the lifeboat. '*Celtic Star*,' someone shouted. 'Where from?' 'Freetown.' 'Where you go?' 'Buenos Aires.' 'Where's the Captain?' 'He's gone down with the ship.' It was the Third Mate speaking. 'What cargo? — how many crew?' The questions petered out, the officer held a conversation with a dim figure with a hat like the Captain's hat leaning on the rail of the conning tower, high above us. Then, 'You want cigarettes? – brandy?' 'Yes.' 'You – come and get them,' and he pointed at one of the crew, a tall fellow with blonde hair. The man looked uncertain – and then he stepped over the gunwale onto the sloping deck, a hand was stretched out to him and he was hauled aboard. We saw him hustled down through a hatch and then the man with the boathook bore off, there was a sudden hiss of compressed air, a thump as the engine fired and the submarine moved quickly away, leaving us alone under the stars.

It has happened to me a few times in my life that some event, or even a chance meeting, has made such an impact as to change everything, so that I could say to myself, 'If I had not done this, or if that had not occurred, or if I had not met this person, nothing in my life would have been the same.' The sinking of the *Celtic Star* was one of those happenings. We were in the lifeboat for four days. We stepped the mast and rigged the sail and set off bravely towards the coast of Africa some 500 miles to the east.

On the day after the Fourth Engineer died there was a

breeze and the boat began to sail with a semblance of speed. We moved some of the men to the weather side to balance her, playful little gobbets of spray flew across the bow, the water sped past her lee gunwale. I felt her come to life as I sat at the tiller. I was the only one of all the crew who knew how to sail a boat. It gave me a feeling of power even over the Second Mate and the Captain. I experienced the fascination of ocean sailing for the first time and I remember casting my mind forward to the day when I would sail my own boat across an ocean. The project moved into top place on my list of ambitions and stayed there for many years.

I soon shook off the emotional shock that all of us must have passed through. A huge volume of experience had been concentrated into a few days. In some ways we were prepared for it in advance because we all knew that it was only a matter of time before it happened to us but even so, it is surprising that it seemed to have such a slight effect on us. We had seen our way of life shattered in minutes; we had seen friends and shipmates dying horrible deaths. We took it as a matter of chance that we had come through and they had not, some quirk of the Almighty's handling of affairs that took others away and left us behind. I suppose we grieved for those who were dead, but not very deeply – even our shipmate who had been taken on board the submarine and who may have suffered agonies as a prisoner, only held our sorrow for a short span of time. Because we were young, we held life cheaply and were always ready to risk it, even throw it away, for causes that may have been dubious at best. An old person, who has less to lose, will hold on to life with a greater tenacity.

The sun was our enemy in the lifeboat; it beat down with unremitting ferocity, there was no escaping it. Water was rationed to half a tiny beaker twice a day, amounting to roughly a quarter of a pint. The boat was provisioned for twenty men – it held forty-five. Ship's biscuits were impossible to eat because they dried out the mouth, Horlicks tablets were excellent. We had the lifeboat's heavy canvas cover on board and we spread this out over our bodies, our heads protruding round the edge like the petals of a withered flower. It was oven hot underneath but it saved our skin from being burnt. Some of the men crouched in the well down the centreline of the boat, never seeing the light of day. At noon on our first day we picked up another survivor – a Maltese fireman, a small, dark, stocky man. We pulled him out of a shark-infested sea. He looked round at us all when we dragged him in, accepted a small drink, nodded to one of his friends and disappeared into the bottom of the boat, not to be seen again until we were rescued.

The sharks were all around the idle boat – she was more or less becalmed except for that one day of breeze. They would nudge their blunt snouts up to the rudder; I could see the little blue pilot fish behind their heads. If I gave a flick to the tiller there would be a sudden swirl and the powerful creature would break the surface and roll on his back, showing the vicious teeth. The Second Mate swore at me, 'Don't do that, boy – it makes me nervous'. I never doubted we would be picked up. 'Sparks' had got the signal out and although distress signals were never acknowledged, I was pretty sure it would have been received by someone.

On the fourth day we saw smoke on the horizon, then the upperworks of a small ship slowly turning itself into the hull of a corvette. We stood up on the thwarts and waved, let off flares. At first it looked as if she would steam past but then we saw her alter course. She was an old corvette, converted from a trawler. She had been on passage between Durban and Freetown to pick up a convoy for home. She had been looking for us but had just given up the search and was back on her course. It was never easy to find a tiny spot in the ocean in the days before electronic navigation. The crew of the *Wastwater* were a kind, generous-hearted lot. The naval ratings helped us on board, gave up their bunks for us, gave us cigarettes, long drinks of water and then a meal. It was a kind of soup with beans, tinned tomatoes, hunks of meat and potatoes. It still rates among the most delicious meals I have ever tasted. I went to the 'heads' for the first time in four days and passed an enormous black

We stood up on the thwarts and waved

turd, then went to sleep in somebody's bunk. The Captain had us standing watches to help the *Wastwater*'s officers until the ship arrived in Freetown. *Celtic Star*'s Third Engineer was awarded the MBE.

I had enjoyed my sojourn in the lifeboat. I had known that it had to come – I suppose I would have been disappointed if it had not come. When it did happen I was able to sustain it without difficulty. If the *Celtic Star* had been in the North Atlantic, in winter, it would have been a different story. The sailors that belonged to the red lights we had seen floating past the ship in the cold sea during U boat attacks only had minutes to live. I might have been below decks when the ship was torpedoed, like the Mate.

The crews of ships caught by German surface raiders, of which there were usually one or two loose in the Atlantic, passed through a refinement of hellfire. The torpedo was a clean weapon as far as weapons of war can be said to be clean. To have the ship raked by shell-fire would have been a horror of a different order. The German surface raiders seldom gave crews time to take to the boats before they sank the ship. It was a slow, miserable death. The ships caught on fire, men were killed trying to launch the boats or left on board with terrible injuries. I have met men who survived it, but there were not many of them. The *Celtic Star*'s lifeboat, on the other hand, was a place I took to naturally and felt at home in. It was crowded, of course, and the sun was scorching and there wasn't much to drink, but for the first time I saw the ocean from its surface, close to, as it really is, as if I was a part of it instead of an alien riding along on its surface. I liked it and began to dream of getting to know it better.

After the sinking of the *Celtic Star* I forgot about Buenos Aires, forgot the smart girlfriends, the bars under the Arches, the *estancia*, Montenegro, Andrea, Guillermo, even Uncle Billy – my life took a new direction.

Part Two

Sail

Iskra
photo by Shirley Orchard

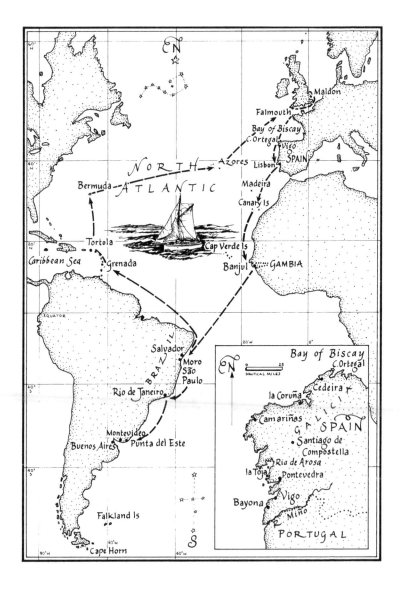

Maldon

Falmouth

Bay of Biscay
C.Ortegal

Vigo
SPAIN

NORTH
Azores Lisbon

ATLANTIC Madeira

Bermuda

Canary Is

Tortola

Cap Verde Is

Caribbean Sea Grenada

Banjul GAMBIA

EQUATOR

Salvador

BRAZIL Moro
São
Paulo

Rio de Janeiro

Montevideo
Buenos Aires Punta del Este

Falkland Is

Cape Horn

Bay of Biscay

C.Ortegal

NAUTICAL MILES

la Coruña Cedeira

Camariñas GALICIA SPAIN

Santiago de
Compostella

Ria de Arosa
la Toja Pontevedra

Bayona Vigo
Miño

PORTUGAL

84

VI

Five Yachts

I stole the first boat I ever owned – if it can be said that I ever did own her. She lay hauled up the white sand beach in Sorrento, with the Isle of Capri off on her starboard side and the volcano of Vesuvius over her stern. She was very beautiful. The little town of Sorrento, its pink and white houses baked in the sun, spread itself up the mountain in front of the beach. The rich people of the town, including the owner of my boat, had run away from the fighting, leaving the starving poor behind – and my boat. If I had wanted to risk syphilis in Sorrento, I could have gone ashore every night with a tin of Irish stew and spent it in bed with any one of half a dozen frightened, half-starved girls. I had never experienced such poverty at first hand.

The people of Sorrento looked at us with unsmiling eyes, hunger their preoccupation. It was soon after the Allied landings in Salerno. The ship of which I was navigating officer was the ocean rescue tug *Weazel.* She had been one of the first in at the Salerno beachhead; we had towed the long steel pontoons that were used for the landings. We towed them from Algiers and ran them up the beach so that the landing ships could roll off their tanks and trucks and personnel. After the landings the *Weazel* was based for a time at Sorrento as duty tug for the fleet salvage officer. There was no one there when we arrived except the wretched inhabitants and the newly installed King's Harbour Master.

I asked an old fisherman I found about the sailing dinghy, in my pidgin Spanish-based Italian. 'It belongs to a *signore* who lived up there,' he pointed to a pale blue villa on the side of the mountain, its paint faded, stucco cracked and splintered. '*Collaboratore,*' he said and drew his finger across his throat. I approached the King's Harbour Master. 'Do you mind if I take that boat?,' I asked him affably, 'We really need a small dinghy we can launch easily for running out our towing lines.' It was true, or partly true and it was plausible. 'Certainly not,' he said curtly. 'You can just keep your hands off it.' I reported this to the Captain who had already had a brush with the King's Harbour Master. The Captain was an old Merchant Navy skipper who had been at sea all his life and had a hearty disregard for jumped-up young bank clerks pretending to be naval officers. 'I see,' he said.

That night I swam the couple of hundred yards to the beach, across the harbour from the mole where the *Weazel* lay alongside, towing a light line from the tug's after-deck. I crawled up the beach when the naval guard was at the other end of his beat, made the line fast to the dinghy's painter and swam back to the ship. We took the end of the line round the capstan on the after-deck, waited until the guard was out of sight and hove away easy. The dinghy slid gently down the beach, cruised slowly and quietly across the harbour, was hauled on board by willing hands and stowed away in the recesses of the *Weazel*'s towing hold, hidden under a 21 inch towing hawser. I slept very peacefully.

A few days later we took a pair of davits from a wrecked Italian trading schooner in a corner of the harbour of Castellamare, a set of teak gratings from another wreck made her floorboards. The old fisherman knew where her sails and mast and rudder were to be found. A few wisely placed tins of corned beef procured them. The King's Harbour Master was furious. We called the little boat *Ratty*, after him.

The *Weazel* went through the Italian campaign and was never touched by anything more lethal than a large piece of shrapnel that fell on the deck one night, grazing her topsides and missing my head by inches. The *Ratty* hung in her davits at the break of the fo'c'sle-head just under the wing of the bridge where I could keep an eye on her. As the *Weazel* moved from job to job on her way to the Pacific I sailed the *Ratty* in every port we went to in the Mediterranean – Tunis, Tripoli,

Bizerta, the Grand Harbour of Malta, Tobruk, Alexandria, Haifa, and then in Port Said. Once through the Suez Canal I sailed her in Massawa in the Red Sea, Aden and then in Cochin in Southern India. Finally I sailed her in Trincomalee harbour, the naval base for the Eastern Fleet on the east coast of Ceylon. She was an object of envy wherever she was seen, particularly in Trincomalee where there was little in the way of diversion. When I had no work I sailed her round the anchorage, in and out among battleships, aircraft-carriers, cruisers, destroyers and up the tropical creeks and inlets all around this harbour, probably the most extensive and beautiful natural harbour in the world.

The spectacle of the battle fleet was something that will never be seen again but Trinco wasn't an enlivening place for a young sailor. There were no bars, no pretty girls except the dignified and beautiful Sinhalese and Tamil girls, who to us were like girls in a glass showcase, unattainable. The Officers' Club was a dreary place as was the ratings' canteen. The *Weazel* was used to tow targets for the Eastern Fleet off Trinco harbour. The target was a lattice structure on a steel hull, 80 feet long and about 40 feet high. We towed it on a set course some twenty miles out into the Bay of Bengal. The battleships could sometimes be seen as tiny dots on the horizon. We could see the flashes of the 16 inch guns, then we would see columns of water leaping up from around the target and then hear the whine and the boom of the huge shells; we would feel the air shake. Sometimes the shells fell alarmingly close to us.

It was a target that wrecked the *Ratty*. The little boat had transformed my span of service from a drudge to something better than bearable. The harbour of Trincomalee was a labyrinth of coves and bays, the fresh monsoon driving across calm water, the bright flashes of strange birds. I lost the *Ratty* through carelessness. I hauled her up on her davits one afternoon when I had been sailing and left her without swinging the davits inboard, so that she was hanging over the water, out from the ship's side and ready to launch again. One of the harbour tugs brought a target alongside for us to take

Santa Lucia

Transcur

Girl Stella

to sea the next morning. The forward span of the target caught the *Ratty* and smashed her. When I came running up she was all crushed to matchwood, hanging from the falls like a shredded garment. It was fifteen years before I could scrape together the money to buy another boat.

Santa Lucia was a real little ship. She was built, or perhaps devised would be a better word, by an old shipwright in Walton, on the east coast of England. He had taken the hull of a ship's lifeboat, chopped off her ends and built on a new bow and a new stern. He gave her a finely proportioned clipper bow and a counter stern with a pretty lift to it so that she had a graceful sheer from forward to aft. She was a real picture, only 18 feet long on the waterline but with her overhangs she looked bigger. She was a gaffer with a long bowsprit. I sailed her to Spain, direct from Salcombe to Santander, a distance of nearly 600 miles.

My next boat was called *Transcur,* I have never discovered what it means. She was an old Essex smack built in 1911 and converted to a yacht in the 1950s. She was built in Brightlingsea at Aldous's yard. A previous owner gave her a new mast and a Bermudian mains'l, spoiling her rig. She still sailed well but not as well as the traditional smacks. She wasn't a classic boat because of her rig but nobody cared much about classic boats in those days. I improved her over the years. I took out the iron ballast and replaced it with lead, making her stiffer and quicker on the helm and giving her an extra 8 inches of headroom. I shortened her counter, cutting out a lot of rot and enhancing her good looks. Good looks and good performance usually go together.

It was a steady progression from one boat to the next. They got bigger as they went along but not much more expensive until I arrived at *Girl Stella.* She had been neglected. I bought her cheap but spent money on her before she was ready for ocean sailing . She was big; an old gaff ketch built in 1896. In her youth she had been a fisherman, a Looe lugger with her mainmast well forward and a small mizzen sheeted to an outrigger. She had been converted to a yacht in the 1930s; 40

feet long and 24 tons, she was the epitome of the classic yacht. There are few comparable yachts afloat now that come near her in terms of real classicism and performance. She looked like a print from the 1890s come to life; a gaff ketch with tops'ls on main and mizzen. In a breeze of wind she would run away from them all.

In retrospect I understand that I overreached myself in buying her. If she had not been wrecked in the Azores she would have broken me. She had an appetite for money which I could never have satisfied without spending my whole life in the pursuit of it. I would never have started sailing by myself if I had not lost *Girl Stella*; I would never have explored the strange ground of introspective self-analysis that comes with solitude.

In the weeks and months of solitude after I bought *Iskra* and sailed her alone across the ocean, I began to understand that the business of amassing wealth is a shallow occupation to engage the best part of a life. My childhood experience of poverty and the poverty I passed through after the war convinced me that it is a state of existence to be avoided at almost any cost. I agree with Bernard Shaw that poverty is a crime, not an individual crime perhaps but a crime society permits against the less fortunate, or weaker of its members. Great wealth is an equal crime, also sanctioned, even acclaimed by society. The secret of life is to position yourself somewhere between the two. To make modest demands on life is to strive modestly to achieve them, thus leaving time and energy for better things. The problem is to know where the optimum level lies.

I found the right boat for myself in *Iskra*, by luck rather than wise choice. I didn't realise until some time after I bought her that she was a jewel among cruising boats. It was a long time before her qualities made themselves clear to me, like a man buying a picture because it suits the wallpaper and finding himself with a masterpiece. I had to have a boat, any boat. I got an *Iskra*. I have never wanted to part with her, I wouldn't exchange her for any other boat. I don't know how many thousands of miles I have sailed in her backwards and forwards across the Atlantic Ocean and round Norway and Iceland and France and Spain. She is exactly right for me and for Wendy. She has insinuated herself into Wendy's affections just as she did into mine.

Iskra isn't grand; she excites no envy, only admiration. She isn't too big, Wendy and I can manage her without relying on the favour of a crew. She isn't too small – we live aboard her in solid comfort. She slides into the great swells and furrows and troughs of the ocean when it is in an angry mood like a sea bird. She is warm and comforting, always a pleasure to come back to, having the charm and simple peace of a well loved and well worn home. We know that she will always give of her best when we ask too much of her, always bring us safely home as long as we grant her the care she deserves.

I found Wendy by luck as well; I doubt whether anything I have ever done, or said, or thought, deserved me of such a break. The association between us came out of a welter of frustration and confusion and unhappiness; it matured into

We know that she will always give of her best

91

something of value for us both. Wendy edged in on my partnership with *Iskra*, happily slotting into our quirks and eccentricities and we into hers so as to make a viable trio. The dolphin figurehead tucked under *Iskra*'s bow is now as much loved by Wendy as by me. He owes his allegiance to us both.

Wendy suffers seasickness. She turns pale green and retches into a bucket. I think she is going to die. Sometimes it takes her three days to recover. She lies in her bunk with the canvas bunk-board fast, to stop her from falling out, a plastic bucket hooked over the brass wing-nut that holds the lid of the cabin stove and is miserable. She sleeps for hours – I have to look at her every now and then to reassure myself that she is still alive. Anything she has to eat or drink comes straight up, sometimes she becomes dehydrated. She isn't sick when we are at anchor in a harbour, however *Iskra* may roll in the swell, but as soon as we put our noses outside it starts, even if the sea is calm. From this one might assume that she is frightened of the ocean but she does not appear to be any more or less frightened than I am. If things get suddenly bad and I need help, she will get up and do what is required of her with the utmost calm and then go back and continue to be sick.

I once had *Iskra* in Boston and Wendy flew out from England to spend a long weekend with me. After the weekend she was to go to a conference in Los Angeles. A man I met loaned me a mooring in the harbour; we always prefer lying off to being in a yacht marina. The day she arrived a big swell set in from seaward and *Iskra* rolled her scuppers under on the mooring. I thought the weekend would be a disaster but Wendy never noticed the rolling and it was bliss. A few weeks later we sailed out of Lunenburg in Nova Scotia and ran into a swell. She retired at once. Then the gaff broke and I needed her help. She came on deck, forgetting about the seasickness until the job was done.

At first I thought we would never be able to make sailing voyages together but over the years she has come to terms with it. At first we tried the usual palliatives; they were useless. The drugs were the worst; Stugeron caused her to have vertigo, she nearly fell overboard. Capsules behind her ear made her really ill, with stomach ache and dizziness. Someone in the Canary Islands gave her some white pills based on tobacco, which he claimed was a homoeopathic remedy but this was another failure. We bought coca leaves in the market in Salta in the north of Argentina. I boiled them up with water, like tea and gave them to her. They were quite good – they put her to sleep and when she woke she seemed better and had no after effects. In the Andes they use coca leaves for altitude sickness – after a time they went mouldy and we couldn't use them.

Next we thought that acupuncture bracelets, or sea bands, were the answer. They worked well when we were round the English coast but their effect seemed to lessen as Wendy continued to use them. They are still better than anything else we have tried and she always puts them on before we go outside the harbour. Now, as soon as she feels ill she lies down and goes to sleep. When she wakes I give her a honey and ginger drink – two dessertspoonfuls of honey in boiling water with a slug of ground ginger. It almost always stays down and it stops the dehydration. After a day, or even half a day now, I give her a lightly boiled egg with a thin slice of bread and butter. If this stays down, which it usually does, the seasickness is beaten – *Iskra* can loop the loop for all she cares. My own diet is greatly enlivened by Wendy's malady. I have full run of the store lockers and am able to fill myself with curried tuna and eel stew, octopus and squid in chilli sauce.

Over the years Wendy listened as I tried to paint her a picture of life in *Iskra* in the ocean; the peace, the freedom, the quietude, the sudden lifting of everyday worries, the infinite space, the awesome beauty of the sea and the sky, the community of birds and fishes and sea creatures, the easy comradeship of other sailors, the happy landfalls, exotic places, the adventure of it, the cleansing of the soul. I may not have told her the other side of the coin in such detail, not because I set out to deceive her, to persuade her against her judgement, but because the consciousness of a lone sailor is so constructed that the unpleasantries fly out of his mind.

Although he knows they lurk in the dark recesses of his memory he discounts them. The gales and the driving spray, the crashing seas, the cold and wet, the dangerous lee shores, are only there to throw into relief their opposites. After all, our judgements are only governed by a comparison of opposites. If there were no thieves, there would be no honest men.

Wendy herself was torn wide apart by the prospect of an ocean voyage. Part of her was frightened, frightened of the unknown ocean, frightened of being frightened. She didn't know that she could ever overcome her seasickness, she didn't know that she wouldn't retch herself to death, become so weak that the terror of the storm would finish her. She knew she was vulnerable because she had come to the sea late in life so that the ocean's moods were not incorporated in her understanding. She had not developed the facility to gauge danger at sea and to know instinctively where is the dividing line between what is safe and what is not. She wondered how she would sustain herself with none of the diverse company she was used to.

Above all, Wendy was frightened and still is frightened of the consequences to her of an accident to me. Suppose I was swept overboard, how would she ever get back? Suppose I was injured, how would she look after me and look after *Iskra* at the same time? Suppose she was left alone in the ocean, hundreds of miles from safety, how would she bring *Iskra* to land? *Iskra* is too heavy for her. Wendy isn't strong enough to hoist the mains'l in half a gale of wind, she wouldn't know how to reef, put up storm sails, to handle the gear, to navigate accurately. It was one thing to sail around the coast where help is close at hand, but the ocean? Mile upon mile of empty space with no succour within sight or sound or imagining? On the other hand, overridingly perhaps, she wanted to do what I wanted to do, to be part of my life so that it was no longer my life but our life. She has learnt a lot since we started sailing together; so have I.

It was all decided for us, inevitably I suppose, when my

cousin Clive, Marta his wife and two or three of their flock of children arrived one day in the bungalow in Maldon. I had only ever seen Clive once or twice since he was young, some time about twenty-five years ago. I knew his brother Julian better from when he was at school in England and worked at my office in London. I liked him. He was a quiet boy but pleasant. Their existence hadn't entered my thoughts for years, I had almost forgotten about Argentina, life had led me in other directions. I had always kept up my Spanish, had even improved it since my visits to Buenos Aires during the war. I had been to Spain in all the boats I ever owned and when *Iskra* was in Cuba I had spoken nothing but Spanish for months on end. I had even been in love in Spanish; there is no better way to learn a language than to be in love in it.

Clive and Marta and their family all speak English. Marta is an English teacher in Buenos Aires. Clive, a confirmed anglophile, has lived most of his life in Argentina. They stayed in Maldon for a couple of days and got to know us. Clive told me that Guillermo was still there, in Napaleofú – he didn't know what had happened to Andrea. He remembered that she had looked after him as a child, after Freda died. Now Clive and Marta live in the *estancia* house and have another house in Buenos Aires, where Clive's business is, where the children go to school and where Marta does her teaching.

Before they left Marta said, 'Would you like to come to stay with us in Argentina?' I thought for a moment, or perhaps half a minute, glanced at Wendy and I knew what was racing through her mind and she knew what was racing through my mind. There is an unspoken language used by people who know one another very well; the flicker of an expression, the blink of a darted glance, the sudden creasing of lines round the mouth and forehead, the tilt of an eyebrow. 'We'd love to come,' I said, 'Then it's settled,' Marta said, 'Tell us when.' I thought again, 'On March the first next year.' I took the date out of my head without giving it too much thought, but I knew that seven or eight months at a leisurely pace would take *Iskra* to Argentina. Marta believed we were coming in an aeroplane.

We showed her *Iskra* while she was in Maldon but she didn't think anyone could seriously consider a voyage to Argentina in such a vessel. 'We'll look forward to seeing you on 1 March next year,' she said.

We started with our preparations at once; there was no time to lose. We had to get *Iskra* ready for the longest voyage she had ever made; in all her travels she had never been south of the equator, neither had Wendy. We decided to leave in early July, giving ourselves plenty of time to sail down-channel from Maldon and leave Falmouth for Spain at the end of the month or in early August. We reckoned to get fine, summer weather all the way to Spain and have time to spend in the Spanish Rías before setting out for Madeira and the Canaries with the last of the Portuguese trade winds behind us. It was to be a leisurely cruise, no hurrying, there was plenty of time.

We planned to spend three months in Argentina, March, April and May, which would be quite enough. Clive and Marta would be tired of us by then anyway. However high in affection and esteem a guest may be, his level of welcome declines with passing time in a downward graph, steepening as the weeks pass. It's better to go home before the graph runs off the paper. If we left Argentina for home in June we should be able to cover the enormous distance, some 2,500 miles, between the River Plate and the corner of the continent by the middle of August. We could then sail home in time to miss the worst of the winter storms, making the whole voyage in just over a year. The plan involved a long sea passage, from Fernando Noronha to the Azores. It was an ambitious itinerary; too ambitious as it turned out.

Argentina was in everyone's bad books since the Falklands War of 1982, or the Malvinas War as the people of South America call it. It had been a singularly unpleasant and unnecessary war brought about by the arrogance and ambition of soldiers and politicians. Britain's claim to the Malvinas was always tenuous, the Argentine case almost as fragile. When the British left the islands after a brief occupation, in May 1774, they made no move to return for sixty years, during which time

Argentina became an independent republic, assuming sovereignty over the islands, which was not at the time disputed. An Argentine Governor was appointed in 1840 and a colony founded, with ninety colonists who set up a fishing industry and imported livestock from Argentina. It might have gone on indefinitely, nullifying the islands' subsequent history, if the Governor, one Louis Vernet had not arrested three American schooners for poaching seals near the islands. The Americans sent a warship at once, the *Lexington*, which broke up the colony, took prisoners and smashed the settlement the colonists had constructed. There followed a period of confusion when the islands were shuffled between France, England and on one occasion, Spain. They were used for a time as an Argentine penal colony. One fine day in January 1853 the British sloop *Hans Clio* sailed in and took control of the islands, overran the garrison, hauled down the Argentine flag and hoisted the Union Jack, shipping the inhabitants back to Argentina. The argument about sovereignty has smouldered on ever since and still smoulders. One fact in the maze of conflicting interests and assertions is that the Malvinas lie 300 miles off the coast of Argentina and 6,000 off the coast of Great Britain.

Before the war the islanders lived happily enough alongside Argentina. Their children went to school in Argentina, they went to Argentina for their holidays, if they were ill they were treated in the British hospital in Buenos Aires. The bottled gas for their cooking stoves came from Argentina, the only fresh fruit they had came from Argentina. A ship, or a fishing boat carrying passengers left Port Stanley every week for the mainland. Now everything the islanders need comes from the other end of the world. Now they must dig peat for their fires, there is no fresh fruit, no holidays in the soft climate of Mendoza or on the beaches of Mar del Plata. Like most wars, it was fought for nothing. At the end of it when the dead were counted and the flag-waving had died down, the original causes of it were still intact.

There is a term still used in Argentina, a hangover from

the past perhaps but still valid, '*palabra Inglés*' – an Englishman's word. People used to say it when they really meant to do what they had promised to do. The day the Argentine cruiser *Belgrano* was torpedoed by the submarine *Conqueror*, *palabra Inglés* was sunk for ever. The British had imposed a 200-mile Total Exclusion Zone; any vessel inside it, Argentina was warned, was liable to be attacked. The *Belgrano* was outside the zone by at least forty miles. The *Conqueror* sent out no warning signal, no challenge. Like the *Celtic Star*, the torpedoes came out of nowhere with no warning. Unlike the *Celtic Star*, the *Belgrano* was in the freezing waters of the South Atlantic. She sank in less than an hour. Three hundred and sixty-eight of her crew perished.

Wendy and I spent the summer preparing for our voyage. *Iskra* is very old – she was built in 1930. She is, in years, as well as in her rig and her appearance, a classic boat, more suited, many people believe, to sailing around the coasts and estuaries near to her home than to voyaging across oceans. But she is the only boat we have and are ever likely to have. If we were ever to visit Argentina *Iskra* would have to take us. The truth is, she has spoilt us. We both enjoy living in her and we know that if we were to go abroad without her, we would soon get tired of the cheap pensions and crummy eating places we would be able to patronise.

It is cheap to travel abroad in *Iskra*; she is basic in her requirements. No big sums of money are needed to equip her for a voyage, she has no expensive electronic systems; my old sextant, a book of tables and the Nautical Almanac are all I need. We eat, of course, which we are in the habit of doing whether we are on a voyage or not. We don't need smart clothes, we don't need to carry luggage about with us, packing it up and unpacking it and hauling it in and out of taxis or trains or ships or aeroplanes every other day, we don't pay fares, we don't stay in hotels. In *Iskra* we find ourselves quartered in the centre of town for free, except occasionally when some modest harbour dues are asked for. We can always accept hospitality from people we meet in the knowledge that we can return it on board. We always have our own bed to sleep in, our own food, our own creature comforts whether we are in Reykjavik or Rio Grande do Sul. We cause as little inconvenience to others as possible, we pollute nothing, we fend for ourselves. We live free, we borrow the wind, use it to our advantage and return it intact.

VII

Bad Beginnings

A voyage in a small boat is an entity in itself, quite separate from everything that goes before it or comes after it. It has a beginning, a middle and an end, and when it is over it can be stored away on the high shelf of memory to be referred to as convenient. It can be taken down occasionally, looked at and put back. It can be titivated by the imagination, bits added here and there to make it better, others taken away and put to one side. It can be dramatised or glamorised, made fearful or made tedious. Make of it what you will, the voyage is still there, carving a niche for itself in your experience so that your thoughts and attitudes are always coloured by it. Once you have it, whatever happens, no one can ever take it from you.

There may be voyages whose passage is so smooth and well grooved that the experience leaves little imprint. Most voyages pass through the whole range of experience from electric excitement to commonplace, from the beautiful to the odious, sublime happiness to misery. The charm of the business lies in the sudden jolt from the easy plateau of normal life to the uncertainties of sailing across an ocean. A voyage that starts badly may end well because the actors in the drama develop wisdom or are lucky. One that starts well may end badly because the same actors are given false confidence. Any voyage can be cut off in its course and finished for all time by an unpredictable blow from the gods. Wendy's and my voyage started badly.

From the Downs boatyard in Maldon, where *Iskra* lay against a wooden staging, we can see our bungalow across the saltings. We were carrying the last of the stores on board, half a dozen boxes of tins from the supermarket. It had been raining, the grass on the slope from the road to the Downs was slippery, I went with the first box and was putting the tins away in the locker when a thought came to me – 'She's wearing those shoes with silly heels, she could easily slip . . . .' I came off the boat quickly, ran along the staging. She was just leaving the house, I saw her through the trees, a heavy box of tins in her arms. I saw it happen, almost as if my premonition had been a trap for her to fall into. As she came down the slope her feet went away from her, she fell on the ground in a scramble of tins and jars – tuna, beans, spaghetti, soup, sardines, pickles, gherkins, fish paste. She broke her ankle. Being a nurse, she stayed still on the ground until I came up. 'I think I've broken something.' I ran into our boat shed, found *Iskra*'s old pipe-cot from the fo'c'sle. A passing friend helped me carry her inside. The doctor confirmed it. I took her to the hospital and they put her leg in plaster. It was the end of a beginning; it put us back a month.

The next misfortune carried no premonition. We were leaving the same staging a few weeks later, Wendy sitting in the cockpit with her plastered foot on the seat in front of her. We were taking *Iskra* down the river to her mooring in Bradwell, some eight miles from Maldon. It was a lovely day, a light breeze, *Iskra* chugged down the river under her engine, past the Queen's Head and the Jolly Sailor where the Thames barges lie to the town quay, their tall masts a tracery of wire and rope and tanned sails against the old tower of St Mary's church, Cook's boat-building yard close beside, a few smacks at moorings along the river bank. It is a happy scene, one that goes back over the years with little change. In the public bar of the Queen's Head there are pictures that show the scene in the 1850s and before. It was much as it is now. We reckon ourselves privileged to live in such a place.

Another yacht was ahead of *Iskra*, slightly to one side of the narrow channel but converging – she hadn't seen us. I shouted a friendly warning, the skipper, on the foredeck coiling down a halyard, looked up, gave a wave and shouted to a young girl on the tiller. She put the helm hard over the wrong way. The yacht's bow swung round and she came straight toward *Iskra*.

She hit the topsides with the steel fitting on her stem. There was a splintering of wood, a confusion of shouts, recriminations, swear-words. *Iskra* limped back to the yard with a broken top strake. Another beginning ended. It put us back another two weeks. A friend said to us, 'Frank, give it up – can't you see you're not meant to go?'

Wendy's ankle mended quickly. Even before the plaster was off I was able to lever her on board where she could supervise the stowage of gear and stores to her liking. I put her through a fierce regime of exercises and swimming and any therapy that came to hand. We even conscripted the services of a faith healer, not, it must be said, with any immediate result. The estate agent up the road let our house to a young couple we thought would be excellent tenants. They came to supper and we showed them where everything was, explained that we would put our valuables in the loft, out of their way. The girl said she would water Wendy's plants, look after the garden. She was fond of gardening, she said. The young man told us he had a small builder's business. He had bought a plot of land nearby and was going to build his own house. They wanted to rent our bungalow until they could move in. They were just the kind of young couple it would be nice to help, we thought. They liked the position of our bungalow, they thought it would do them very nicely. We were not to worry – they would look after everything as if it were their own. We were delighted.

The time came nearer for us to go. We had made all the preparations, done everything we could think of to make smooth our absence. True, we had not spent much time sailing the boat to get ourselves accustomed to her ways after the winter lay-up. She had not been fitted out the previous season, we had hardly sailed her through the preparations for leaving. Never mind, we would soon be getting plenty of practice. I forgot about my dictum, that it is folly to embark on a voyage, fresh from the winter's lay-up, without first sailing around familiar waters for a week or so to loosen rusty senses, sharpen perception, limber up the brain and flex the body for a voyage.

We were exhausted by the time the day came for us to leave. We were now very late in starting; it was 1 August 1987; we had wanted to start in May to catch the fine weather across the Bay of Biscay and to pick up the last of the Portuguese trades to take us to Madeira. As it was, we might be lucky with the weather and we might not. I don't like leaving things to chance on these voyages – on Wendy's first exposure to the ocean I didn't want to run into bad weather. At least it was fine enough the day we started. We sailed the five or six miles from our mooring in Bradwell across to Pyefleet, an anchorage round behind Mersea Island from where we could leave with the tide the next morning on the first hurdle of our voyage – across the Thames estuary.

Iskra was heavy with a full load of stores, full water tanks, full fuel tanks and all the extra gear necessary for a long voyage; awnings for the tropics, an extra anchor, spare sails we didn't normally carry. All the space under the bunks in the cabin was filled with tins and bottles and packets, carefully purchased by Wendy, their quantities and positions entered in a small brown notebook. We had bought charts for the coast of Africa and for the eastern side of the continent of South America from Cape Horn to the Caribbean. I already had the charts for Spain, the West Indies and the east coast of North America. I brought them for good measure in case we changed our plans.

Iskra's gear was in good order. I had spare wires and spare ropes on board and all the equipment needed to improvise repairs. One of the virtues of an old boat, like an old car perhaps, is that when things break it is usually possible, with some imagination and some inventive skill, to devise a makeshift repair. I had lengths of chain and lengths of wire and bulldog grips and all manner of rigging screws and shackles and thimbles and grommets all hung round the fo'c'sle bulkheads. I had sheets of copper and sheets of lead and copper fastenings, caulking cotton, bags of sand and cement, the towing hawser I had for the schooner *Integrity* years ago, clamps, vices, cold chisels, bolts, nuts, screws, odd pieces of stainless steel, canvas, terylene. *Iskra* was down to her marks. Our dolphin was newly painted, a wide grin spread over his chubby face in happy expectation of the ocean.

Wendy had accomplished a feat of compression. Her clothes for the whole voyage were on two shelves in the lavatory, carefully wrapped in polythene against deck leaks. As a concession she wrung out of me a small shelf in the hanging locker opposite, hanging in name alone because there is now a bilge pump in way of the single hook that gave the locker its name. She had a gas iron so that she could be turned out in pristine condition for dinner-parties or visits to the opera and she had three folding hangers, another concession. A small mirror in a plastic frame with a special hook to position it on one of the cabin portholes was added to *Iskra*'s amenities, a special hole was made in the lavatory shelf to accommodate her toothbrush. The ultimate concession which hurt me hard, allowed her to bring a hot-water bottle and an umbrella, without which, she said, she would refuse to come. Her foot had been out of plaster for just four weeks. When she was tired it was still painful to her but it was better in the boat than ashore because there wasn't much walking and she could put it up on the settee or on the cockpit seat. She had finished with the crutches but we bought her a folding-walking stick.

A gentle breeze propelled us across the River Blackwater into the Colne and to a quiet anchorage in Pyefleet. The sun set with a tinge of yellow lurking under low cloud across the horizon. It didn't look specially good, but it didn't look specially bad. The forecast was good, there was a gentle north-west breeze. The darkness came round us as we lay at anchor. There was no other boat in the anchorage, no other person. From the saltings up Pyefleet the gulls and terns set up their evening sibilation; close by, the hollow call of a heron echoed round the anchorage. *Iskra*'s riding-light fixed her in a yellow pool, faintly flickering as the breeze eddied round the lamp, her portholes sending shafts of brightness into the opaque night. We ate our supper in silence, sat in the cockpit, mugs of coffee cupped in our hands. We could hear the plop and gurgle as the ebb tide slid down the mud.

'Are we really going to South America? – It's ever such a long way.' I said, 'We'll try.' We looked round at our boat, all of 30 feet long, a fraction short of 10 feet wide, her wooden planks 1 inch thick. She looked frail and small. It was hard to believe it. How could she take us all those thousands of miles across half the world? Surely it was a conceit, a dream that had somehow inflated itself into reality. 'I don't know how she can do it,' I said, 'All I know is that she has done it before – not quite so far perhaps, but no more in principle. I have never known how she does it.' Wendy said, 'It's a lot further than Ipswich.' She judges all sailing voyages in terms of the distance between Bradwell and Ipswich. We often go there for a weekend jaunt, a shopping spree or the theatre. 'It's only four hundred and seven times as far,' I said. She was encouraged.

The day broke grey and brittle with the same light north-westerly wind, the same favourable forecast, the barometer down a little. 'The wind's still fair,' I said, 'We'll go.' I hauled up the anchor, Wendy stowed chain in the locker as it came in over the gypsy. We set the mains'l, the stays'l, unrolled the jib. On the way down the river we had breakfast. We sailed out through the Spitway, the wind freshening, a light mist cutting visibility to less than a mile. Very quickly the weather began to look nasty.

I have sailed across the Thames estuary dozens of times through the years. It is a kind of Rubicon, to be crossed before and after every voyage through the English Channel. The sandbanks fan out like the branches of a rugged tree, the swatchways between swept by the ebb and flow of the tide so that the boat makes a crab-wise course, difficult to calculate or estimate accurately. *Iskra* bumped across hard sand within yards of the Barrow Beacon – my chart was out of date, the sand had closed a gap I had always used. She came clear of it quickly but the wind was freshening again and backing, the visibility shutting in. 'I'll have to reef her.'

Wendy came and sat at the tiller with her foot up on the cockpit seat, I gave her the course, scrambled to the halyards and began to reef the mains'l – pick up the topping lift, lower throat and peak, heave home the reef pendant, fasten the forward cringle, tie in the points, square up and coil down. It took a quarter of an hour. It was thick when I came back to the cockpit. 'I can see nothing,' Wendy said, 'A ship went past a few minutes ago.' I peered into the murk, *Iskra* rushing through the water, easier now with the reefs in but sailing fast with the wind on her quarter. We ought to have seen the No. 9 Barrow to starboard but there was no sign of it. The No. 8 should be ahead, slightly to port. I could see nothing. I went below to check the chart. As I switched on the echo-sounder she hit the sand with a crunch, slewed round and keeled over on her side. Wendy was thrown off the cockpit seat, I lost my balance and fell against the galley stove.

In seconds our ordered world was pitched into chaos, sails flapping, spray lashing across the deck as the vicious estuary waves crashed against *Iskra*'s side, almanac, chart dividers, parallel rulers flying off the chart table to the lee side, *Iskra* picking herself up and banging herself on the hard sand so that she must break soon, 'Are you all right?' I shouted. 'Your foot – is it all right?' 'Yes – I'm OK.' I crawled along the sloping deck to the halyards, lowered the mains'l. It lay half in the water on the lee side. I threw the anchor out, hauled down the stays'l. 'Roll up the jib.' Wendy hauled on the tripping line and the sail rolled itself away.

Iskra was helpless and in danger with the sails lying all over the deck, ropes trailing overboard in confusion. She banged on the sand with sickening jolts that shook every frame and fastening. Her head began to swing to the anchor. 'Start the engine,' I shouted. The engine is always left in gear. It always starts at the first push of the button, but the order was given without proper thought – would never have been given if it had not been our first sail of the season, if I had used my head. Wendy reached her hand into the cabin where the switchboard is, felt for the starter button and pressed it. The engine gave a cough and a splutter and then came to life. *Iskra*'s head began to turn away from the sand, I began to take in slack on the anchor. 'She's coming,' I shouted. Then the engine stopped – a stray rope with twenty turns round the propeller. Her head fell to leeward. The banging started again.

The rope that fouled the propeller was one of the vangs that run from the end of the gaff to the boom. As the propeller wound the turns round itself the vang pulled the gaff down into the sea. The peak halyard had been left loose and as the sail was pulled down the bare end snaked up the mast out of reach. Now we were aground on a lee shore in a rising wind, unable to hoist the mains'l or use the engine. There was no possibility of getting her off unless the wind dropped and the tide came up enough to float her. In the meantime, she would break herself to pieces. I said 'I'll have to go overboard and clear it.' Wendy looked at the sea breaking against *Iskra*, the brown estuary water swirling round her stern, the bleak seascape. Our boat, this ordered, logical machine was now a heap of confusion. 'Oh my God,' she said.

I took my clothes off, she fetched my mask from the cabin. The water was cold, I could hardly see the propeller but I could

I could hardly see the propeller but I could feel it

107

feel it. I began to cut at the turns with my knife, every time the boat lifted and fell I banged my head against her side until I was nearly senseless. The rope was wound tightly round. The knife made little impression. I had to rest and draw breath after a minute. 'Try this,' Wendy shouted and passed me the bread knife. It was better. I got half the turns off, cut the ends of the rope. I worked for ten minutes I suppose and then I was cold. 'Come in,' she shouted again, 'You can't go on – leave it.' I cut one more turn and then the stern lifted and crashed down on the sand – my foot was an inch away from the keel. I got scared. 'OK.'

I climbed back, shivering, half with cold, half with fright. Wendy made me drink brandy. The spirit flushed through my body. I gave a prolonged, involuntary shudder – my strength came back, at least temporarily. The end of the halyard was waving in the wind half-way up the mast. I climbed up on to the sidelight screen but it was still just out of my reach. I was too weak to climb the shrouds after the months of winter idleness. Wendy came to the pitching, shaking foredeck. I fastened a spare halyard round my waist, took the other end to the winch and Wendy helped pull. I went up the mast inch by painful inch, the rope cutting into my back, cutting into Wendy's hands until I touched the end of the halyard and then grabbed a hold. It was all tangled round but by luck it came free and I dropped with it to the deck. 'We've got a sail,' I muttered, 'We might have an engine.'

The tide was flooding now but *Iskra* was being driven back on to the sand by the wind and the run of the seas, her bow held up to the wind by the anchor. Wendy cleared the ropes away from round the stern. I half hoisted the mains'l until it had wind in it, 'All right – try again – start her.' This was the last chance. If it failed we would be calling for the lifeboat. She pressed the button again. The engine fired again, coughed again, spluttered again and then it ran, its sweet tune raising our hearts. I hove the anchor and *Iskra* began to move ahead. In a moment she was afloat, 'Break out the jib' – she began to sail. The bilge water was over the cabin floor.

By one of those unlooked-for dispensations, as if the gods had admonished us, shaken a finger of warning at us, reproached us, given us a serious caution, they relented their anger and yielded to compassion. The wind unexpectedly eased, the mist cleared showing us the No. 8 Barrow buoy close ahead. We must have passed no more than a few yards from it and hit the very tip of the Sunk Sand. We soon picked up the Knock John, the Tizzard Bank and the buoys of the North Edinburgh channel through the sands. I was able to get warm and dry and dressed while Wendy steered *Iskra* from buoy to buoy, the wind now a sunny breeze on our quarter. We picked up the North Foreland and shaped our course for Ramsgate. I glanced at Wendy, half expecting to see disenchantment, distaste in her expression. There was none, only concern and relief.

The alarms and near scrapes we pick up in the course of sailing must have left a tough skin over Wendy's spirit. They seem to leave us much as we were before – a little contrite perhaps and aware yet again that disasters and near-disasters are brought about only by our own lack of care and concentration. If we had been calmer, less hurried, more prudent before we started, we would have been spared this one. As it was we were unscathed, for which we offered a small hymn of thanks. But *Iskra* was hurt – she was leaking.

At first she leaked quite badly so that I was pumping her every half hour; not a lot of water but enough to suggest that if conditions got bad, she would leak more. As time went on she began to take up. I was convinced that she had sprung one of the garboards, the planks that run right through the length of the boat beside the keel, but I could see no water coming in from the inside. When she sailed hard to windward she leaked more. 'We'll have to get it done before we go over any ocean,' I said. *Iskra* had always leaked a little – most old wooden boats do, it's something I have always lived with. Some leak a lot and contrive to do so for year on year without anyone being able to find where the water comes in. *Iskra* is particularly difficult in this respect because she is sheathed in copper. This is a wonderful protection for the hull but it complicates any real investigation of the bottom because if there is a leak, the water will run along inside the copper before it comes in or out of her. Consequently, if you see a dribble coming out of the hull when she is hauled out of the water there is no telling from which spot it is actually coming. We determined to have her slipped before we left England.

We went to a dozen yards along the south coast. At home in Maldon I know of at least five shipwrights, any one of whom I would have entrusted with work on *Iskra*'s hull but the south coast, once the mecca of wooden boat-building, is now a wilderness of plastic. There were some yards who told us their shipwrights were on holiday, others who for one reason or another could not take on work 'just at the moment,' others in which I had no confidence. I almost contracted to have her slipped in a famous yard in the West Country but when I went and looked at the work that was being done and the state of confusion and disorder in the yard, I changed my mind. I could envisage her being pulled to pieces in a random, haphazard way on some hunch about the source of the leak and ending in the same state when she was put back in the water. We sailed all the way to Falmouth without finding a yard that could or would do the work and that we trusted. By this time the leak seemed almost to have stopped, at least when she was quiet in harbour. 'We'll go across the Bay and try in Spain.'

In truth we had little alternative; having let our house we had nowhere to go. The voyage round the coast was slow, with fickle, light winds alternating with hard blows from the south-west. If we had started a month earlier we would have had brisk northerly and easterly winds; the passage to Falmouth would have been over in a week. As it was, it wasn't unpleasant creeping down the coast, sometimes becalmed for days, sometimes sheltering from hard westerlies. We met friends, who delayed us, and spent fruitless days trying to find a yard to mend the leak. South America began to look further and further away. We put *Iskra* against the quay wall on the concrete slip in Falmouth, poked about underneath her while

110

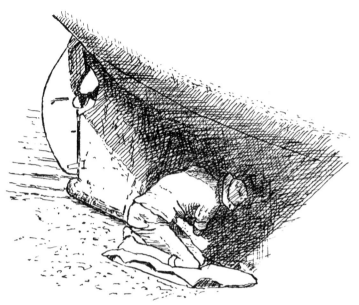

*... poked about underneath her
while the tide was out*

the tide was out, stuck in various concoctions of patent gunge
and gave her a coat of paint. It made very little difference.

We waited in Falmouth for the wind to shift out of the
south, as sailing vessels have done for hundreds of years. We
never told anyone of our plans; as the days and weeks passed
they began to look more and more unreal, we didn't want to
invite ridicule. The project begins to seem ridiculous when
you look with an impartial eye at the size of the boat, at her
speed, something approaching the pace of a queue for fish and
chips and at the vast tract of ocean to be crossed. Sometimes
when the wind howls round the chimney at home and rattles
the halyards of the yachts in the yard across the road, we
wonder how *Iskra* can survive for five minutes.

When our own puny strength is considered against the
forces of the ocean, when our frail contrivance of wood and
rope and wire is set against the fury of the sea, the voyage looks
like a fantasy. On our walks across the low hills outside
Falmouth, Wendy still with her folding stick, we would catch

fleeting glimpses of the horizon, an infinity away, retreating further from us as fast as we sail to catch it, an illusion always to be pursued, never to be captured. It makes me frightened every time I see it at the beginning of a voyage; I never admitted fear to Wendy and never really considered whether she was not as frightened as I. She *was* as frightened – more frightened. I didn't know then, or didn't wish to discover it perhaps, but now I do know because she confessed it to her log, which I never saw until the voyage was over.

One day the wind changed, the barometer began slowly to rise. 'This is it,' I said to her, 'Are you ready?' 'Yes – we are ready to go.' A fleeting look of apprehension came across her pale blue eyes. It was gone in an instant.

VIII

Spain

The north and west coasts are the unsophisticated, unfashionable parts of Spain. There isn't much of a tourist industry, the sun cannot be guaranteed to blaze for all and every day, there are no yacht marinas, few night clubs, the cars are older and slower, there are no more ghetto-blasters than you could shake a stick at. From La Coruña to the north round Cape Ortegal and Cabo de Bares to Ribadeo is the wildest coast in all Europe, perhaps the wildest anywhere. The massive rock capes jut out into the Atlantic and the Bay of Biscay, battered by storms as fierce as the Atlantic can hurl against them, the rocks to seaward stand in jagged rows like decaying teeth, ready to strip the soft belly out of any ship that falls foul of them. The coast is known to the fishermen of Galicia as the '*Costa de la Muerte*', the coast of death. The great harbour wall of Castro Urdiales, to the east in the bight of the Bay of Biscay was famous among square-rig sailors. It was their last hope as they ran from the westerly tempest. 'Castro or death . . .' was in their hearts as they rounded up close to seaward of the wall, let go their hooks in good holding ground and prayed. Between the capes the *rías* of Galicia offer a refuge to those with the knowledge and courage to pass through the twists of rock and the crashing surf into the haven behind.

It was to the ría of Cedeira, right up in the north, near Ortegal itself, that *Iskra* brought us after our crossing of Biscay. It had been an unusual crossing. We started from Falmouth in bright sunlight and a brisk south-easterly wind just before the beam, so that *Iskra* sailed at her top speed. It is a point of sailing where speed sacrifices comfort. The steep Channel waves smacked her bow, half in play, half in anger, just forward of the chain-plates, sending a hail of stinging spray across the deck. Sometimes they struck her hard, an edge of spite turning the smack to a blow and then she would give a faint shudder, the top of the wave would roll over the deck and thunder across the coach roof. The sea was a bright patchwork of sparkling white crests and the pale, cold green of the English Channel. Dark clouds hurried across the sky, over the horizon towards the coast of Ireland.

In the cabin it was noisy and uncomfortable. Sometimes *Iskra* would lift and roll and then fall into the trough of a wave, upsetting the even rhythm of her motion. Drips of sea forced themselves into every unsuspected crack and fissure, releasing themselves with devilish ingenuity above the napes of our necks. The barometer was high, the wind fresh, with two reefs in the mains'l we made 160 miles in the first day to bring Ushant abeam. We passed close to a fine ship sailing across our course, the barque *Belle Nantes*. It was a wonderful, invigorating day to remember. Wendy was below, flat on her back.

We were both disappointed. I had convinced myself that the sea bands were the answer; we thought she had conquered it, that it was all in the past. She hadn't been sick since we had left Bradwell. Now, I could see it wrecking our venture; it was hard to imagine that anyone could persist with a voyage in a small boat and continue to suffer the humiliation, the misery, the anguish of this affliction. As one who has never been ill, or seasick, I always found it difficult to equate to the sufferings of those that are, until Wendy started sailing with me. I had the gut feeling, deep inside me, that if people are ill, they ought to snap out of it and get better without delay or fuss. I would go through the motions of sympathy and sorrow but I had to admit I didn't feel these admirable sentiments deeply. Wendy changed all that. She was ill as we sailed across the Channel, at first so ill for so long that I feared for her.

The other threat to the voyage was the leak. I had decided, or I told myself I had decided, that I would not take *Iskra* across the ocean with a leak. I knew there was no logic in this. She could leak just as much and just as dangerously in the Channel as in the Atlantic and sink just as inexorably. There is a nagging worry about a leak that hammers away at the consciousness day and night, week in, month out. I had already experienced it once before when I owned *Girl Stella* and I had no wish to carry it with me on another Atlantic passage. Somehow the leak must be fixed. I would try again in Spain, surely a good place for a wooden boat and if I failed, I would abandon the notion of Argentina, sail about in softer latitudes for the winter and then take *Iskra* home. She leaked enough on that short stretch across the Channel to convince me that this was the only course I could follow.

After Ushant the wind fell light and veered to the south so that our fine progress was all but stopped. Wendy got better as it became calm. The sunshine left us, giving way to low cloud and a thin mist. Sometimes the wind died altogether and then we started the old engine and thumped along slowly but steadily towards Spain. I kept *Iskra* inside the shipping lane which runs in a straight line between Ushant and Cape Finisterre; hundreds of ships pass up and down every day all day, a conveyor belt of ships. A few miles to one side or the other of the line there is nothing but empty ocean.

Dolphins played around the boat, snorting and splashing, diving under the keel and turning on their backs to show us their white bellies. With their smooth, graceful movements, their bodies perfectly suited to their element, the slightly humorous expression that plays round their snouts and eyes, they are the charmers of the ocean. We want to shout and sing with pleasure when they are around. A little green bird came and perched on the rigging, this one far away from home and doomed to drown. It would accept no comfort or food or even the offer of a ride to land. It went on its hopeless way, swerving and twisting over the waves in the direction of America. In the calm of the night there was a strange loneliness in the air, no sound except the soft rustle of the yacht's gear as she rolled easily in the swell, none of the endless song of wind and sea that goes with a sailing vessel. Nothing was to be seen or heard outside the pool of light round the boat, not the cry of a bird or the splash of a fish to offer company. Beyond was darkness and mystery, a black void, reserved for the secret doings of the ocean. Beads of moisture ran down the sails in sudden spurts, gathering themselves under the boom until they were too fat to hold on and then plopping down into the sea. Wendy's soft hand slid into mine as we sat and watched and listened.

We saw no sun and no stars after leaving Ushant; instead, a thick, opaque mist. There is a radio beacon on the Estaca de Bares, in the north of Spain, which we picked up on our direction finder when we were fifty or so miles off shore. We continued towards the coast, this bearing together with our dead reckoning our only guide. Visibility was down to no more than a few yards and we could only guess how far off the coast we were. It was not easy to decide how to proceed, La Coruña was still more than twenty miles distant and it would be a long thump with the engine. There are several *rías* on the coast but it was impossible to know with any accuracy how far we had come and how far off shore we were. The entrances to many of the *rías* are strewn with rocks. If we hung about becalmed off the coast in fog we could be run down by a ship or a fisherman in a hurry.

We motored towards the shore, gingerly, peering through the fog and listening. The swell steadily increased in size, we must be close to it. *Iskra* began to roll her scuppers under, hurling herself from side to side as she chugged through the calm. Wendy had come through her sickness, she was unaffected by this mad rolling. Suddenly we saw the rock cliff quite close, towering above us, seagulls wheeling about its face. We seemed to be in a shallow bay but there was no break in the rock wall. I had a strange feeling that it was familiar to me; something about the place touched a string of memory. I went below and looked at the chart, leaving Wendy at the tiller. Cedeira, that was it, I was sure it was the ría of Cedeira. It was years since I had been there but the familiarity of it came flooding back. 'Look,' Wendy pointed ahead of us a few yards, 'a fisherman.' We came up close to him. His boat looked tiny; she was probably as long as *Iskra*, an open boat all painted bright red and blue. Two men were streaming a net. They looked round as we came up with them. One moment they were high up on a swell looking down on us, the next we gazed down on them as if they were at the bottom of a well. 'Buenos dias, señores,' I shouted, 'Cedeira, es aqui?' One of them stood up, balancing himself against the boat's roll and gave a wave towards the rocks. 'Sí señor – por aqui – keep over to port, close to the north shore.' I remembered it. We turned towards the cliff. I have never known such a swell. We had to cling to the cockpit sides, tied in with our safety harnesses, or be hurled overboard.

Close under the cliff the swell was overlaid with a confused sea, making *Iskra*'s motion jerky and uncomfortable. It crossed my mind that if the engine failed we could be dashed against the shore in seconds. We didn't speak, only watched and waited and listened as the engine's even beat was thrown back at us from the vertical cliff face. Slowly we saw that the mountain folded in ahead of us; there must be a gap, another cliff curving out from the south. As we moved forward they slid apart, offering first a slit of light, then a wedge of the sky, then the *ría* opening out from behind. It was like coming out into another world. In the *ría* the sun was shining, it was calm, the motion stilled. We saw a quay wall, fishing boats at anchor in a calm roadstead, an old, bent man rowing a skiff. As we glided in we came to the town of Cedeira scattered up the mountainside, red roofs all in a jumble, the church, pink stucco cottages scattered along the harbour side, a donkey cart with a load of hay, children on the sand beach, a new enchanting world. A bell rang out for matins, it was Sunday. Wendy looked at it all with bright eyes.

Wendy had never been to Spain. Before I knew her she had travelled in America, Russia, Japan, Pakistan, Italy, Czechoslovakia, Morocco, Korea, Hong Kong, all down the Rhine to Geneva, but the Iberian Peninsula had always slipped out of her path. I came to love Spain, especially the coast we were now on, when I first started to make sailing voyages. I was able to build on the Spanish I learned from Guillermo and

As we moved forward
they slid apart, offering
first a slit of light...

Andrea with language tapes and to shake off some of the coarser aspects of the language and its grammar as it is spoken in Argentina. I had picked up the accent as a child so that now, although my vocabulary and grammar are weak, I am often taken for a native. This is a two-edged asset; Spanish people assume I am bilingual and set off at such a lick that I can only pick up half of what is said.

Spain had changed out of all recognition since my last visit. Then, we were forced to go through a grim charade with Franco's police. There used to be more policemen per head of population in Spain than in any other country. In every tiny port or anchorage they would come on board, usually sculled by a small boy in an ancient skiff, with a form to be completed as their excuse. 'What armament does the ship carry? . . . How many torpedoes?' They were dirty, unshaven, with stained uniforms, cigarettes hanging from avaricious lips. It was difficult to get rid of them without a bribe, they had the power to search the ship, even put you in prison on the slightest provocation. They were hated by the ordinary people. 'Todo por la patria' was their motto, but it meant something different. In the seclusion of back-street bars the locals would stick out their stomachs, 'Todo por la patria . . .,' they would say with a huge wink and rub their hands over their paunches. Failure to register in every port carried a heavy fine. Not many yachts went to Spain in those days.

We went ashore in the evening, sought out the Captain of the Port's office. We found a young man on duty. 'Report the ship's arrival?' he said, 'come and see the Commandante in the morning. He'll put you in the book. In the meantime welcome to Spain. Enjoy yourselves – this is a free country." We have both been to many countries under many forms of government. Some feel free, some do not, there is no mistaking the atmosphere. Spain is now a free country. It never was before.

To Wendy it was like a fairyland full of enchantment. We wandered up the steep, cobbled streets, inspected the church, the Ayuntamiento – the town hall, drank the thick Galician wine out of small earthenware bowls. We ate *tapas* of squid and fresh sardine and *percæves*, goose barnacles, looking like hens' feet, a delicacy of the coast. We watched the children playing a kind of hopscotch on the pavement. In the old part of the town there was a stone cross, all ivy and moss, by a well high up a steep alley with spectacular views of the harbour every time we turned round. We nodded 'good evening' to a group of women and old men, some sitting on a stone seat in the evening sun, others leaning over the half door of their houses. We climbed to the top of the village, saw where the countryside begins with small, stone walled fields and the Galician *hoóreas*, grain stores raised from the ground against the rats on stone pillars. There were bullock carts with big wheels and a stacked load of beet or maize. The air was soft, we could hear the rustle of the sea across the mountain.

We walked back a different way, turning and twisting down towards the harbour. Round an unexpected corner there was the stone cross again. They greeted us like old friends, we sat on the seat and they asked us where we had come from, what could have brought us to this place. 'We are from England,' I said, pointing to the north. 'We came in a small boat – nosotros dos, solos,' – we two alone. They had never heard of anyone doing such a thing. We spent half an hour with them, they insisted on knowing everything. 'The señora – she's so fair – so beautiful. And the señor – he speaks Spanish like us.' An old lady took us into her house, sat us in the kitchen in front of a wood stove, gave us steaming cups of coffee with hard bread to dunk in it. She wanted to give us potatoes, onions,

They greeted us like old friends.

120

until we protested. 'You must not give us these things – we can buy them for ourselves – we have money – you are poor. She wagged a bony finger at us. 'It is good to give,' she said, 'good to receive. When you are poor like us you can give because you have nothing. It is only the rich who cannot give . . . .'

The *rías* of Galicia are split into two sections, the *rías altas* to the north of Cape Finisterre, and the *rías bajas* to the south, ending with the *ría* of Vigo. There are six or seven *rías* in each section. The *rías altas* are bare and bleak, the little towns cowering behind the capes for protection against the westerlies. The *rías bajas* are wider, less precipitous and softer with medieval cities like Pontevedra, lush countryside round the Ría of Arosa and the old castle of Bayonna. They form one of the most rewarding cruising grounds in the whole of northern Europe, comparable to the west of Ireland but warmer and drier. For some reason the *rías* are little known, tourists deterred by bad roads and the yachts all hurrying south or north, only stopping for fuel and stores at La Coruña or Bayonna. To Wendy they were a salvation, the much needed assurance that the pain and fright of cruising in a small boat has some redemption. She loved the little towns, the wild scenery, the birds, the peasant markets, the friendly welcomes when we anchored for a day and a night behind a harbour wall or in some quiet roadstead. We sat in the pavement cafés in the morning sun, drinking coffee from tiny earthenware cups or sipping our vino and watching the life of the town go by, with a *tapa* of toasted shrimp or fried squid.

We explored La Coruña, the 'Cuidad de Cristal', with its glass frontage to the harbour reflecting the early sun, wandered through the paved squares, into ancient churches, up the steep streets of the old town. We climbed the Tower of Hercules, the world's oldest lighthouse, built by the Romans, saw the garden on the battlements of the town where Sir John Moore, hero of the Battle of Elvina, is buried. The words of Charles Wolfe's poem, 'Not a drum was heard, not a funeral note . . . ' are engraved in English on the wall of the garden. Sir John Moore was one of the great English soldiers. The

Spanish revered him for his fair treatment of the civil population during the Peninsular campaign. The British retreat to La Coruña saved Spain from Napoleon, the glorious battle of Elvina on 16 June 1809 in which Sir John received his death wound saved a British army from certain destruction. He was a born leader, loved by his officers and his men. In an age of brutal military discipline he would have none of the lash and the gallows.

We sailed into the *ría* of Camariñas, where I had old friends, round the grim lighthouse of Cape Villano where I once made a landfall, in fog, from Bermuda 3,000 miles away across the Atlantic. From *ría* to *ría* we went, soaking in the delights of each one. In Corrubedo we met my old friend José del Sol, a fisherman I have known for twenty years. He greeted me like a lost son, Wendy like a new daughter – took us to his house where his señora gave us lunch in the stone kitchen with its deal table, oilcloth and smell of new baking. We met the whole family, were shown the new fishing boat and all the new prosperity that has come to the coast in the last ten years. They all came to tea on board *Iskra* anchored in the harbour.

We took the train from the ría of Arosa to the cathedral city of Santiago de Compostella, the tomb of Saint James, visited by waves of English pilgrims since the fifteenth century. The city is still like a medieval city with ancient courtyards and hidden gardens and sudden glimpses of the towering spires. We saw the Goya tapestries and the portico of Master Mateo, sculpted between 1168 and 1188. We embraced the vocation of tourism with enthusiasm, knowing that we always had our homely, familiar boat to go back to when the day's sightseeing was over.

In Pontevedra, perhaps the loveliest medieval city of all, where Columbus's ship the *Santa María* was built, we met a professor who was so delighted with my Spanish that he took us on a conducted tour of the city. We met an English girl in El Grove, married to a Spaniard, who saw *Iskra*'s red ensign and invited us to her house, took us round the *ría* in her car and to the island of La Toja where the healing water is said to cure

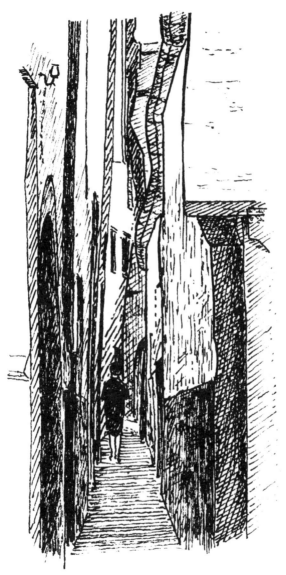

The city is still like a medaeival city

arthritis. An old, sick donkey was once left on the island by his owner to die peacefully after a lifetime of service. When the owner went back three years later, so far from having died, he found the donkey in excellent health. He had been rolling in the thick, grey mud. People have been rolling in the mud of La Toja ever since, not always, perhaps, to such good effect as the donkey. A smart hotel with shaded terraces and a swimming-pool has been provided to help them. We didn't see any donkeys – we doubted whether they could afford the cure now.

We spent five weeks cruising through the *rías* to Bayonna from where we would set off on our next ocean crossing. It blew two hard westerly gales while we were there. We weathered them both, one tied to a buoy in El Grove and the other in Murjia, where *Iskra*'s anchor held her through a force 9 wind. As we sailed into the harbour of Bayonna we glimpsed the ocean between the islands over to starboard. I saw a flicker of misgiving flash across Wendy's face like a brief cloud across the sun.

Bayonna is one of those crossroads of the ocean where yachts gather themselves together, prepare themselves and wait for fair weather for their venture. There are a number of these havens dotted about the world, where sailing ships, now yachts, have always gathered for the same reason – Falmouth, Horta, The Downs, English Harbour Antigua, Newport Rhode Island, Sydney Cape Breton, to name a few in and around the Atlantic. The weather was unsettled when we arrived; there were a score of yachts at anchor and alongside the yacht club pontoons, English, Dutch, French, German, Danish, Swedish and some from further afield. We already knew some of them, we got to know others during the two weeks we waited for a break in the weather. Bayonna is an old town; it has a walled castle, now a *parador* (a state run hotel), and walks over the hills behind. There is a coastal bus ride to Santa Teckla, on the banks of the River Miño. The river forms the Portuguese border with Spain.

This was my last chance to get the leak repaired. It had

been bothering me all down the coast but no more or less than it had bothered me since the day it happened. It was as if the leak was a kind of conscience pricker, reminding me of my folly and admonishing me not to repeat it. We had been through no real bad weather and this had to some extent lulled my anxiety. We heard there was a good boatyard in Vigo, we took the bus up the side of the *ría* to the big city, the commercial capital of Galicia. A few years ago, before Bayonna was the fashion, Vigo was one of the yacht crossroads and I got to know it well. We went to find my old friend Caruso, who used to sing Italian opera in the Mosquito Bar and on board *Iskra* when the bar chucked out, but he was gone. We walked, Wendy still with her folding stick, along the docks until we found the yard.

It was a jumble of a place, all sandwiched between great shipbuilding enterprises, no yachts to be seen. A nice man assured me that the last had just gone and the next was just expected. He quoted me a stiff price and said he would take her up in three days. There was a slip that must have come from a second-hand railway junkyard, a few nondescript sheds and no workforce that I could see. I reluctantly agreed; the man told me he was vastly experienced and I had heard good things about the yard. He took pity on Wendy's lameness and gave us a lift back to the bus. When we got on board *Iskra*, *Wanderer III* was at anchor beside us. We rowed over, met the owner, Thies Mantzen and asked him to supper.

Wanderer III is one of the prettiest boats I know, and also one of the bravest. She was built in 1952, designed by Laurent Giles for Eric Hiscocks who made her famous by sailing her round the world and writing a fine book about her. I met Eric and Susan Hiscocks, in *Wanderer IV*, in Bayonna some time in the 1970's. *Wanderer III* is only 8 tons against *Iskra*'s 10, 26 feet on the water-line against *Iskra*'s 28 feet 6 inches, but she is much the same build as *Iskra* and, like her, she is copper sheathed. It was a delight to have her at anchor beside us.

Thies came on board and we soon got to know him, finding him at once convivial company and having a good brain and a wide understanding. He is a shipwright. He had carried out basic, structural repair work on *Wanderer*, who by the time he came to own her had been round the world twice and was showing signs of it. Thies put in new floors, refastened her, strengthened her and made her better than she had ever been. He was bound, in a leisurely fashion, for Samoa, earning his money as he went by working on yachts or in boatyards. There was a job to do on *Wanderer*'s bottom, a minor repair to the copper and he was arranging to put her on the travel lift in Bayonna. We watched her come out of the water on the lift, observed the similarity between her and *Iskra* and took note of the unhurried, professional manner in which Thies went about the repair. 'You could do *Iskra*'s leak,' I said. It was agreed. I cancelled the arrangement with the yard. 'I'll do it when we get to Madeira,' Thies said. There was a window coming in the weather, neither of us wanted to miss it. We agreed to leave Bayonna together, not to sail in company but to see which of us got to Madeira first. Thies has no VHF on board, we wouldn't be able to communicate with him on the voyage.

Wendy set about the business of laying in stores. We loaded *Iskra* down with tinned delicacies from Galicia which can be bought in such variety and so cheaply nowhere else. There was a squid or an octopus in its own ink or the claws of a lobster or a pickled scallop lurking in every locker, our casks were full of cheap Galician wine, fuel tanks brimful, water overflowing and *Iskra* deep down to her marks. The Portuguese coast is well known for calms when the barometer goes up; I carried two extra cans of diesel fuel as well as every drop the tanks would hold. The club at Bayonna was alive with activity as the yachts prepared to leave, only waiting for the southerly wind to ease, as it surely must. 'Even if it doesn't,' I said to Wendy, 'we'll certainly find a different wind offshore – there'll be a strong northerly fifty miles out from the coast.'

There was a large collection of yachts in Bayonna, those bound north were already moving out, most of them English yachts homeward bound. The people of the club were not sorry to see them go. The Spanish are a formal people, they like things to be nice. The yacht clubs are mainly social

126

establishments; there isn't much sailing as we know it, a bit of dinghy racing, some rowing in the *rías*, the odd yacht belonging to a wealthy Spaniard. The club is a place for dancing, dinner parties, formal gatherings. Foreign yachts are invited to use the club free of charge, as guests, but this privilege, sadly, is not much respected. We saw people from English yachts monopolising the bar, drinking too much, shouting in a foreign language, scruffily dressed, generally behaving in a way which was anathema to Spaniards. We could see them cringing away in distaste, their innate courtesy preventing them from making any complaint. In Brazil, where the clubs are of a similar ilk, the Rio de Janeiro yacht club banned all visiting yachts when the Round-the-World Race crews behaved disgracefully. In a drunken spree they seized an elderly member in a wheelchair beside the swimming-pool and pitched him in, roaring with laughter at their bravado.

After two weeks of waiting the weather window opened itself a crack. The sun came out for a spell, the strong wind that had been blowing for weeks fell light and shifted into the south-east. 'This is it,' we said with an optimism born only of impatience. 'We'll go in the morning.' There were four of us. *Iskra, Wanderer III*, a powerful ketch with a big engine and *Fair Winds*, owned by an American called Randy Martin. We all set off from the snug, calm protection of Bayonna Bay, round the rocks clear of the entrance and away into the ocean.

IX

Storm

The barometer had gone up fast over the past twenty-four hours, too fast perhaps. 'Quick rise after low,' the adage runs, 'foretells a stronger blow.' As soon as we got outside the harbour we ran into another big swell, like the swell off Cedeira. *Iskra* began to pitch and roll violently. Wendy steered while I hoisted sails, striving to keep my balance on the heaving foredeck. I set the steering vane and she went below. In minutes, the plastic bucket was in position on the knob of the stove. I fastened her canvas bunkboard and tried to comfort her. 'Don't worry – it'll soon get better – as soon as we're clear of the land we'll lose the swell – the wind will go to the north.' I must have believed it myself. There comes a time when you are weatherbound waiting to set off on a voyage when you have to go, even if the weather isn't exactly as you would wish it. We had been in Bayonna nearly two weeks, it was already late October, it would only get worse the longer we waited. The wind was from the north-west as forecast. I could see the tip of the little *Wanderer*'s brown sail dancing over the swells ahead of us. The ketch had already disappeared, Randy was leading us, sailing fast with his engine on I guessed. The barometer began to fall as we left the mountains of Spain behind.

Wendy and I both write a daily log of the voyage. It is private, even to each other, until the voyage is over so that both of us can say what we really feel without fear of hurting the other. Writing a log is a soothing and calming therapy, helping us to put our ideas and feelings about the voyage into perspective. When we were in the swell in the Bay of Biscay, Wendy wrote, 'I feel utterly miserable and long to be back in my bed. I keep thinking how lovely it would be to wake up there, open the curtains and look out on the calm, beautiful

128

river. All I ever do is cling to the tiller for dear life or cling to the side of my bunk. I hate every minute of it, regret my job and the way of life I have abandoned for a rolling and pitching boat. I feel so frightened surrounded by terrifying, rolling seas.'

At sunset a black, moonless night wrapped itself around the boat, the wind died so that the gear slatted and banged. I started the engine and ran it for most of the night to keep some forward movement, to ease the motion and to get as far offshore as possible. With a falling glass the land is no friend of mine.

At dawn a breeze came from the south-west, the barometer fell a little more. There was no sign of the other yachts. I should have known what was coming but for some reason the notion of a gale never occurred to me. I had persuaded myself that we would soon pick up our Portuguese trades and nothing would shake this conviction. By mid-morning the sea was rough, we were sailing with two reefs in the main, the working staysail and small jib, making good speed offshore to find that northerly wind. I had been promising Wendy the Portuguese trades since we left home.

By midday it was blowing force 7 and there was a big sea with breaking crests. Still I wasn't worried. True, the motion was wild, true the barometer had now fallen from 1023 millibars when we left Bayonna to 1014, true we were down to staysail only, the mainsail tied to the boom gallows, the Wyckham Martin jib furled. But *Iskra* was going safely enough, quite fast towards the west with the southerly wind a point before the beam. She was taking a wet one over occasionally, she was heeling far over to starboard, burying her lee rail, she was leaking more. I was pumping every half hour, which worried me. I reefed the staysail. The wind continued to freshen. Wendy was flat out on the lee bunk – all palliatives to seasickness submerged in the overwhelming motion, the sense of alarm.

By 1400 the wind had increased to beyond force 8. I was pumping every twenty minutes to keep the water off the cabin floor. *Iskra* was built with cement in her bilges, making them shallow so that a small amount of water in her will splash over the floor. She has an inside bilge pump and an electric pump; it is no great labour to keep the bilge clear. All the same, to pump three times an hour is too often, she must be eased.

Reluctantly, I turned her to starboard bringing the wind and the sea aft, pointing her back towards the north. I clawed my way to the foredeck, one hand for the ship, one hand for myself. In a gale, it's a long way from the cockpit to the foredeck. When you get there, the foredeck is a bleak, lonely place. I let go the staysail halyard, made the bare end fast to the pin rail, moved deliberately and with great care from hold to hold to the eyes of the ship, a tiny triangle of leaping deck in the vast, angry ocean. I dragged the staysail down the forestay, making it securely fast with a line to the bitts, trying not to look at the surrounding fury. I would have left the staysail set, to give her some speed through the water so that her vane can operate efficiently, but now that she was heading north my preoccupation was to slow her down, to lose no more distance than I had to. When I turned to go aft the gale was in my face.

I have never worried overmuch about gales in *Iskra*. I have always known that she would pull through them. She is so heavy, so strong, she gives off confidence and security. I believe Wendy feels the same about her. Provided I am strong enough and careful enough and sensible enough to do the right thing for her and provided she is well clear of the land and provided she doesn't run foul of some obstruction in the ocean, there isn't much that can harm her. In a hurricane, she would probably be safer than a big ship. But I know I can afford to make no mistakes – the ocean does not suffer fools gladly. Because Wendy worries that I should have an accident, or fall overboard, I sing at the top of my voice so that she can hear me. If it's calm I whistle or hum a tune. She lies in her bunk for hours with her eyes closed but I know she is awake, her brain racing round, keyed up and aware of every sound.

When the staysail was safely lashed down and I turned to

come aft, the song was snatched from my mouth. Now the seas were building up, the crests were already torn from the wave tops, the sky was a deep black, no redeeming patch of silver or grey, the noise of the wind and the sea was enough to drown my feeble air. The ocean and the sky had a look of absolute desolation. The barometer was down to 1008 millibars – no Portuguese trade here.

It was a bleak, oppressive seascape, low cloud racing across the waves, bearing down on them as if to merge ocean and sky into a single, furious amalgam of anger. I looked out, first to port, then to starboard. The edge of our world seemed close at hand, only a few boat's lengths away, an insubstantial ribbon of blown spume and racing cloud where the horizon had once been. We were quite alone, at the centre of a diminished world devoted only to violent chaos. I looked again to starboard – something was there. I lost it and then found it again – so we were not alone. Perhaps half a mile off there was a tiny brown triangle. Surely I must be mistaken. I kept looking on the

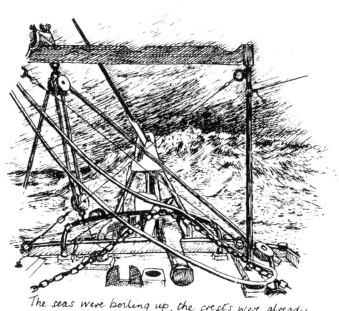

The seas were boiling up, the crests were already torn from the wave tops

same bearing and saw it again and then again – *Wanderer*, hove-to on the port tack, a patch of mainsail and her white mast above – quite unmistakable. I shouted to Wendy, '*Wanderer* she's over there – not a mile away.' I watched the brown triangle move slowly across our stern, regretting that she has no VHF – Thies is a purist in these matters. Then I lost her.

Minutes later a ship came up on our starboard side heading south, a big container ship. She passed us close. I made no wave or signal and received none from her. The danger with ships is that they will try to save you whether you want to be saved or not. I watched her as she passed. A few minutes later I glanced astern and saw her turn through 90 degrees and head west just where Thies and *Wanderer* were lying hove-to. Then she was gone in the mist, leaving us puzzled and worried, wondering why the ship had turned towards *Wanderer* in that way.

For the first time I smelt diesel from the cockpit. I knew at once what had happened. I had filled the tanks too full before leaving Bayonna because I had convinced myself that it would be calm. *Iskra* had heeled so far that oil had spilled out of the air vent in one of the tanks and was all over the cabin floor. It was like a skating-rink. I looked in through the hatch – the cabin mat was saturated with diesel, the boat smelt like a garage sump.

The wind was now a shriek with squalls of rain driven horizontally. The tops of the waves were drawn into a mist of blown spume which seemed to be about six or eight feet above the level of the sea. I sat at the tiller, my eyes shifting between the compass and the burgee. The wind was too strong for me to turn my face into it. The spray and spume drummed against the back of my oilskin hood. I guessed the wind's strength at 11 on the Beaufort scale. Wendy had got up and was working the inside pump, amidships in her hanging locker.

Lightning forked into the sea, thunder clapped with explosive crashes, the seas were flattened by the rain and the scouring wind. As I steered with all my concentration, striving to keep the wind fine on *Iskra*'s quarter where it can do her little damage, I saw that she was turning to starboard. First the course went to north-by-east, then north-east then east, right round half the compass in the space of half an hour until she settled on south, the reciprocal of what she had been steering for the past four hours. The barometer was at 1002 millibars, a drop equivalent to nearly half an inch of mercury.

On this new course the seas were rougher and more uneven, the new waves thrusting themselves against the momentum of the old to produce columns of water, leaping out of the ocean, sometimes to a height of eight to ten feet before they were blown into mist. The wind kept its force through the change of direction until well into the night. Wendy passed hot soup to me followed by hunks of bread and cheese. At 0200 on 10 October it had eased back to force 7 or 8. I was able to set a small triangle of staysail and put *Iskra* back on her vane steering. The barometer began to rise; the worst of the storm was over.

I left the helm to the vane and went below, cold and stiff and wet. Diesel had been spread in a thin film over the cabin floor. Wendy had pumped the bilge dry with the inside pump leaving the oil behind. She was back in her bunk, still convulsed with sickness. As soon as my feet touched the cabin floor they slid away from me and I fell in a heap. The oil lamp swung on its gimbal with the yacht's motion, throwing a yellow shadowy light across the confusion. A locker had burst its catch, letting go its contents in an avalanche to the lee side. The chart, the Almanac, had flown off the chart table and lay in an emulsion of dirt and oil and tins and spilled packets. A mug of wild flowers Wendy had gathered before we left had slipped its stowage spreading over the mound of confusion like a funeral bier. Wendy lay behind her bunk-board, her eyes half closed, hoping for a quick end to this perversion of her life. She had been happy in the *rías* and in Bayonna, now, within hours, she was reduced to despair. I soaked a rag in detergent and cleaned the floor, restoring those rogue-parts of our lives to their proper places and cleaning off the oil. I swilled more detergent round the bilge to get rid of the smell, made Wendy a honey drink, assured her that the end had not yet come. I found some dry clothes and opened a tin of soup.

With the dawn the wind eased again, resolving itself into fierce gusts which could be seen skimming across the waves. In a brief glimpse of bright morning sunshine the ocean was suddenly lit with gaudy colour, the great white coamers a dazzling pattern of brilliance across a sea of intense blue, the clouds still scurrying overhead like racing chariots. It was beautiful; I forced Wendy to rise from her bed and observe it. The sight seemed to do her good. The gale went with rain. 'When the wind comes before the rain,' runs another sailor's rhyme, 'soon you may make sail again.' The rain pounded down on *Iskra* as if she had strayed by some error under the Falls of Iguazú. It flattened the waves, filled the side-decks, cascaded out through the scuppers, drummed on the cabin top like galloping horses. It was such a downpour of water that it was hard to define where was rain and where was sea.

When it eased in the evening the wind began to go slowly back from north to west; I looked at the chart, calculated a rapid DR and saw that Lisbon was under our lee, not more than thirty miles distant. This was confirmed by a radio bearing and we decided to go in, clean the ship and lick our wounds before continuing the voyage to Madeira.

Lisbon swung the balance back as always happens, sooner or later. We washed the oil out of the cabin mat, laundered the whole boat and counted our blessings. It was a delightful week in a lovely city – it was some months before the centre of Lisbon was destroyed by fire. The castle, the old city, the sixteenth century Tower of Belem where the Portuguese navigators started and ended their voyages, the ship museum, one of the finest in the world, coffee in pavement cafés, cheap meals in secluded restaurants, rattling trams, bustling markets, friendly people. There was the usual gathering of long distance sailors, yarns in smoky cabins far into the night, tales of storms and calms and far-away places. *Fair Winds* came in a couple of days after us. She had been some way ahead of us, had missed the worst of the storm, had sheltered in Figueira on the Portuguese coast. Randy told me the dial on his wind-speed indicator had been hard against its stop at 50 knots, or force 10. The yacht we lay alongside in the marina had her coach roof split by a sea, the big ketch was towed in by the lifeboat. A freighter had limped into Lisbon, her containers swept overboard and her upperworks damaged. It blew another hard gale while we were in Lisbon and we spent an uneasy night keeping *Iskra* clear of damage. We heard vaguely about the great gale in England and wondered how our house had fared.

The weather seemed to settle after a week; we did our shopping for another voyage, collected a grand weather forecast from the Portuguese meteorological office, all bound in a smart folder and set off down the 10-mile estuary of the River Tagus to Cascais at the entrance. We had a fine sail down this wide river with a pleasant, fair wind. It was evening when we got to Cascais; we anchored for the night, to give ourselves a good long sleep rather than cross the shipping lane in darkness. When we woke next morning the barometer had fallen. There was something about the look of the weather I didn't like. The wind was strong now and there was swell in the anchorage. I called the Harbour Master at Cascais on VHF, asked for a weather check. I didn't want Wendy to have another nightmare voyage. The same story that was in my smart folder came again – moderate easterly, veering to north, fine and settled.

There wasn't much I could do but go. Cascais is an open anchorage, it has no harbour; if we returned to Lisbon we would have a 10-mile beat up the river against tide and current; I would be a fool if the forecast turned out to be right. We left. This time Wendy had taken Stugeron against seasickness. It made her dreadfully ill. It began to blow hard as soon as we cleared the land; now we couldn't go back against half a gale and a big sea.

I had been a fool to trust a weather forecast against commonsense and the movement of the barometer. I reefed the mainsail, changed to a small jib. Soon we had a storm trysail set, another gale was blowing and it was backing round to the south-west. This time I was really worried about Wendy. She lay in her bunk moaning gently and bringing up a noxious, yellow bile. *Iskra* flogged through the gale for three days, making little progress with much travail. It was cold and wet. It was our wedding anniversary. I said, 'All right – we'll pack it up – we'll abandon it in Madeira – just stay there and then go home in the spring.' We had taken enough punishment – it had been all swings and no roundabouts.

The gale petered out, leaving an uncomfortable chop and the wind went round a little more to the west, enough to allow *Iskra* to fetch Porto Santo, the island beside Madeira, 20 miles to the east of it. That would do. I had been there before, years ago, and I knew there was reasonable anchorage behind the island in any wind except from the south-east. I began to wean Wendy on scrambled egg and thin slices of brown bread and butter. We set full sail for the first time since leaving Lisbon, even to the topsail. A fleeting sun showed itself for long enough for me to catch a sight and work a position. We both got some rest. Pumping became less frequent; in the gale I had been working the pump almost continuously. Whenever there had been a moment of peace Wendy or I had pumped; it was like a conditioned reflex. Then another gale came upon us, this one of a different order.

No two gales are the same. There is infinite variety in the ocean, it rings the changes of wind and sea and sky and rain and fog and thunder and lightning in a varied carillon, seldom repeating itself, always offering surprises, new terrors, sometimes joys. It wages a kind of psychological warfare, or perhaps only a game, designed to sap the will and the nerve of poor sailors in small boats. On this bright afternoon the wind freshened from the north-west in jumps. The barometer dropped as if someone had pushed it over a cliff. Vicious squalls set *Iskra* racing across an ocean knocked flat by the wind, so that I had to scramble for the halyards. As soon as the sail was down the wind left her and she would spring to life; with the pressure on her sails released she hurled herself about in the confused seas like a demented creature. I would hoist sail again to steady her and the performance would be repeated.

It got dark. We saw the lighthouse on Porto Santo. We would have to weather it to get into the anchorage. Wendy steered, I tended the sails, hauling the close-reefed mainsail up and dropping the peak of the sail to spill wind as the gusts came and went. They were so strong that even without the mainsail *Iskra* was hard pressed. Between them, unless the mainsail was set again, she rolled her rail under. Next it started to rain and hail. We pursued a stop-go course towards the light, *Iskra* sailing so fast in the squalls that she surfed on the seas – I had to fight the tiller to keep her from broaching. Soon the mountainous island could be seen, a black lump on our lee bow. Then it started to hail, big painful blocks of ice thundering on the deck, hammering on our oilskin hoods. As we came close to the shore vivid flashes of lightning lit the panorama with brilliant light, followed by claps of thunder echoing off the mountains. The sky was black, low clouds tinged with grey raced across. For an instant the lightning flashes brought the shore and the jagged line of rocks round the lighthouse close aboard so that it looked as if we must run ashore. Wendy was frightened.

'We're going to hit the rocks,' she cried. 'We're not, we can't – the lighthouse is on the end of the point – we must be clear of it.' She wouldn't be mollified. 'We're going towards them – I can see them,' she was near weeping, a note of panic in her voice I had never heard before. I checked again with the chart. 'Keep the course, we're on a safe bearing. We must be clear.' I had to be right, yet everything in these crazy glimpses of black mountain and saw-edged rocks spelled destruction. Sometimes the lightning concentrated itself into a ball of brightness, like the fireball of an explosion and then the rocks would increase their size, shift their perspective, so that they seemed to tower up ahead as if to leap on top of us. Only the winking lighthouse gave the assurance of sanity. We passed a few hundred yards clear of it, rounded up in sudden peace under the lee of the mountains, felt our way into the anchorage and let go. We were at peace. We drank tots of brandy and slipped exhausted into our warm, dry bags.

We stayed for a week in Porto Santo waiting for the weather to ease, cowering at anchor off the beach as the wind roared over us, or tied up in little more comfort to the pontoons of the yacht marina. I was impatient to find Thies – he was beginning to grow larger in my mind with his almost casual offer of salvation from the penance of pumping. We met old friends in Porto Santo and made some new; we rode our bicycles all over the island. At one time it was a dry island, the pattern of rain always missing it in favour of its big sister Madeira. This has changed and the island has become green and more populated, more as it was when Columbus visited it on his first voyage to the Americas. Now there are gardens, the little town is much bigger, there are fruit and vegetables to buy. We were asked to dinner in a splendid restaurant.

When the wind did ease it went altogether, leaving us to motor for 10 miles along the south coast of Porto Santo, then across the uncomfortable strait between the islands. For 20 more miles we motored, in the lee of the mountains and cliffs of Madeira with their toy houses and plantations way up above us, the terraced fields all carefully cultivated. Finally, we saw the long harbour wall of Funchal, the cruise ships alongside, the town spread up the mountainside and the new yacht marina tucked into a corner behind a new stone wall. We motored in, found a berth and tied up fore and aft. In moments there was a shout of greeting, a waving figure running along the harbour wall, 'Hullo – glad to see you.' It was Thies.

X

Triumph

The little *Wanderer* fared better than *Iskra* in the storm. By jogging through it on the port tack Thies moved his boat out of its path and soon passed into calmer winds. I would have done the same if it had not been for the leak. Thies divided his time between sleeping and reading books, while *Wanderer* quietly got on with the job. He cursed the big freighter. It woke him up by taking his wind and causing *Wanderer* to roll in the unnatural calm she created. The ship may not have seen *Iskra* or they may have thought she looked quite safe running before the gale with a person to be seen in the cockpit. *Wanderer*, on the other hand, from the vantage of a big ship's bridge, must have looked tiny, frail and apparently deserted. The officer on the bridge, far above the level of the sea, would have no notion of the feeling of security given off by a yacht safely snugged down in a storm. With a sound boat and good gear a man alone has no need to fear provided he has sea room. By turning and bringing the wind aft to ease the pumping, *Iskra* was carried into the storm's centre – we must have sailed close round it. But Thies ran into bad weather again, just as we had done. It took him nearly ten days to reach Madeira.

Iskra has been through worse storms since I have owned her; never with a stronger wind perhaps, but several with heavier and more dangerous seas. One storm at least, stands in my mind and is the yardstick I offer to all storms. It was in the Bermuda Triangle on my way back from Cuba on my first ever single-handed voyage. Then, the destructive force and size of the seas was of a different order. The waves were high, sometimes over thirty or thirty-five feet. It is hard to estimate the size of waves exactly and impartially from the cockpit of a yacht but it was clear that when she was in the troughs, the wave tops were way above the top of her mast. I was in a gale off Cape Horn, not in a yacht, where the waves were up to forty-five feet high, which is about the maximum except in winds of hurricane force. In our gale between Lisbon and Porto Santo I don't believe they were more than fifteen or twenty feet high. Wave height depends on many factors in addition to wind strength – the nature of the sea bed, the depth, the direction of the current, the wind pattern over a long period, the state of the barometer.

We found, surprisingly and contrary to what we expected, that there was no proper slip for yachts in Madeira, only a concrete ramp at the end of the harbour among the fishing boats where yachts could be hauled out on wooden cradles dragged up the slope by a powerful forklift truck. There were some boats already hauled out, as big as *Iskra* if not as heavy. Before any action could be taken there was a bureaucracy operating within a complex maze of forms and people and rules and regulations which must be negotiated with infinite patience and perseverance. A shadowy figure somewhere at its core called Mario, whom we never saw, wielded the power necessary to start the system going so that those who wanted work done and those who wanted work could be brought together. We started, as simpletons, at the bottom. Language was an added problem. The Portuguese refused to understand Spanish, I believe because they have no love for Spain or for Spaniards. They spoke to me so fast in their island dialect that I could seldom fathom it.

We were supposed to see Mario to arrange *Iskra*'s slipping. We worked our way through an array of people we found in the yard, always being referred from one to another, each one having to be found and identified, until we got to the yard foreman, who was Juan Santos. Santos listened to our request and told us that we could see Mario the next day at 12 o'clock. But 12, 1 and 2 o'clock all came and went while we stood about; then it was passed on to us that Mario would not be available until the next day at 12 o'clock. This went on for three days until I managed to get past Santos and see a serious looking

140

girl in an office at the top of the ramp overlooking the yard. She filled in six forms, made me sign them and told me it would cost £150 in escudos. There were a huge number of escudos to the pound – something over a thousand. Then there was the question of a cradle. There was a cradle, but it belonged to someone else and his permission had to be obtained. It needed a repair, which I would have to pay for. Thies would repair it, I offered. No, it would have to be the carpenter in the yard. I paid, in cash. Then the cradle was in a different place and had to be brought to the yard on a truck. This would cost a little more – I paid. Mario would be there the next day at 12 o'clock and he would authorise the whole business. He wasn't, or at 2 or 4. Then it was the day of one of the saints that hold sway over the island and no one worked, then the truck driver's mother-in-law died and he had to go to her funeral. After nearly a week of sustained effort, Santos told me to bring *Iskra* round to the slip the next day.

There was a big swell at high tide, fishing boats were tied up all across the ramp, we came from our marina berth round the corner of a tumbledown dock but there was no one about, no sign of a cradle or a forklift, no sign of Santos. I went ashore, leaving Wendy and Anne to fend *Iskra* off the dock as best they could. Anne had come out from England to stay with us for a week or so. The serious girl was at work in the office. There was a strike, she told me, but she couldn't afford to go on strike because her husband was already on strike. I mustn't worry, she said sympathetically, they would all be back tomorrow. The three of us, Wendy and Anne and I, went out that night to the bars along the docks. I got drunk on sangria and when tomorrow came I had a hangover.

Thies thought he had found the leak. He stuffed roll after roll of lavatory paper into every corner and cranny of *Iskra*'s bilges. The cabin floor was taken up, we crawled round with rags and a bucket squeezing out and mopping up every drop of water and Thies followed with the lavatory paper. No sign of a leak showed itself until he came to the engine. Squeezed under the bearers, with the oily sump against his ear, his arm

He stuffed roll after roll of
lavatory paper into every corner
and cranny of *Iskra's* bilges

stretched out into the murky intestines of the engine, he stuffed the lavatory paper into the darkest recesses of the bilge. It began to soak up water. He stuffed in more, more water came – not a lot but a steady trickle, 'When the boat is sailing and heeled over to the wind,' he said, 'and the weight of the engine is to one side, she will leak more.' Triumph.

Two days later it was calmer on the slip, the strike was over. A man sculling an old dinghy cleared us a space between the fishing boats, the cradle was put in position – I had stood over the carpenter until it was finished. Now there were dozens of people, some pulling on ropes, some pushing the cradle with the forks of the truck, some standing round in an advisory capacity, all shouting instructions with commands and counter-commands flying from side to side like grapeshot. The cradle didn't fit the hull – someone would have to dive into the oily water and insert wedges under *Iskra*'s keel. Everyone looked at everyone else. I dived down through the oil and grime, putting the wedges in as best I could. The truck began to pull. *Iskra* jerked ahead a foot. The strain came on the rope again, she jerked another foot, her mast and rigging shaking and shuddering, my dolphin with a disenchanted look across his face, Wendy and Anne watching with awful trepidation. Then the rope broke, the truck shot ahead, almost dismasting another boat in its path. *Iskra* came sulkily to a standstill. Santos waved his arms – 'Multo pesado, multo pesado . . .' he complained, very heavy. 'Get another rope,' I shouted, 'outra corda.' Someone produced a rusty wire from behind a pile of lumber. I found two big shackles in *Iskra*'s fo'c'sle. The truck started again – the wire stretched bar tight, *Iskra* jerked again, then again. She was half clear of the water now, slewed round at an angle to the ramp. At the next jerk she threatened to tumble off the cradle, the wheels of the truck spun against the ground, she would budge no further. 'Multo pesado,' shouted Santos, 'no mais – no more.' Thies said, 'OK – we can do it now,' they all went off, it started to rain.

We were on the slip for two days – there was no lavatory, Anne and Wendy peed into a bucket, we washed in the marina lavatory which was filthy and ten minutes walk away. It went on raining. At low tide Thies worked. He stripped the copper where the leak was, found where the water was coming in, exactly where he suspected it round the engine holding-down bolts, caulked it, put on a neat lead patch, replaced the copper. He was fast, methodical, thorough. Anne and I went round after him, squatting on the cradle under the bilge in the mud and grime, filling the old nail holes in the hull with wood splines made from Portuguese matchsticks. The tide came almost up to the repair but not quite. At high water we had to stop. It rained.

We slept uphill, *Iskra* at a steep angle on the slip; by morning we had all slid down to the bottom of our bunks. It was a struggle to keep the boat clean, the muck came up the ladder on our shoes every time we went ashore. We were overlooked by a line of spectators who could see into the boat from the high side of the slip. We would hear them discussing every aspect of our lives, our ablutions, our toiletries which seemed to afford much interest and amusement. Emptying the pee bucket, I slipped on the seaweed and mud at the bottom of the ramp. I fell backwards, my feet flying away from me, hit my head a sharp crack on the concrete, staggered back on board up the ladder almost insensible and pouring blood. I was in good hands. Wendy and Anne are both nurses; Anne was once Matron of Barts Hospital.

We slept uphill, Iskra at a steep angle

Thies worked on the hull as soon as the tide went down. We finished the job, painted *Iskra* with anti-fouling. Somehow we marshalled Santos's forces for the reverse procedure and they all came back at low tide to persuade *Iskra* down the ramp. This time the truck pushed the cradle, first on one of its runners to get it straight, then with a baulk of timber across the front of the cradle. She trembled at every encounter, jumping backwards in little leaps, shaking so that we thought every fastening in her would be loosened. They stopped before she was properly down, Santos sending them all away in spite of pleas, threats, promises – everything my pidgin Portuguese had to throw at him. 'Multo pesado, multo pesado . . .' was all he would say. When the tide came up she wouldn't float out of the cradle. By luck, Wendy found a fisherman with a powerful motor boat, persuaded him to take our line from *Iskra*'s stern. She came off. We disentangled her from the fishing boat lines, spent an hour in the outer harbour cleaning the muck and grime off the decks, off ourselves, Anne and Wendy scrubbing her out inside.

We went back to the marina and waited until the next morning, refusing to look in the bilge or touch the pump. Thies came on board. I said, 'Now – the crunch. We'll see what kind of a shipwright you are.' He betrayed no unease. I took the pump handle in the cockpit, pulled a stroke. At the second stroke the pump sucked air. Wendy and I looked at each other, our faces relaxed into happy smiles, the strain and anxiety of months, the doubts and apprehensions falling away in a single moment. When I went to pay the serious girl in the office and we converted the escudos to real money, the bill was for just over £5. They had made a mistake with the decimal point – the bureaucracy had found itself a saving grace. *Iskra* has never leaked since.

Anne came with us from Madeira to the island of La Palma in the Canaries. As soon as we cleared the land a strong northerly wind took us in its grasp and sent us skimming south at last. It was rough, boisterous, exciting sailing, *Iskra* under her twin stays'ls for the first time on the voyage. The twins are designed for trade-wind sailing. I had them made when I first bought *Iskra*. I love them. With twins the whole business of sailing a boat with fore and aft rig is transformed. *Iskra* becomes light, nimble, swift. The mains'l is furled away, the heavy boom lashed amidships, the twin sails spread like wings on their booms, lifting her as if they would have her skim the wave tops, wafting her smoothly, gracefully onward. She rolls easily in the following sea, her motion at once even and relaxed. There is no strain, no apparent effort to inspire this happy gait. White moustachios plume out on either side of her bow, she snugs herself between the rushing crests, twisting and turning her way through them to find the easy water, her wake zipping up the sea behind her so that she leaves no record, no hint of her passing. The steering vane stands erect and quivering in the wind, transmitting its mute instructions to the tiller, checking, correcting, coaxing her to the course. She is at one with the ocean, prancing across its surface beside a million white crests all hurrying on beside her. The sun lights the sea with bright warmth, the white trade-wind clouds all fashioned into fairy castles and mansions of fantasy, take up station around the horizon's rim. It is good to be alive.

After a day and a half the island of La Palma rose out of the ocean like a black lozenge. Slowly it changed its colour as we approached; first a deep green, then pale green, then bright as the morning sun matured. We began to see houses perched on the side of the mountain, roads snaking up and away into the forest, then plantations, fields, villages and at last the long harbour wall of Santa Cruz. We entered in the afternoon, tied to a buoy, rowed ourselves ashore to the fleshpots of a new place – coffee, sticky cakes, glasses of wine, *tapas* in the balmy evening air, watching the girls and their *novios* along the marine parade, wandering through the alleys and squares and secluded gardens of the steep little town.

Anne went home from La Palma, her senses purged of shoreside drudgery for a spell, richer in experience, poorer for buying us an expensive dinner ashore. She came again, later in the voyage when her bank balance had recovered. We stayed for a month in La Palma, correcting the proofs of a book. Every afternoon we went for a long walk through and around Santa Cruz. It is a lovely unspoilt island, we felt very much a part of the place. The girl in the post office, the waiter in our favourite café, the lady in the bookshop, even the policeman were friends with whom we could pass the time of day for half an hour. A few yachts came and went but La Palma is an off the track island, not popular with itinerant yachtsmen. Therein, to us, lies its charm. It has no beaches with golden sand, another feature to its inestimable advantage. We hired a car and drove all over the island. The northern peak rises to 8,000 feet, making La Palma the steepest island in the world, according to the guidebook. It is a beautiful island, the mountain roads breathtaking. The crater of Taburiente is the largest in the world, again according to the guidebook.

The Guanche indians were slaughtered by the Spanish invaders in the fifteenth century but not before they had implanted their blood and features into their conquerors. Guanche descendants with blue eyes and brown hair can still be picked out in La Palma. In prehistoric times the Guanches lived in caves and were still Stone Age cave-dwellers when the Spanish arrived. Their staple food was *gofio*, a finely ground and roasted maize and barley flour which can still be bought in La Palma. It is nourishing, health giving and, according to the guidebook, a considerable aphrodisiac. I found it a splendid breakfast cereal, Wendy tolerated it.

Gomera is another favourite island, as charming and as beautiful as La Palma and even less touched by civilisation. Not only has it no white beaches but it has no commercial airport. We sailed there through a night, watched the dawn unfold over the volcano of Teide, on Tenerife and anchored in the wide bay of San Sebastian. Gomera has no safe harbour; I had always wondered why Columbus had used the place as a starting point for three of his transatlantic voyages. Some say he conducted a love affair with a notorious beauty, Beatrix de Bobadilla, who lived in a *castillo* overlooking the strait between Gomera and Tenerife. Just below the house there used to be a natural

147

spring gushing out of the rock face. Now the spring provides water for a swimming pool at the new yacht club. The water from the spring was far and away better than the noxious stuff on offer from any other of the Canary Islands and this, I have always thought, was the reason Columbus started his voyages from Gomera – to water his ships with clear spring water. I have always filled my tanks from the spring before crossing the Atlantic. On my first voyage I still had more than half *Iskra*'s tanks full of Gomera water when I arrived in English Harbour Antigua. People came on board *Iskra* especially to taste it.

We went into the interior of Gomera; it is even more spectacular than La Palma. Agulo, a bus ride towards the north of the island, is a town from another age with steep cobbled alleys, donkey carts with solid wooden wheels, swarthy peasants with honest, open faces, girls with dark eyes, flashing smiles, bright embroidered skirts. We drank our vino in the sun on a stone seat outside the café in the main square, a view over the valley and away to the sea. An old lady told us, 'I have lived in this house all my life and I will die in it. I like the view.' She had never been off the island. We had soup flavoured with a herb unknown to us, Spanish omelettes, beans and flan and Canary Island wine. We lay in the grass and went to sleep until the return bus came by.

We had to up anchor in a hurry when the wind went to the south and the glass plunged down, leaving the bay open to the gale. Outside the harbour wall where the ships berth and round a promontory on the corner of the island we found tenuous shelter and lay anxiously at anchor in a rockbound cove until the wind shifted. We spent the last of our money in Don Louis's bar. He had become a real friend. We got to know everyone in the little town, everyone took a keen interest in provisioning *Iskra* for the next part of her voyage. We bought fruit and vegetables, all fresh from the land, exotic tins. The people seemed to be convinced that we were mad. 'Qué barbaridad,' the lady who sold us the vegetables said, shaking her head 'La señora tan guapa, tan pequeño el barquito, tan ancho el oceano.' 'How terrible! – the señora so pretty, the boat so small, the ocean so wide.' Don Louis gave us a rare send-off on our last evening. We left him the last of our pesos, which were not nearly enough for the huge dinner he gave us.

We went off into bad weather, leaving the island in a calm so that *Iskra* rolled, sending Wendy to her bunk. Soon it started to blow from the south and *Iskra* was close hauled, pitching and banging into the seas. Then it blew again from the west, sending her helter-skelter on her course with storm trys'l and small jib. After two days Wendy was better, it was warmer as we sailed south and at last the trade wind established itself and *Iskra* began her tireless dance under her twin stays'ls. Wendy had never sailed in *Iskra* in these conditions. We settled into an easy routine so that the days and nights slipped happily by, the days bright with sun, glittering with white crests, the bright ocean alive with interest, nights full of stars, the silent moon observing us with a sombre gaze, my dolphin smiling happily. We set watches at night. We sailed well clear of the coast of Africa, kept a good lookout and left our VHF switched on.

At noon on our seventh day at sea we were in the same latitude but far to the east of the bones of the *Celtic Star*, on the bottom of the ocean for almost forty-five years. I sometimes wonder how it is that my own bones are not yet in the locker with her – I spared a thought for the Fourth Engineer, the Mate.

There are pirates on this coast. Some yachts have disappeared, others have been found drifting with no one on board, or with the crew murdered. One we met later in Banjul had been chased by a suspicious craft. When she came up close our friend sent out a mayday on VHF which was picked up and answered by a French patrol boat. The pirate, if he was a pirate, turned and departed. Using fast rubber boats the pirates come up on ships in the night and climb aboard unobserved. They make their way to the bridge, hold up the officer of the watch or the captain at gunpoint, killing them if they offer resistance. They smash the radio, take the contents of the safe and any valuables and depart, leaving the ship still on course under her automatic pilot.

Iskra covered a thousand miles in ten days without conscious effort. Wendy had never enjoyed an ocean voyage before, soon she was loving it. All that I had been telling her for years could at last be seen as the truth. When we came close to the Gambia which is on the westernmost bulge of the African continent, the weather became hot and humid, the trade fell light as we approached Cape Vert. The last ninety miles of our passage lay close to the shore, within ten miles of the steaming jungle. Strange insects invaded the boat, wafted from the shore by a faint, scented breeze. Long cigar-like creatures with folded wings, spindly legs and weaving proboscises; fat, waisted insects like huge wasps with purple bodies and scarlet heads; creatures like large earwigs arrived in droves, appearing to have no wings; butterflies, white and pale green, decorated with a blue design, fluttered round the cabin lamp. The sun sank in a scarlet bowl, the stars unusually bright, the sea black, mysterious.

In the night the silence was broken by a faint swish, the dip of paddles. A long shape glided silently past, three or four figures working their arms with rhythmic precision. We saw others ghosting through the starlight, heard strange cries and echoing answers through the silent night. They were the fishermen of the Gambia, working the rich grounds with their dug-out pirogues.

XI

Happy Voyage

There are degrees of poverty, all of them relevant to the place, the circumstances, the moment. The threshold moves up and down with people's expectation of what they should receive from life. The tycoon whose enterprise tumbles so that his mansion must be exchanged for a suburban villa considers himself to be in poverty. The cardboard box dwellers of London, when compared to the poor of the Gambia, are wealthy. Their shelters are palaces in comparison to the hovels of Banjul. In the conurbations of the Gambia, acre upon acre of mud and adobe dwellings, with no services but a weak tap to every hundred families, house half a million souls. Our cardboard boxes are an indelible stain on our national conscience; a simple reallocation of resources could sweep deprivation to one side. We have the poor because we choose to have them, not because any financial or economic quirk of fate decrees them. They are victims of politics.

The Gambia has poverty beyond any remedy that could be contrived by financial or political jugglers, or even by the sacrifice of the few rich families who manage to exploit their pathetic economy to their advantage. This poverty is caused by over population and by the irresistible failure of the rains. But even these people are on a different plane from their starving fellows across the African continent; Gambian tummies may seldom be full but they are not always empty. Most of the people eat, some more often than once a day. Wendy and I are aware that within the world's pecking order we are part of a minority of a minority of a minority. Chance has placed us in a rich society, in the affluent class of that society and in a corner of that class which has leisure and resources to live in the way we wish to live. We are aware that our good fortune is made possible by the lesser fortune of others. In spite of our position in the upper echelons of the poverty league we do not regard ourselves as wealthy people.

The Gambia River follows a swathe of green valley some 200 miles long and 30-odd miles wide which juts into the area of Senegal. Banjul is at the entrance to the river, on its southern side. It is not an easy place to approach, with a low, sandy coast, a considerable current running out of the river and haze over the horizon throwing doubt on the accuracy of sights. We picked up the entrance buoy a mile off, perhaps by luck as we have no electronic machines to give pin-point positions. Our ancient methods of navigation usually bring us to a safe landfall.

We sailed into a wide estuary, close along the shore past the nondescript town, a palm-fringed beach, a few ships lying

Close along the shore past the nondescript town

alongside the quays and others at anchor in the roadstead. The big pirogues were drawn up on the beach, a colourful mob jostled and shouted; tall straight women in flowing robes, men with red fezzes, long, gaily coloured coats. Already we could hear it and smell it – Africa. We dropped anchor off a tumbledown shipyard. The heat hit us as if someone had opened the door of a furnace. We set *Iskra*'s awnings; they cover the boat from stem to stern, protecting her and us against the direct rays of the sun and encouraging the faint breeze to flow through the boat. It was Sunday evening. Wendy and I savoured the stillness of the boat at rest after the tumble of the ocean, sat in the cockpit with a glass of wine, sniffed the perfumed air, watched strange birds wheeling and diving, listened to the subdued hum of people, the muezzins calling the faithful to prayer, another day turning itself to a night of stars. The fishing pirogues came home, paddling past us with long, graceful strokes. We slept a full night, undisturbed by watches and the need to be alert.

My friend Bill Howser went to the Gambia in his boat some fifteen years ago. He told me stories about the place which made me want to go there. The people were gentle and friendly, he said, there was no violence, the boat was always safe with no one on board, food was plentiful and cheap. The Gambia River was a paradise, crocodiles lurked in the shallows, scarlet and green birds flashed over the river, troops of baboons swung through the forests. I should go there at once, he said. I had been there in fact, during the war, in the old *Celtic Star* when Banjul was still called Bathurst. I remembered little about it except that I got very drunk on some unmentionable spirit which gave me a hangover for a week.

Wendy has a friend in Banjul; she met Pierre in London when she did her Health Education Diploma. Pierre was on the same course, his address was scribbled on one of the bits of paper that Wendy never throws away. I have another friend, Sainey, who works on the African service of the BBC. The next day we met Abdullah, a longshoreman whom we contracted to look after our affairs. 'I take you immigration Master,' he said affably, 'I take you Customs, Harbour Master – very quick, very easy.' He had a pleasant smile. Abdullah conducted us through the jungle of officials with good humour and without fuss. The money changers sat cross-legged in a line outside the post office, wads of notes in their hands which they flicked through with forefinger and thumb. They gave us the black market rate for our pound notes, as quoted in the local paper.

Banjul was teeming, noisy, smelly, colourful, sweltering hot, dusty, black. The bazaars were stuffed with rolls of cloth, gay prints to funereal black. In the Hermitage arcade, men with sewing machines would make you a shirt in as long as it takes to drink a couple of gin-and-tonics on the verandah above. People were selling everything, everywhere. Thin women sitting beside the road in a patch of shade with a few tomatoes or oranges or bananas on the ground in front of them, tall men with bundles of towels or cloth on their heads, children offering live chickens, snake-charmers with reedy pipes, their partners in the act coiling themselves up off the ground, looking round with inquisitive eyes, flicking tongues; beggars, thin, maimed, held out their hands and gazed at us with feeble hope in their eyes. Nothing could be bought without an argument about the price — it was expected, even demanded. We were pestered to buy or to give or to look, on all sides, without pause, as if we were the fount of all riches suddenly appearing in their midst to dispense the white man's wealth. In a way that is what we were. Often there was an edge of threat in their importuning; we were rich, they were poor, we must redress this at least in part. We could see the justice in it.

The threats increased as we strayed away from the main streets into the maze of humble dwellings behind, the press of human souls never diminishing. Our search for Pierre, with Wendy's scrap of paper beside us, took us deep into the vortex of this sprawl of dwellings where white people do not go.

Our progress was accompanied by a considerable party, some leading the way, others following, outriders on the perimeters to ensure that news of our progress was properly spread about. Pierre's name clearly meant something, which was probably the best insurance for our safety. As we penetrated deeper the streets became narrower. It was dark now, the pools of light from oil lamps threw grotesque shadows against the mud walls. We came to a kind of bar, or perhaps the verandah of a lodging house, which our guide triumphantly identified as Pierre's residence. We went in with him while our escort waited outside. People were drinking beer out of bottles. Pierre's sister was there, slightly tipsy.

Pierre, it transpired was no longer in residence, he had moved to another part of town. She rustled about in a drawer behind the counter and came out with a telephone number. We spent half an hour in small talk, money for our beer was refused. Then we began to retrace our twisting path back towards the boatyard, which was itself in a slum area of the town. The crowd behind us thinned as we took them further from their base. We gave our guide money, but not enough he said. As we got nearer home his aggressiveness increased. Only when we invoked the name of Pierre did he consent to leave us. He may have enlisted an accomplice because we were attacked a few minutes after he went. A large man came up behind us, quietly, like a cat and made a grab for my watch. He grabbed my arm, wrenched at the watch and hurled me to the ground. Wendy kept him off for long enough for me to get up and he ran off.

The Atlantic Hotel was one of several scattered round the white beaches of Banjul. The hotels were financed by the World Bank in its wisdom, in the belief that they would bring prosperity. Hotels are not a labour-intensive industry. To the general population of Banjul, like Pierre's sister and the people we met in her house, the hotels are objects of ostentatious wealth contributing nothing to their welfare. Instead, they generate bitterness and jealousy, sometimes even hatred and violence. The tourists flaunt wealth and invite envy as they are followed through the poor streets by hungry eyes. Now, for their safety, they are not allowed to stray from the hotels without a guard with them who shepherds them round the markets and bazaars of Banjul and then delivers them safely back to their hotel. European men wandering about in shorts and women in scant bikinis are an affront to Muslim puritanism.

The anchorage off the old shipyard wasn't a safe place to leave *Iskra* alone although Abdullah looked after her as well as he could. A Swede in the only other yacht in the anchorage had his outboard motor stolen very quickly, followed by a break-in when he was ashore and the loss of his radio and all his money. Wendy left her washing on the line all night – it was gone by morning. Instead of locking *Iskra* when we went ashore, we left her wide open with lights on and radio playing and this seemed to keep her safe. We decided to move out of Banjul when we were attacked again on our way back to the boat one evening. We always walked warily, one eye behind our backs. I called 'Watch out' as a shadowy figure stepped behind us and made a dive for Wendy's bag. He made a lunge with a knife glinting in his hand, missed the strap of her bag and her arm by inches. We got our backs against a wall, near the dock gate, fortunately, and both of us started to shout at the top of our voices. The watchman came out, the man stood in front of us undecided, the knife in his hand and then he shrugged his shoulders, turned on his heel and walked off into the darkness of the narrow streets. Wendy did not carry a bag again and I gave up wearing a watch.

Abdullah found us a pilot and we moved *Iskra* 6 miles up Oyster Creek to Denton Bridge. The pilot was Abdullah's father, we found out. *Iskra* wound her way up a green mangrove stream, the pilot taking her carefully from side to side round tight bends and through narrow cuts. 'No crocodiles now,' he said, 'all handbags for tourists now – all gone to London. No baboons – they all gone to the Abuko Nature Reserve.' There were still a few green parakeets that flew across our bow, low over the muddy water and a few white herons standing on one leg in the shallows, fishing with the studied patience displayed by all fishermen. There was at least one crocodile left in Banjul whose acquaintance we made. He lay motionless in a turgid pool in the middle of the dance-floor of a local nightclub, observing the dancers with a solemn eye.

We found Sainey, who greeted us with great enthusiasm and came on board *Iskra* with his tape-recorder for us to make two recordings, one for the BBC and one for Banjul Radio. The anchorage at Denton Bridge was quiet and clean. There were a couple of local boats there, looked after by a watchman who was not quite as honest as Abdullah, a police post by the bridge and an hotel we could go to if we wanted to walk along the road for 2 miles.

Sainey was proud of what was happening in the Gambia away from the hotels and the tourists and the degeneracy of Banjul. He took us to a women's garden project outside the urban sprawl of Sukutan, a few miles from Banjul. The women were given strips of land, they were given seeds, irrigation was supplied and they were taught how to grow and tend crops. If they looked after their strip and it produced, which most of them seemed to do, their surplus produce was sold through a co-operative. If they didn't, the land was taken away from them and given to someone else. The land is good and the scope for this type of development is enormous. This project is financed locally, not by the World Bank.

A red dust from the Sahara blows over every living and growing thing in the Gambia. It gets into hair, eyes, ears and lungs, causing a form of catarrh which Wendy soon picked up. 'What we need,' Sainey told us, 'is not hotels for tourists – they bring us no help in our struggle against underdevelopment. We need a programme of tree planting round the perimeter of our country, where the fertile river valley meets the desert. The desert is encroaching, the rains are less and less regular and less and less prolific. Trees would be better than hotels if they really want to put money where it is needed.' It is all desperately hard work in the stifling heat.

Sainey took us down the coast to another project run by caring, thinking people, the fishing co-operative at Brufut, 15 miles south of Banjul. We saw the big pirogues come surging in through the ocean surf, a tall, robed figure in the stern with a long steering oar, men paddling for their lives. They were met by a hundred laughing, shouting helpers who ran waist deep into the waves as the pirogues came, grabbed the gunwales and ran the big canoes up the beach. The fish were distributed by the co-operative, every person receiving his share with no unearned profits to middlemen.

Sainey took us home to dinner with his girlfriend Adele, who had driven us to the women's garden project and for miles around Banjul in her car. Sainey has three wives as well as Adele. 'I haven't any money,' he told us, 'but I have a lot of wives and this makes me very happy.' He was proud of another girlfriend he once had in Singapore who has his child. He showed us a picture of the boy. Sainey lives in a simple hut in the centre of a compound somewhere in the depths of Banjul, his wives living all around him, all of them with children. We met several of the children and one of his wives; they were charming, the children polite and well educated. As well as working for the BBC Sainey is a writer, contributing to African

The fish were distributed by the co-operative...

magazines and newspapers. He and Adele, assisted by various children who were despatched for supplies, cooked us a fish supper – a strong curry with a delicious sauce.

We spent another day with Wendy's friend Pierre, who came on board *Iskra*, very dapper with goatee beard, malacca cane and a black suit. He asked us to spend the day with him and picked us up in his truck. The two of us squeezed in on the front seat and we threaded our way to his home on the outskirts of the town. Pierre had been a Public Health Inspector in Banjul when Wendy knew him but a few years ago he started his own butchering business which had clearly prospered. We spent the morning in his house, listening to his tapes and talking to his wife Ailse. She is a Nigerian. As well as looking after Pierre and the four children — again, all of them delightful — Ailse is the headmistress of a Catholic girls' secondary school.

The house was spacious, simple and informal, the garden inhabited by several sheep, two sows with piglets, various assorted ducks and a dog. There were a number of grapefruit trees. The children filled three hessian sacks with the fruit. 'This will last you to Brazil,' Pierre said. Ailse cooked a stupendous meal – rice, fish poached in hot sauce made of chile, garlic and black and white pepper, steamed egg plant with tomato sauce and a salad. We loved Pierre and his family. As we drove round Banjul he showed us how the weather is changing. The winters used to be colder with more rain; he showed us dried-up ponds and watercourses, stretches of barren land which were once productive. 'The Sahara is creeping in year by year,' he said, 'we need trees,' echoing Sainey. 'The World Bank can think of nothing but profits – hotels – bah!'

Wendy got the same story from Dr Zaballala, in charge of the World Health Organisation in the Gambia. She was struggling to bring medicines and health care to the villages. They needed a boat with an engine to bring people to hospital. A sick woman from a village on the north side of the river might be lucky enough to get a lift to hospital in a dug-out canoe, or even a pirogue. If she had a haemorrhage in childbirth, she would almost certainly die on the way. They need drugs such as Chloroquinin for malaria, antibiotics, aspirin, disinfectant – all in short supply because they have no foreign currency. Notices are put in hotel rooms asking the tourists to leave behind any spare drugs they may have.

Dr Zaballala had very little money for training staff in health care. She recruits workers from the villages and trains them in her clinic in Banjul, sending them back with at least a minimum of knowledge about hygiene, diet and the recognition of symptoms. The health workers are paid by the villagers in kind; an hour's work on his plot, a repair in his house, a gift of food. Many of them are illiterate. The villages are given graphic charts which illustrate likely symptoms in grisly detail. The patient brings a marked chart with him to the clinic. Dr Zaballala's primary health care programme is well known and respected in many African countries but she has to perform a constant juggling operation with inadequate resources, using imagination and improvisation where money cannot be found. Wendy spent a day with her and wrote an article about her work which she sent back to *Nursing Times* magazine in England.

By the time we left the Gambia we had tired of the heat, the red Sahara dust, the noise, the smell, the constant fending-off of robbers. A boy of about twelve whom Wendy had been kind to the first day we went ashore became our main tormentor. He met us on the jetty every day we were in Banjul, asking us for money and following us wherever we went. We were shot of him while *Iskra* was in Denton Bridge but he contrived to find out when we came to town on the bus. Finally, Abdullah piloted us back to the anchorage off the shipyard where we lay for a day before we left. As soon as we went ashore the boy was there, with astonishing persistence asking us for money and offering all manner of spurious services.

Even walking along the beach between the Atlantic Hotel and the spot where the pirogues were built we were plagued by importuners. They usually became aggressive no matter how polite and understanding we tried to be. Before we left I went for a wash in the very dirty shower in the boatyard. I hung my clothes, my wallet in a pocket, on the back of the door. When I finished a large, muscular individual came and told me that he had watched me having a shower, could easily have stolen my money but, being an honourable man, had refrained from doing so. Therefore, in view of his virtue, would I give him money? When I declined he became aggressive. I was lucky to regain the dinghy without a fight.

Our friends Julie and Dave, whom we met later, had an opposite experience in the Gambia. Having a good engine and a shallow-draught boat they had gone far up river to Georgetown. There were no baboons or crocodiles but the people in the villages, they said, were lovely. They had seen the old Portuguese trading posts from the early eighteenth century, the stone circles at Wassu, the huge, unexplained V-shaped stone at Kerrvatch.

It may be that we receive the treatment we deserve, that our approach is wrong, or our standards of behaviour off-key or our expectations too high. It is naive to expect people in foreign lands with different cultures to behave as we behave. If we had never strayed from the beaten tourist path, or even the yachtsman's path, we would probably have suffered no inconvenience to our European susceptibilities. We would then not have met the many delightful Gambians, whose friendship we value. I would have stayed longer in the Gambia, seen more and met more Gambians but our voyage had to proceed. Wendy was tormented by the heat and the never-ending wrangle over the simplest shopping transaction, both of us by the dirt and the duplicity of Gambians. Gambians do not seem to have derived much grace from their association with Europeans, nor Europeans much discretion from their exposure to Islamic culture.

We left the Gambia on Christmas Day bound for Salvador in Brazil, 2,100 miles away. *Iskra* was once again full of stores. Pierre's grapefruit were in sacks under the cockpit floor, we had bought each other Christmas presents in the market, nicely worked things in leather and wood. The tin-locker was replenished with whatever was available from the sparse supermarket shelves of Banjul. We left Abdullah with a suitable reward for his service and a letter of recommendation to show to other yachtsmen. We sailed out of the great wide muddy river with the last of the ebb, down along the beach where the blond English and Danish and Swedish ladies were exposing their skin cells to the sun's cancerous glare, past the palm thatched shacks on the shore where the pirogues were drawn up and the master shipwright was directing his chippies, away from teeming humanity into the quiet ocean.

It is the wonder of sailing that whatever amalgam of experience we may pass through, however concentrated the impact of a new place, new emotions, new problems, new friends, it is all cut off at a stroke the moment the anchor is hove home. The world is transformed to a place of space and peace where our prosperity, our destiny even, is thrown into our own hands. No person will dictate to us here, only the brute force of nature which we have learnt to accept with an even mind. We are governed by our own skills, our own wisdom which will rebound on us, either to our advantage or against us according to how we conduct ourselves. The world for us is reduced to an essential simplicity where cause and effect lie close alongside one another and where we win or lose only by our own judgement. The sun shone, the sea was calm, a cool breeze set *Iskra*'s bow-wave to chuckle under her forefoot, our dolphin turned his blunt snout towards the ocean once more, the shore slipped away from us, we were at peace.

It was *Iskra*'s ninth crossing of the Atlantic Ocean. Before, I had been by myself and on those voyages I got to know myself well – aspects of myself that I had not been familiar with, some perhaps to my credit, others not. The way people behave and think and react when they are under prolonged strain and pressure often shows them in an unsuspected light. On this voyage Wendy showed me aspects of herself that I had not been fully aware of, as no doubt I revealed myself to her. The ocean shows us up for what we are, the facade we present to the world is a frail garment, soon stripped away when the horizon of life is expanded to infinity.

Iskra's cabin is about 10 feet long and perhaps 8 feet wide from the back of one settee across to the other. The fo'c'sle is almost the same length but, of course, it converges to a point at the bow where there are racks for rope and spare tackle and sails and gear. The fo'c'sle is a repository for gear. There are tools, a vice that fastens to the bench on the starboard side, shelves for ready-use lashings and blocks and shackles. There are varnished wooden slats fastened across the frames where all manner of things are lashed – spring clips, bulldog grips, track slides for the twins, spare strops, tyers for the mains'l, the handle for the mast winch, the lead line. At sea the gear rattles and jingles, adding to the music of the ocean round *Iskra*'s bow and the soft voice of the wind. The fo'c'sle smells of tar and linseed oil. There is one bunk in the fo'c'sle, quite a wide bunk at its after end but narrowing as it stretches forward into the bow. Our folding bicycles are stowed on the fo'c'sle bunk when it is not in use.

When I was alone in *Iskra* I often slept in the fo'c'sle bunk. Through the porthole set in the hull by my head I can watch the ocean, almost be a part of it. When *Iskra* rolls to port the sea comes racing up across the glass, hinting at the green mysteries below. When she rolls to starboard, the porthole breaks out into the cool air. Wave-tops, the horizon, flash across my vision, the trade wind clouds and the pale blue sky are my companions for a few seconds before I am pitched back into the ocean. I was always asleep in minutes.

Wendy is another who goes to sleep in minutes. Her bunk is on the port side of the cabin, mine on the starboard. The chart table is over her feet. One oil lamp swings in its gimbal above her head, the other above mine. There are two small paintings and a photograph on the bulkhead over her bunk, one of *Iskra* by an old sailor we knew, the other a small nostalgic oil painting of sea and sky, and the photograph is of *Iskra* in an Icelandic fjord. The ship's radio is on Wendy's side, bookcases and a good luck charm given us on this voyage by an old Indian in the Andes, are on mine. I can stand upright in *Iskra*'s cabin, it is a roomy, airy place for us to live in; we never feel cramped or restricted. The chart table is the ship's nerve centre; the clock and barometer are above it, the switchboard for navigation lights and the electric pump on the aft bulkhead, a hand-bearing compass and my sextant stow beside it. There is a bookcase with navigation books, pilots, reference books, a rack for chart pencil, dividers. A small drawer under the books holds the chronometer, parallel rules. The ready-use charts are in a locker under the chart table, spare charts under the fo'c'sle bunk.

The galley is Wendy's domain although I do cook when she is sick and occasionally to give her a rest. We cook on a two-burner gas stove, with a grill, slung in a gimbal against *Iskra*'s roll. We have no oven, Wendy bakes bread, better than any bought bread, in an old pressure cooker on a gas ring. The plates and mugs and china bowls are in racks over the galley. When she has found her sea legs Wendy conjures wonderful things out of the galley from our store of tins, from the fresh vegetables stowed in slatted boxes in the cool of the fo'c'sle bench, from plastic jars filled with beans and split peas and rice and barley, sometimes from the sea when a fish accepts our hook. The worse conditions are, the better the food becomes. She is inspired by adversity.

In the trades we sit in the cockpit watching *Iskra*'s progress for hour on hour, a weather eye toward the horizon, the configurations of cloud, in case they might harbour a squall or call for a trim of the sails. She may demand an adjustment to the gear to get the last fraction of speed from her – set tops'l, change stays'ls, ease or check the twins' guy-ropes. We live the life of Riley, eating and sleeping and laughing like passengers on a liner.

For a week the north-east trade wind had us in its firm, friendly grip. Once we got clear of the African coast and across the busy shipping lane *Iskra* reeled off 120 miles a day with effortless ease. The twins were set, the mains'l lashed to the gallows leaving the deck clear. We rigged a sun awning over

The north-east trade wind
had us in its firm, friendly grip

the cockpit, opened the fo'c'sle and the main hatches so that a cool breeze flowed through the boat. We read books, played music – Mozart, Beethoven string quartets, and Schubert songs for me, ballet music for Wendy with occasional jazz and Beatles for good measure. Our tastes are catholic.

We watched flying fish skim the wave-tops, marvelled at the dolphins' easy grace, sorrowed at tiny, lost land birds clinging to the rigging with a last, desperate grip, flung greetings to the storm petrels that weaved and swayed across our wake. We saw no ship, no human presence to defile this all-embracing wonder. *Iskra* rolled herself towards Brazil, day and night, night and day, shouldering her way through the endlessly varied hills and dales of the ocean with steady purpose, a magical coming together of all the art that goes to fashion a sailing ship. She is a miracle of ingenuity, the rounded sails full of silent power, the subtle lines of her hull, the web of rope and wire sharing the strains between them, the mute vane carefully guiding her progress, all the age-old systems of a sailing vessel brought together to smooth her onward movement.

The nights were as lovely as the days. We watched for a green flash when the sun met the horizon, but never saw it. We lit the oil lamps in the cabin, oil navigation lights, the soft, warm glow giving off confidence, bringing us closer together. Our tiny capsule, which seems to us so spacious, moving purposefully across the world. Sometimes the moon hovered over us, regarding us with patient forbearance. Soon we saw the Southern Cross, low on the horizon ahead of us. We sat and watched it all, marvelled at it and were happy.

It all changed, as we knew it must, when we reached the doldrums. The trade wind faltered, losing its consistency and the truth of its direction. New Year's Day was squally from the north-west with sudden calms, so that *Iskra* rolled in the swell,

We sat and watched it all,
marvelled at it and were happy

her twins flat and empty, like washing on a line. It was my birthday. Wendy found me a cake, candles, presents, goodwill. We laughed, I swam overboard, diving into the deep, mysterious bowl of ocean until I was frightened by its vastness, its latent energy, its overwhelming authority. Wendy doesn't like me to swim in the ocean, it frightens her. We ran the old engine for a spell sometimes, putting on a few miles and helping our spirits.

It took a week of anxious coaxing and constant vigilance to get *Iskra* through the doldrums. Sometimes the squalls would come out of nothing, out of the darkness or from a rogue direction, catching us with the twins aback or with the mains'l guyed out to windward. Sometimes we could see them coming, guess their strength and scramble to douse the tops'l or to drop the stays'l or scandalise the main by letting go the peak halyard. Sometimes pounding rain washed *Iskra* clean, cascading down the sail in cataracts of sweet water. Sometimes the squalls sent her racing through a flat sea, every rope, every wire bar-tight, tensed with strain. The squalls would come from any direction, with little warning, but as we progressed south they began to swing more and more to the south-east so that the weeks of sailing with twins were forgotten, *Iskra* close-reaching or hard on the wind on the port tack. Soon we were picking up the powerful direction-finding transmission from Fernando do Noronha, a group of islands way out into the Atlantic off the north-east coast of Brazil. I was able to cross these bearings with my sights, giving a valuable check.

It took longer than I expected to get through the doldrums. Two or three times we thought we were clear of them, only to find ourselves once more with an oppressed, overcast sky and a calm. Wendy was given a gentle ducking when she crossed the Equator. Sights of the sun were often taken through a screen of light cloud and with a hazy, insubstantial horizon but they were always within a small margin of accuracy whenever they could be checked. Sights were taken every day; it is a routine I was taught to follow by Captain Macay and I have never neglected it. We saw no ships in all the 2,000 miles until we came within 50 miles of the coast of South America. Pierre's grapefruit gave us a juicy treat every day, putting us in good humour. On 9 January we had our worst day, only making good 55 miles in a hot, humid ocean. Then it all changed again.

A steady breeze came at last from the north-east to our surprise, the horizon went all firm, the sky cleared and fine-weather clouds came back. Slowly the wind went round to the south-east where it was supposed to be and *Iskra* began to move with her old purpose. The big, light sails were put away as she felt the weight of the south-east trade wind. It blew hard for a while, up to force 7, and then it settled itself down, the breeze taking the heat out of the sun and the boat alive with movement again. We began to realise that our adventure was ending with a kind of nostalgic regret, mixed with the excitement of a landfall. As we got closer to the coast *Iskra* began to race, as if impatient for harbour, like a horse coming to the home paddock. We began to feel the benefit of the Brazilian current in our favour and one afternoon the great city of Salvador came up fine on our starboard bow. I felt the flush of happy satisfaction that comes with a good landfall. The business of navigation is a recurring magic. That a pale star or the fleeting sun, caught for an instant in the sextant's cunning arrangement of arms and shades and mirrors, can resolve itself into the certainty of latitude and longitude is a never-ending surprise to me. I wouldn't change the fun of it for an electric box for all the coffee in Brazil.

It was nearly dusk when we arrived. We sailed across the front of the city as the setting sun threw its skyscrapers and towers into sharp relief. We passed close to the lighthouse on Cabo São Antonio, past a fisherman tending his lines who gave us a grave salute, rounded a rocky promontory until we came to the ancient town with its churches and spires and jumble of red-tiled roofs, all among palm trees and the dense green tropic foliage. A shower of rain swept across with the evening, soaking us and everything with its renewing vigour, as it does every evening and every morning in Salvador. We spotted the light on the harbour mole, lowered and furled our sails as *Iskra* rounded into the wind off the pier-head and made her way to anchor. This was a fairy city, lights twinkling, the waterfront alive with movement, a high cliff topped by the cathedral, the old fort built on a rock in the centre of the harbour, yachts and trading schooners at anchor. The chain rattled over the fair lead – *Iskra* was at rest.

XII

Journey's End

Brazil is a riddle, a vast, sprawling enigma. It holds everything within its bounds, the best of everything, the worst of everything, the kindest, the cruellest, the most beautiful, the ugliest, the richest, the poorest. Our first day wasn't our best, our second was worse. We went ashore, unwisely as it turned out, as soon as *Iskra* was safely berthed to find ourselves a meal. We found nothing open at 8 pm except an indifferent café where we ate an indifferent meal at a high price – Wendy would have prepared a nicer one for nothing. We were ripped off, effortlessly, by the affable young man who changed our dollars. When we got back to the quay we found it all locked and barred, our dinghy on the wrong side. We had to climb a high fence. Wendy got stuck on top, her skirt ripped by the barbed wire, to the delight of a ribald gang of layabouts outside the dock gate.

We slept late the next morning and went ashore in the heat of the day to clear ourselves and the yacht. We discovered that we had to pass through no fewer than four different bureaucracies: police, customs, Captain of the Port, port medical officer, each one a good distance away from the next. At the police office, which we found in a back street behind a disused church, I was refused attendance because I was wearing short trousers. The official was inflexible. I was free to leave the country, he said, if I did not wish to comply with its regulations. As it is more than a thousand miles to the nearest other country we went back on board and I changed. The office was closed for lunch (three hours) when we got back.

We went up the cliff in an elevator, to the old market place behind the cathedral, the square surrounded by fifteenth and sixteenth century Portuguese houses and churches. Brazil has operated a strict conservation policy for its ancient buildings for fifty years. There were money changers in the square, just as there had been in Banjul; one of them offered to change 50 dollars at a good rate. He counted the money out with studied care, turned round for a second to talk to a friend behind him, gave us the notes done up with an elastic band, took the 50 dollars and vanished into the crowd. The notes were worthless old currency from before the last devaluation. We went sadly back down the elevator.

The police took nearly two hours; forms to be filled in, lists to be prepared, questions to be answered bearing no possible relevance to our situation, undertakings to be entered into. The customs we found in an office near the docks – another two hours. We were asked to give a list of every piece of equipment and every item of stores *Iskra* had in her. Dealing with the Captain of the Port (one hour) was comparatively simple. We waited in a queue of supplicants for some favour the Captain of the Port had at his disposal and then our names, ages, places of birth and other important details of our existence were entered in a large ledger together with details of our boat. We baulked at the port doctor, risking immediate expulsion from the country. Some of our friends fared worse. Unlike the British, the French need visas for Brazil. Our neighbour in the anchorage had obtained his visa before leaving France but it had expired by the time he reached Brazil. He and his crew were made to fly to Paraguay, get a visa from the Brazilian consul and fly back again – or leave the country in forty-eight hours.

The purpose behind this bureaucracy seems to be to make it as difficult as possible to visit Brazil in a yacht. For those who come by plane, we were told, there are no problems. It was hard to imagine the real reason for it. It is self-perpetuating, perhaps because so many people depend on it for their livelihood, not so surprising in a country with an increasing middle class, largely unemployed. Another Englishman we heard of was fined 500 dollars for failing to comply with one or other of the regulations that haunt visiting yachts. Rather than pay the fine he upped anchor and went, sailing some 3,000 miles to the Caribbean without a stop.

In the main, Brazilians are a friendly, welcoming people. We got to know how to comport ourselves; we found that there was an official black market currency rate and we found a man who was prepared to understand my Spanish and who changed our money honestly. 'Change a little at a time,' he advised us, 'the rate goes up every day.' When we came to Brazil the rate was 70 cruzados to 1 dollar. When we left ten months later it was 1,000. We never fully understood and still do not, how people living on a fixed income are able to survive. Surprisingly, Brazil gives generous refuge to fugitives from other lands. The train robber Ronald Biggs was happily making his living as an indoor decorator while we were in Rio, there were left wing refugees from Chile as well as ex-Nazis wanted for war crimes. An American we met could eke out his Vietnam veteran's pension in Brazil because he had a Brazilian child, and could in consequence stay in the country. Another, from Surinam wanted to start a business in Santos. 'It's no problem,' he told us, 'I'll find a Brazilian wife.'

It was Wendy who pointed out the curious mixture of Portugal and Africa that makes Brazil. The architecture is Portuguese. The pavements in the street are decorated with the same mosaic we found in Lisbon, the profusion of fifteenth and sixteenth century churches and buildings is remarkable. Cities like Ouvo Preto, which we visited, are more Portuguese than many cities in Portugal. The language, even the bureaucracy which touched us so close, are Portuguese. The food is African, the music has the beat of the jungle, the dance is African, a large minority of the people, especially in Salvador and Rio and the eastern coastal strip, are direct descendants of the five million slaves brought to Brazil between the sixteenth and eighteenth centuries. The Catholic religion, which the Portuguese colonists imposed on the native Indians and the imported slaves, has been modified by the waves of heathens to include their own imagery and belief. Voodoo and heathen rites still mingle uneasily with the established Catholicism.

Some of the churches are decked out with such profusion of gold and silver as makes even churches in Spain or Portugal look like Calvinist chapels. The gold and silver cloy the senses; too much extravagance succeeds only in being vulgar. The church of the São Francisco convent in Salvador, the inside structure all covered in gold, seemed to us one of the ugliest churches we had ever been in. Even villages in remote corners of the long east coast often have an ancient church as centrepiece. Some date from the seventeenth or even the sixteenth century like the tiny church on the beach at Parati Mirim. No other part of the Americas has anything to compare with Brazil's architectural heritage.

Brazil was cheap for us, not for the people who happen to be Brazilians. Our money was in dollar notes, in a concealed compartment under a bookcase in *Iskra*'s cabin. Twenty dollars lasted us a week; all our food, the odd meal ashore, the odd garment that took Wendy's fancy in the shops. Every week when we went to see our friend the money changer the rate had gone up, keeping our stipend stable. The supermarket near the dock was stocked with everything anyone could think of. Plenty of Brazilians could afford to fill the giant trolleys, twice the size of a supermarket trolley in England, until they were heaped like Guy Fawkes bonfires with tins and packets and boxes and great sides of meat. There were plenty more outside, hungry eyes glued to the windows. There is always a guard with a gun at the supermarket door. Twice we were at the checkout when the woman in front of us was short of enough cruzados to pay her bill; Wendy chipped in a few coins or a few dirty notes, receiving a faint smile and a murmured word of thanks in return. Poverty lies close to shame. We wondered what she would do next week when her cruzados would buy less.

We wandered all over Salvador, by bus round the skyscraper part we had sailed past where the tourist hotels are, through glass arcades alongside golden beaches. Tourist cities are all much the same wherever they are, offering little insight into the real life of the place. We took an ordinary bus instead of the tourist bus. The old part of Salvador is a different world; narrow, winding, cobbled streets, jumbled up red tiled shops and houses, ancient churches, poverty cheek by jowl with the tall hotels. It is hard to imagine how the two extremes can live together in such close proximity.

It was late when the bus put us off in the cathedral square. 'Let's walk down instead of the elevator – it can't be far.' The lights dimmed as we progressed down the side of the cliff, the streets grew meaner. Ragged children gazed at us and disappeared into a labyrinth of criss-cross alleys, there were no women to be seen, the men observed us, some with incredulity, others with sly envy in their eyes. We were conspicuous, not through our clothes or even our fair skins but because we didn't fit and couldn't fit. No matter how simply we were dressed, how devoid of any outward sign of affluence, the human condition showed through. We were rich, they were poor.

We began to feel uneasy. We passed a couple of cheap drink shops, a pool of light, a low hum of noise that seemed to stop as we walked past. 'I'm not sure this is very nice,' Wendy said. It didn't seem that we had far to go but the streets were now full of people, some lying on the ground, drunk perhaps, some sitting with their backs against the house walls. Suddenly a plump, middle aged woman dressed in black ran out in front of us. 'Go back," she said urgently in Portuguese, 'muito perigoso – muito perigoso— mafioso, mafioso.' She turned us, pushed us back in the direction we had come and disappeared. We hurried back, glancing warily behind and from side to side until we found the wide, lit streets again. We made our way to the elevator, paid our 10 cents and were transported back to bright lights and shop windows and the safety of the environment we were accustomed to. It was a relief to get back to *Iskra* and be reassured that our lifeline to the familiar was still there.

We often went through the old quarter of Salvador, never

174

the part along the face of the cliff, but the old city where there were fascinating shops and churches and houses among the twisting alleys. We went in the daytime, still objects of interest but in comparative safety. As in Banjul, we got used to being alert, wary, like small animals or birds, eyes darting in every direction in constant vigilance. We found a cheap restaurant where we had wonderful food, the best we had in Brazil, strange spices, unfamiliar vegetables, hot sauces, curried fish and beans and mounds of feathery brown rice. The dish was called *bejoada*. The *suco*, fruit juices, of Salvador are like nothing else in the world.

We were in a hurry on the outward voyage to Argentina because we wanted to be there with the autumn weather, from March to May. We only called at Salvador, Moro São Paulo, a small place 20 miles down the coast from Salvador and Rio de Janeiro. Like all cities, the charm of Salvador soon wore thin; Moro São Paulo provided the contrast we always felt we needed. Moro was refreshing, a brisk sail across the wide bay of Todos os Santos. It has a seventeenth century fortification, the same lush vegetation of this rain-washed climate, a village of considerable charm having a lovely beach, fishing boats and friendly people. It was quite a sophisticated village where people from Salvador came to spend holidays or weekends but there were no tourists or hotels. It boasted a vegetarian restaurant. There were chickens running about the unpaved roads in and out of the houses, an old pig snorting about the ancient stone gateway to the little quay. We had dinner in a café on stilts over the sea, fishing boats drawn up below, the beach in a crescent of palm-fringed sand.

A couple of yachts lay at anchor in Moro; a wealthy German doctor and his family, his wife missing her home as sailing wives sometimes do and a Danish ketch on continuous charter to rotating groups coming from Denmark. She was owned by a commune which sent the charters every two or three weeks; the skipper was a professional. He had an eye for old boats and fell for *Iskra*. We had dinner with them; the skipper said he would give us sailing directions for Rio, 'Nothing to do with getting into the place you understand – that's easy. I'll tell you how to drive the bureaucracy once you get there.' He gave us a street map of Rio, marked on it the position of the offices we would have to visit to pass police, customs, immigration, Captain of the Port and health. 'You can easily spend three days getting clearance in Rio,' he said, 'I think you will thank me.' We did.

We took a ferry in Moro for an hour up the river through the forest to the town of Valença, another surprise in this country of surprises. Valença was seemingly untouched by commercialism, a simple, small country town with a splendid vegetable market, no cars that we could see, ox carts, donkeys, chickens in the streets, a pleasant bar where a smiling girl served us lunch. We would have stayed longer but there was only one ferry. On the way back most of our shopping was stolen by a smiling boy from beside us on the ferry seat. The moment the ferry docked he slipped ashore with our bag before I noticed and was gone in an instant.

We were ten days on the way to Rio, sailing down a thousand miles of flat coast, the mountains behind sometimes visible in the evening light. It was slow and hot. If we used the engine we got some breeze blowing across the boat but the engine made the cabin unbearable. At midday the sun was overhead. We passed under it one day, the true altitude at noon 89 degrees 27 minutes and it was bearing north. We tried to keep the deck cool with buckets of sea water, but there was no shade; *Iskra*'s varnished bridge deck was so hot that we couldn't walk on it. The canvas covered deck and the cockpit floor, which is scrubbed wood, were marginally cooler. The nights were a relief.

Breeze came after a couple of days, as it always does and *Iskra* was soon rolling along under twins. It is not an easy coast, which may account for the paucity of yachts. There are few safe harbours, the current is strong and sometimes sets inshore so that the greatest care must be taken. We knew we were on the easy leg of the voyage, going the other way we would have to contend with a contrary current and probably a headwind.

We passed through an extensive off-shore oilfield to the north of Cape Frio, clearly a new development because it wasn't on our charts. We sailed for a full day with the rigs all around us and were lucky to be clear of them by nightfall.

Cape Frio, a few miles north of Rio, was all calms and squalls from every direction, overcast and with rogue currents so that navigation was more by guess than by art. We spent a whole day with the cape in view, rolling in the calms so that *Iskra*'s insides were tumbled out of her and battling with sudden gusts of wind, the steep, confused swell stopping her dead the moment she tried to gather her way. Having worn our nerves to Irish pennants, this perverse coast played us a last trick, convincing me, when I saw the False Sugar Loaf Mountain, some eight miles to the east of Rio harbour, that we had arrived when we had not. Even bearings of the shore seemed to fit this false picture until I saw the mistake and put *Iskra* back on course with a curse.

We were both getting tired, a dangerous state to be in when entering a new harbour. We pinned in the boom to stop the worst of the slatting, dropped the heads'ls and both went to sleep for two hours, leaving *Iskra* to roll her guts out. Then we slept for another two hours until Wendy announced that there was wind, a headwind from the south. We'd had enough of it all by the time we sailed inside the island of Pai into the bay of Guanabara, the real Sugar Loaf Mountain in front of us, the granite mass of Christ the Redeemer high on the Corcovado Mountain behind the city, caught by the early sun on a bright, crisp morning. It was like waking from a bad dream. Rio is one of the most beautiful approaches to any harbour in the world, high mountains all around, the city on the port hand, another city almost as big, Niteroi, to starboard.

Soon we could distinguish Copacabana, Ipanema, the big suspension bridge over the harbour to Niteroi, the bays that indent the foreshore, each with its forested point and its honey coloured beach, the untouched jungle close behind. The city has excitement in its air, anything can happen here, and often does. We began to hear it and to smell it. There seemed to be flowers everywhere, flowering trees, flowering bushes, laid out gardens along the shore, avenues of tall palm trees. We passed close under the Sugar Loaf, gazed up at the crazily swinging cable car, avoided hurrying ferries blaring out music and full of laughing people. We sailed past the Rio Yacht Club, with its rows of immaculate dream-boats that never go to sea, past the Gloria Church, all blue and white and gold on a mountain of its own by the shore, like a baroque birthday cake.

As we turned to enter the Gloria Marina we noticed the pollution. The surface of the harbour was covered with a deep slick of oil, islands of refuse floating dejectedly, baulks of rotting timber, soaked cardboard, the ubiquitous plastic in every variety of bottle and box and crate and coloured rubbish. We found an empty mooring in the marina and tied our own rope to it, to avoid bringing the filth on board.

With confidence inspired by our Danish friend's map and his explicit instructions we located the office of the Naval Police; it was across the city in a mausoleum where thousands

We passed close under the Sugar Loaf

of people were queuing for permits or identity cards or some document demanded of them by the bureaucracy. We threaded our way through this multitude, dodged under a counter, down a passage, third left then through glass doors, clutching the instructions. Immigration was in another building, presided over by an ample lady who reluctantly granted us permission to stay in Brazil only after she had sent us out to have all our documents and our passports photocopied. Our Danish friend had been right.

We found out in Rio that our affairs at home were in a shambles. Our house had been pillaged by the tenants, we had employed an agent to look after it who had not looked after it, our furniture and valuables had been stolen and sold, our garden neglected, the roof was leaking, the rent had not been paid. It was the disaster that everyone told us had happened to them but which we didn't believe could happen to us.

Rio de Janeiro was the hub of our voyage, a watershed. The city seemed to contain all that is best and all that is worst in Brazil. Our knowledge is only gleaned from our voyage along the 3,600 miles of coastline with a few visits inland. We did not go to São Paulo or Brasilia or Manaos in the Amazon, or any of the cities in the north; the purpose and destination of our voyage was Argentina. We found Brazil so beautiful and so fascinating that we extended our homeward voyage to spend more time there. We made this decision on our way back from Argentina in July 1988.

Now that the voyage is over we tend to look back on it as having been all honey and fun. It was for much of the time, perhaps for all of the time we wish to preserve in our memories, but there were periods when it was all ruin. The first part of the passage from Rio to Uruguay was ruin. The weather was overcast, hot and humid. It rained for day after day before we left Rio, pouring, pelting rain that soaked into ourselves, our boat, our belongings. We did our shopping in pelting rain, traipsed round the flooded pavements of Rio to the customs, the immigration, the secret hideout of the Captain of the Port, to clear *Iskra* out, slogged on board in our waterlogged dinghy with our sodden purchases. Neither of us had ever seen such rain. We left in a gap between downpours. Soon a breeze came to take us out past the Sugar Loaf, through the patina of pollution, close inside the island of Redonda off Copacabana Beach and into the open sea. Our joy to be free of the city and on our own again was short lived.

The wind fell light and began to box the compass in a baffling display of perversity. Squall followed calm followed fierce gust that laid *Iskra* over. Wendy was sick, I fell in the cockpit and hurt my hand, the teapot upset itself over the galley stove. *Iskra* made 38 miles in the first day, most of it due to the south-going current. There was traffic about so that I couldn't sleep. I became more and more fatigued as one day of torture extended itself to three days, more and more bad tempered; we were still only 60 miles on our way, the coastal mountains still visible over to starboard. Then the wind came from the south, an unheard of direction for the time of year and we were close-hauled, struggling to make some headway through perpendicular waves which stopped *Iskra* dead. In one of the calms I hit my head on the boom, such a blow that it knocked me out in a heap on the cockpit floor. Wendy managed to get me into the cabin and onto my bunk, she thought I was concussed.

I recovered quickly but with a headache that lasted another day. We began to quarrel about stupid things, building up resentments over nothing, hurling cruel innuendos. Then we heard on the radio that Rio had suffered serious flooding the day after we left, there had been a landslide, one of the *favelas* had tumbled down the mountainside with appalling loss of life, shacks, tin hovels, people, rolling to the bottom of the mountain and burying themselves in a terrible heap of earth and rocks and muck and bodies. Everyone knows that the *favelas* are unsafe, that the mountainsides are unstable. To build their wretched houses the people cut down the trees, clear the vegetation, so that the rain sweeps the land away. There is no authority strong enough or with the compassion to harness Brazil's overflowing wealth to relieve the plight of *favela*-dwellers. They are poor, beyond the pale of society and therefore their lives are of no consequence. In a strange way, an unkind quirk of the human condition, hearing of the disaster made us feel better, cleverer for having got out of Rio just in time.

We had passed through bad patches before but always because of adversity, bad weather or some external threat which had the effect of pulling the two of us together, combining the rejuvenative sides of our minds to defeat an outsider. This latest attack on us was different, a divisive, continuous series of pricks and jabs of real or imagined importance that put us against each other. I found it difficult to sleep and whenever I did sleep Wendy would find it necessary to wake me for some reason. Wendy was sick, again and again. I made it worse for her by cooking strong-smelling concoctions for myself. My lips got burnt by the sun – it was her fault because she had bought the wrong sort of cream. She was almost tipped out of her bunk by a sudden squall – why hadn't I tied up her bunkboard for her? Stupidities built themselves up on more stupidities until there was an explosion. Harsh things were said, soon to be retracted in remorse.

Nothing goes on forever and at sea the balance of life always tips, sometimes so far that you nearly fall off the end of the plank, but always, in the end, back the other way so that purgatory is replaced by Nirvana. It happened when I glanced over the side on the fourth day of frustration. The wind had come fair for the first time, the humid umbrella of cloud had been folded up showing us the blue expanse of the sky for the first time since we left Rio. There in the sea, no more than a few inches from *Iskra*'s side, perhaps two or three inches below the surface of the ocean, keeping strict formation like guardsmen on parade, were six yellow fishes. 'Hey', I shouted, 'come and look at these chaps.' We kneeled side by side on the cockpit seat craning our heads overboard. They swam with effortless grace, slim long fellows with a black stripe down each side against their yellow bodies. We could see their eyes, their little mouths, the occasional flick of a tail, the imperceptible quiver of tiny fins which kept them riding along with *Iskra*, always in exact station. We watched them for an hour. They made us laugh, they brought us joy that swept away all resentment, all frustration.

Iskra was moving again. The northerly wind was freshening, twin stays'ls were set, the sea gurgled under her bow, sheets were taut, the sails fat and firm like the bosoms of a robust girl. She was alive, moving, rolling off the knots, our little fishes the harbingers of good fortune. They stayed with us for five days, always six of them, always in the same position. We couldn't see them at night but as soon as it got light there they were, swimming along beside us with a kind of desperate urgency when the wind freshened and *Iskra* picked up speed, meandering when the wind fell light. We couldn't understand what kept them there, what, if anything they found to eat, what extraordinary twist of the eternal wisdom that allows nature to flourish, should induce them to visit *Iskra* and fill our world with magical happiness.

With a fair current and a fair wind *Iskra* made short work of the thousand odd miles between Rio and Punta del Este in Uruguay. The slow progress at the beginning of the voyage was amply made up as the twins took her south at 150 miles or more a day. Wendy was much enamoured of two cream-coloured insects, some two inches long with wide, enquiring faces, spindly legs and beautifully formed wings, like the wings of a bat. They flew into the galley and settled themselves one on the kettle and the other in a plate-rack. The kettle one she transferred to a yoghurt carton providing him with a cabbage leaf to eat, the plate-rack one escaped into the bilges where I was afraid he would eat *Iskra*'s frames. I found him and launched him into the air, wishing him luck and happy landings. Wendy brought the kettle one to Uruguay, releasing him where the breeze would take him to the shore. 'You're upsetting nature. You've probably introduced a terrible pest to this country – they'll arrest you.'

In ten days we picked up Lobos Island, a few miles from our destination, the lighthouse on the island emitting a radio signal we could hear on our direction-finder. This is an invaluable instrument and was of great use to us all up and down the South American coast. The main headlands have radio lighthouses which can be picked up as much as a hundred miles distant. They offer a secure bearing, leaving no excuse for a vessel to run ashore even in thick weather. Yachtsmen are strangely reluctant to use radio direction-finders which are cheap and easily obtained. They prefer to rely on satellite navigation sets which are subject to error and can be wrongly interpreted. A Japanese yacht drove ashore at Cabo São Thomé and was lost the week before we came past the cape. There is a dangerous inshore set of the current at many of these capes which cannot easily be detected. The direction-finder shows it up at once. Fishermen, even ships, always use them.

The plank tipped again as we approached the land, the barometer dropped, the wind freshened so that we came up with the narrow channel between Lobos island and the mainland of Uruguay under our storm tri's'l and stay'sl, with a gale of wind behind us. It was just before dawn, we heard a loud honking noise coming from the island, wondered what it could be. 'Lobos Island,' I said to Wendy, '*Lobos de mar* – wolves of the sea – sealions.' The island is a sanctuary for them. As it got light we saw the harbour wall of Punta del Este, the skyscraper city behind with black clouds scudding through the tall buildings. The shore soon gave us a welcome lee, Wendy started the engine and we rounded up and made our way to a wooden quay. 'Nearly there – only one more leg – a couple of hundred miles up the River Plate.'

It was pleasant to be in a Spanish speaking country again where I could speak the language and Wendy could readily understand it. We found we could clear the ship easily and quickly, all in one place. We walked into the town, unsteadily until we found our land legs, bought ourselves coffee and a sticky bun in a pavement café where we could watch the world go by. Punta del Este and Buenos Aires are not like Latin American cities. The atmosphere hit us at once; this was a

European city. It was clean, cool, there were flower gardens in the squares, the shops opened at 9 in the morning, the men were dressed in suits, the women carried handbags, wore jewellery, money was changed at the bank, at the official rate, there was a spotless, pleasant fish shop on the quay, showers and a drink in the yacht club. We had experienced nothing like it since we left the Canary Islands. Punta del Este is, as we had been told, the Riviera of the south.

The harbour was full to the brim with expensive yachts, all lying at moorings. Remarkably, almost all were flying Argentine ensigns. 'I thought Argentina was a poor, Third World country with an economic crisis,' Wendy said. We saw a man rowing round and round *Iskra* in a dinghy, looking her over with a knowing eye. 'She's beautiful,' he said, 'wonderful.' Jorge told us he earned his living delivering yachts, mostly between Uruguay and Buenos Aires but sometimes further afield, to or from Brazil. 'They keep them here and use them to live on in the summer – it's only a few miles to Buenos Aires by plane. Sometimes they even go sailing, but mostly when they want the yacht moved I do it.' Jorge was a real fancier of old boats. 'We don't see many like this,' he said. His girlfriend in Buenos Aires was a teacher of English.

Jorge looked at our charts for us, showed us the way we should go up the river. We had bought our chart of the River Plate in England but because of the Falklands War chart corrections had not been notified and it was out of date. 'You are the first British yacht to go to BA since the war,' he said. We had been told to expect trouble. An Argentine friend we had met in Rio told us he had experienced difficulties with the British when he wanted to go to Gibraltar. They had refused entry to his yacht. He thought we might have difficulty with *Iskra* and might have to take her across the river and leave her in Uruguay, commuting backwards and forwards to Buenos Aires by ferry or plane. 'You may find some Argentines who are violently anti-British,' he said.

Punta del Este is a queen among seaside resorts – smart

hotels, lovely beaches, long cool drinks on the sidewalks, a discreet but perceptible air of people enjoying themselves, most of them from Argentina. We went on the bus to Maldonado, some ten miles distant, where we found a country town, prosperous without being vulgar and immensely cheaper than Punta del Este. It cost us the same to have our lunch as it had cost for a coffee the day before in one of the smart hotels. I was able to buy a new saddle for one of our bicycles, an efficient gas lighter and Wendy bought some clothes. Uruguay is an unpretentious country, where people are used to making do with what they have. We saw old motor cars, collectors' pieces in England, used for everyday transport: Model T Fords still in splendid running order, old Austin 7s, Dodges, Chevrolets. Nothing mechanical is allowed to decay for lack of care.

There are some fine old towns in Uruguay. It is a little known country, the smallest state in South America with a population of three million. We would have liked to have seen more of it. The Uruguay River, another noble waterway, flows for a thousand miles into the River Plate and forms the border between Uruguay and Argentina. It is said to be beautiful and is navigable for yachts in the lower reaches. We went to Colonia on our way home from Buenos Aires, all cobbled streets and squares and ancient buildings, a friendly, pleasant place. Between Colonia and Montevideo we sailed past the wreck of the *Graf Spee*, still visible in the shallow, muddy waters of the river after nearly fifty years. When I first saw her, soon after she was scuttled in December 1939, her hull, upperworks and the massive control tower could all be seen, the mute guns pointing to the sky.

Wendy bought woollen blankets in Uruguay so that we would at least be warm when we returned to our pillaged house. Uruguayan woollens are top quality, the workmanship in leather second to none. Uruguay may be an underrated country, but not to wealthy Argentines who spend their money in Punta del Este.

We rode our bicycles to explore the outskirts of the city and came upon a dream land. There were tree-lined avenues of enormous houses, many of them empty. They were like palaces built for a 1930s film set, mansions with turrets and battlements and landscaped gardens, spacious lawns, clipped hedges. Some were decorated with brightly coloured tiles on the roofs and cladding the walls, coloured paving in the front, many were thatched, plastic gnomes on the lawn. They were pink and blue and purple and yellow, occasionally a modest brown. It was a kind of extravagant Disneyland.

We enquired at a greengrocer's shop we found nearby. 'They were built by the Argentines,' he said, 'when the Generals were in power. They came here and bought everything with the money from the World Bank.' Uruguayans are not over-fond of their neighbours across the water, and regard them, especially since the time of the Generals, as arrogant, overbearing, tasteless. Uruguayans tend to be unpretentious, well educated, industrious and tolerant, with a relaxed manner, in contrast to the unstable, emotional Argentines. Not that they escaped the political and social turmoil common to Latin America. The guerilla war of the *tupamaros* was as bitter and divisive as any conflict the continent has seen.

Refreshed and rejuvenated we left Punta del Este for the very last stint that would take us to Buenos Aires, another 200 miles to go. It was 28 February 1987. 'We won't be there on 1 March,' Wendy said reproachfully. 'Yes we will – it's Leap Year.' There wasn't much wind when we left, no more than a breeze from the south-south-west so that we could just point a course between Punta del Este and Montevideo. It was all beginning to feel familiar and nostalgic. I had seen the city of Punta del Este often enough before. In the old *Celtic Star* it had always been a splendid landmark. Once we came to the skyscrapers we knew we were safe from U boats, even raiders. We would be allowed to switch on our radios and sink ourselves in the luxury of tango music during our watch below. The ads. on the radio were a delectable foretaste of the plenty we would find in Buenos Aires after austere, wartime England. The real moment of excitement always came when we spotted the Argentine guardship at Recalada where we used to pick up the pilot.

I had dreamed of sailing my own boat up the River Plate ever since I was a small boy; alone at first and then, as my metabolism matured, with some golden haired girl draped over the cockpit or in a seductive pose on the cabin settee. *Iskra* was the first part of the dream, Wendy the second, filling the role admirably. She was draped on the bunk at this precise moment, not in a seductive pose, it must be said, but being patiently sick in her bucket.

By evening it had calmed down and she had recovered, the lights of Montevideo were clearly to be seen ahead and to starboard. Soon we picked up the light on Flores Island to the west of the city. Now it was a lovely sail, the wind backing and freshening, a smooth sea, *Iskra* racing for her journey's end. The island soon came on the beam, the lights of Montevideo to starboard, Recalada blinking twice every 12 seconds on our bow, the Banco Inglés, a notorious sandbank, under our lee. We must have been spotted, or reported by a ship, because we were called up by Recalada when we were no more than a mile off, bearing down on it at our best speed.

'Brazilian yacht, Brazilian yacht,' they called. I answered in Spanish, 'This is the English yacht *Iskra* bound for Buenos Aires.' I repeated it slowly and deliberately, spelling it out, India Sierra Kilo Romeo Alpha. There was a long silence – it seemed interminable. Then, 'Please repeat.' I spelled it out again. Now we were getting close. Recalada is at the seaward end of a buoyed channel, 110 miles long, the deep water channel to the port. There was already a ship coming up astern of us. We looked at each other. 'Suppose they won't let us in?' Wendy remarked, 'What then?' 'Wait' I said, 'have faith.' Then they came through again, loud and clear, 'English yacht, English yacht – bienenidos a Buenos Aires – bienenidos . . . .' Welcome to Buenos Aires.

We decided to keep to the buoyed channel so we would always know where we were by the numbers on the buoys. They were 5 kilometres apart. There was plenty of water for us outside the channel but the river is strewn with unmarked wrecks. 'We'll play it safe,' I said. Recalada was helpful. 'Keep just outside the buoyed channel,' they told us on VHF. 'When you come to the entrance channel to the port you will be told where to berth. We'll keep an eye on you.'. This was VIP treatment we hadn't expected. As we sailed through the night a few ships came past us, markedly fewer than in the old days when the port of Buenos Aires was one of the world's busiest. In those days there were ships in and out day and night, like the Pool of London or Liverpool used to be.

Each time a ship came up with us the pilot would call us on VHF to check that we were all right. The wind freshened from behind us so that I had to take in the mains'l and set twin stays'ls to ease the steering. We came up the channel so fast that we arrived at the inner, dredged part of the entrance, where another buoyed channel goes off to Colonia and the Uruguay River, before daylight. There was a plethora of lights and flashing buoys, none of which matched my chart, the lights of the city of La Plata already astern and Buenos Aires winking and twinkling ahead of us, a great rosy glare across the sky. 'I'm lost – we'll have to ask the way.' As soon as I called they knew who we were and they knew our position from their radar. They gave me a course to steer, we still had another 20 miles to go. We were told to berth in the Yacht Club Argentino in the Darsena Norte, the north basin. When it got light the city was in front of us, tumbling into perspective. I remembered it after forty-five years, the tower at Retiro Station built by the British in 1908, the dome of the Congress, the Arches along the Paseo Colon, the pink Casa Rosada, even the Shell-Mex building; many more skyscrapers now than in 1943. The sun came up behind us turning out the sparkle of the night, lighting the city with the shades of daytime; greys and browns and greens. The river took on the strange, flat metallic colour from which its name derives.

The wind eased again, I took in the twins, set mains'l and tops'l to speed us in. We saw a motor cruiser behind us,

188

... set main and tops'l to speed us in

bearing down on us at top speed. It was Jorge from Punta del Este with another delivery. 'She looks wonderful,' he shouted, 'wonderful.' He brought the motorboat carefully alongside, I jumped on board with my camera, photographed *Iskra* with the city behind her. In the early sunlight the mains'l made a dark shadow across the silver river. Jorge disappeared towards Olivos and San Isidro where he was arranging for us to lie in a yacht marina. He told us we would be able to stay as guests at the Argentine Yacht Club for three weeks. We took down sails, stowed away in neat harbour fashion and tried to make *Iskra* look smart like a yachty yacht, with a new red ensign, the blue and white Argentine ensign flying from the crosstrees as a courtesy flag, our yellow Q flag to say that our vessel was healthy and that we required free practique. Soon we came up with the stone breakwater and passed into the basin.

The yacht club was immediately ahead of us, a dignified, official looking building with a tower, an arched verandah, a flagpole, a round, green tree at either end, a white painted gangway down to a pontoon alongside the stone wall. We saw lines of immaculate yachts at moorings.

There were ships berthed alongside the quays behind and we could see the masts and yards of the Argentine training ship *Libertad*. 'This is a posh place,' Wendy said apprehensively. We motored slowly in, the fishermen on the harbour wall gazing at us with studied indifference as is the habit of fishermen. A white painted motor boat with a flag on the bow put out from the yacht club steps, the cox'n motioned us to a buoy. We pottered up to it, the engine running slow. Wendy took the boat hook and walked to the foredeck. The cox'n picked up the mooring and handed it up to her. 'Buenos días señora – bienvenidos a Buenos Aires.' Wendy dropped the bight over *Iskra*'s bitts, 'Thank you,' she said – 'Muchas gracias.' 'Please wait on board,' the cox'n said. 'The port officials will come out to you.'

We sat in *Iskra*'s cockpit marvelling at our reception. This was not the Argentina portrayed to us in the press during the Falklands War. There was no bitterness here, no hostility, no hint that because we were British we would not be welcome. Every Argentine we had met so far, the consul in Rio, our friend who had been denied entry for his boat in Gibraltar, the river pilots and half a dozen others, had been delighted to hear of our visit to Argentina. We had already been given a list of people we must be sure to visit. The old bond between the English and Argentina, forged over many generations, had clearly survived intact, the conflict over the Malvinas no more than an irrelevance brought about by political opportunism.

Soon the motor boat came back with three officials on board, one a police officer with a black book under his arm, one the customs officer and one from the immigration, a sallow man in a light grey suit. The business was done quickly and efficiently, the policeman writing our details in his black book, the customs man taking a cursory look at *Iskra*'s lockers. The Immigration officer was much interested in Wendy's passport. It showed her maiden name, Patricia Slack and under it, 'now

Mrs Mulville see page 5'. Page 5 said, 'The holder is a British citizen under the provisions of the British Nationality Act 1981.' This clearly cast doubts in his mind. 'It doesn't say she's English,' he complained. Wendy referred him to Page 2, 'Place of Birth, Torquay.' 'Oh yes – Turkey,' he said triumphantly, 'part of the British Empire.'

They asked us whether we would mind going ashore to see the Captain of the Port. The motor boat took us all to a flight of stone steps in the main harbour and we walked a few yards along the quay. While we were waiting we talked to one of the Captain of the Port's assistants, a young conscript sailor. 'I saw you come in,' he said, 'what an adventure. I would like to sail to England.' We told the Captain of the Port that we would move up the river after a few days in the port. 'Ah yes,' he said, 'Barlovento Marina – Dumas used to keep his boat there.' Vito Dumas was a great Argentine single-handed sailor. During the war, in 1943, he sailed his ketch *Legh II* round the world single-handed by the so-called 'impossible route' from east to west. The business of clearing had taken about an hour.

We were tired, we had been awake all night coming up the river. We wandered slowly back round the dock. The port was a shadow of the busy place I had known, most of the activity to be seen came from two Russian fish factory ships lying in a repair yard with a small fleet of trawlers alongside. The Russians have a contract to use this part of the port, negotiated at a knock-down price, it is said. The fishing fleet works the banks round the Malvinas and off the southern coast of Argentina, using the base in Buenos Aires to tranship fish for the Black Sea ports of the Soviet Union. It was a long walk, one of the lock gates was open so that we had to make our way right round the dock and across the other end, then back to the entrance to the yacht club along a pleasant tree-lined avenue that runs beside the river. The yacht club occupies the eastern arm of the port entrance. The docks in Buenos Aires are in the middle of the city, the quays stretching along its frontage. In the *Celtic Star* we used to lie in the South Dock, past the Boca, the mouth of the Riachuelo River where the city of Buenos

Aires was first settled by Juan de Garay in 1580. Now, meat for export no longer exists because of lower production and the increased appetites of a growing population.

'It will be nice to have an early supper and go to sleep,' Wendy said. 'I'm exhausted.' We were both exhausted. For the past six months we had been keyed up, always with the voyage as a taskmaster, forcing us on, occupying our concentration. Now that it had stopped we were bemused, not quite sure what we were going to do next. We had come to see Clive and Marta, we had come to see El Choiqué but we were not clear in our minds what other missions we had to fulfil. The voyage wasn't an end in itself, rather the means to move ourselves to Argentina, which we would otherwise never be able to afford. We were in anticlimax, not sure what was to happen next. 'We're here,' I said to Wendy, 'what do you make of it?' 'I don't know yet,' she said, 'we'll see if we can find Marta tomorrow.'

As we came up to the gates of the club a black taxi drove up and stopped with a scream of tyres. The door was flung open, out in front of us stepped a blonde lady, a striking figure, slim, glamorous, hair over her face, a big, generous smile. 'Wonderful to see you,' she said, giving us both a big hug. 'Marta! – how did you know we had arrived?'

'How did I know?' she asked in surprise. You said you were coming on 1 March – well, it's 1 March isn't it? We've booked a table for dinner.' We had arrived.

XIII

El Campo

When I left the *estancia* as a child the young eucalyptus trees in Uncle Billy's avenue lodged themselves in my mind and never left it. Over the years whenever my thoughts have rambled back to the *estancia* it has been the trees that have flashed up on my memory screen; the way they were positioned, the way the bark flakes off their trunks, the way Guillermo and I used to move the old horse in and out of them. Guillermo was a meticulous worker. If one of the trees was damaged, or showed any sign of distress he would put a blaze on an adjacent fence post with a block of chalk he carried with him. Antonio or Montenegro would be told and some action would be taken. Uncle Billy was fussy about the avenue, wanted it to equal or better those of neighbouring *estancias*. There would be few avenues as grand or as noble as the one that led to El Choiqué.

The tank wasn't big enough to water the whole avenue. Eucalyptus are thirsty trees, taking a lot of water from the soil and needing a lot of water when they are young. A fully grown tree will transpire 80 gallons of water a day into the atmosphere. When we trotted the mare home for lunch we always took the cart to the water-mill in the garden and filled the tank. The job took us two days every week. I was proud of the trees. They grew fast and by the time I left they were already above my head. Apart from the refreshing shade they give and their pungent aroma, the eucalyptus gives an excellent, durable hardwood. It splits straight and easily, makes fencing, is good material for the simple camp houses and can be polished to an attractive finish. It contains medicinal oils, all kinds of riches are distilled and procured from it; the wood can be used for boat building. It is an admirable tree.

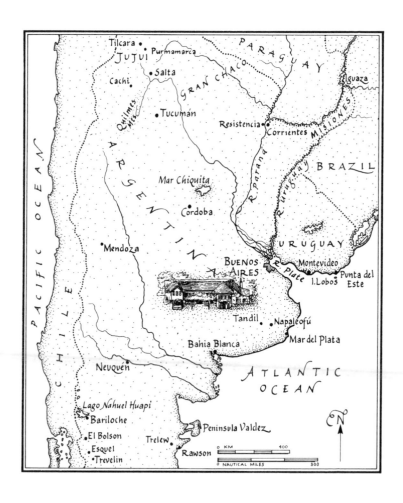

Buenos Aires, indeed all the parts of Argentina I had known as a child, seemed not to have changed. It was even familiar territory to Wendy from what I had told her about it. As soon as we walked into the city I knew the way, the street names were familiar. If it hadn't changed, it was certainly a run-down city. Signs of weak administration were on every side. The pavements were in disrepair, the buses were old, car exhausts were non-existent or corroded to nothing, the underground trains shuddered along, ancient carriages on ancient track. We had to make telephone calls to England in an attempt to keep ourselves in touch with events at home as the drama surrounding our house unfolded. The delays caused by the overworked and under-financed telephone system were very apparent.

It took us most of the next day to recover from our first evening in Buenos Aires with Clive and Marta. As soon as we had digested our surprise at seeing her we took Marta into the yacht club. In a few minutes Clive arrived with a selection of children. We drank a lot of wine and then we all piled into the back of an open truck and Clive drove us at breakneck speed through the city to a restaurant he knew of, where we enjoyed a hilarious dinner-party. We arrived back in the club late, slightly drunk and so exhausted that we could hardly stand, to find it was blowing a violent gale. It was a *pampero*, a wind that blows up with great suddenness on the *pampa*, sometimes drifting across the city.

The club motor boat was broken down and the *sereno*, the old nightwatchman, wasn't strong enough to row us out to *Iskra* against the wind. 'You can sleep in the club for a little while,' he said. 'When the wind drops I'll take you to your boat.' We did as we were told, too weak to argue, found some cushions in the club lounge, spread them out on the floor and went straight to sleep. The old man came and shook us at 4 in the morning and took us back on board as good as his word. 'I'm an old fisherman from the Adriatic – I know how to row.' When we recovered in the morning we gave *Iskra* a special stow, took off her sails and put them below out of the sun, rigged an awning to keep her cool and left her in the good care of the club.

Tandil is the nearest town to El Choiqué. It is six hour's drive along the new road that has been built from Buenos Aires to the seaside resort of Mar del Plata. The *estancia* is an hour's drive on from Tandil. We went by bus; the railways, once Argentina's pride, have fallen into such neglect that they are little used. We arrived in Tandil in the evening and waited for a few minutes for Julian to arrive from the *estancia*. Wendy and I had met him in England a year before we left but I remembered him best from much longer ago, when he used to work in my office during his school holidays. He had been a shy, quiet young man, but big and tall. We had always got on well although he had not been an easy person to know. He was a different man when he walked into the café in Tandil, at once self-possessed, confident and sure of himself. We packed into his car, Wendy and I in the front, Marta and Julian's wife Marilyn in the back and drove off to El Choiqué. Clive was driving to the *estancia* from Buenos Aires in another car.

As often happens with brothers, Clive and Julian are very different from each other, Julian still reserved, Clive ebullient, extrovert, full of ideas and imagination. CB and Uncle Billy had been similarly different. Julian had made himself into a knowledgeable and efficient farmer, taking agricultural degrees in New Zealand and putting into practice all manner of innovations on the *estancia*. Clive did not take any part in the running of the *estancia*, leaving its management in the capable hands of his brother. Clive used the house for weekends and school holidays when all the seven children, six girls and one boy, Billy, were in residence. Julian had built a new house for himself and Marilyn at the other end of the camp near where the original *estancia* house had been before the big house was built back in the 1920s, before Uncle Billy's time.

It was a clear night with a sky full of stars and half a moon over the camp. We saw the avenue, a splodge of dark against the pale moonlight as the car turned into the old road that runs alongside the *estancia*. We came up to it and turned in, the car stopping before the white painted gate. I jumped out to open it, as I had always done. It was the same gate – I recognized its squeak. The trees I had known from their infancy were like the aisle of a cathedral, the pillars standing in staggered lines, arching high above, dark foliage made mysterious in the car headlights. Bright, silver trunks, swathes of bark peeling back, each one of greater diameter than I could encompass with my arms. 'You take the car, we'll walk.' The car left us in deep darkness under the trees, its diminishing lights soon lost in the drive up to the house. We heard a door slam.

We walked hand in hand, gazing up at the branches 60 feet above, patches of starlit sky glimpsing through, the grass edged road soft and springy under our feet, a gentle rustle above us

The trees I had known from their infancy
were like the aisle of a cathedral

like the sea round *Iskra*'s bow. I found the tears rolling down my cheeks. This avenue was part of me. Uncle Billy and Guillermo and I had created it, or at least we had caused it to be there; it was something of real and enduring value, a thing of beauty. To nurture a tree must be to make the world a better place. We walked through the avenue without speaking until we came to another gate. The trees ended, we stepped into bright moonlight. There was a white painted board with bold, black letters, 'El Choiqué'.

Everything in England seems to change from decade to decade, from year to year, almost from day to day. We go back to a place, sometimes even in the deep country, always in towns and cities, to find it unrecognisable. Even in our own road everything changes with bewildering speed. The view of our town has been transformed in the few years we have been resident, new houses, old houses pulled down, a new road, factories built, footpaths altered, the salt marshes outside our window eroding before our eyes.

In El Choiqué nothing had changed, the house, the garden grown up of course, trees and bushes planted by Freda now grown to maturity. The guest room was the same, still no more than a trickle of water in the bathroom tap, Uncle Billy's billiard room the same, the painting of Colonel Charles Blood and the family tree still there, even the same furnishings, the same view over the garden and away to the miles of open camp. I climbed to the top of the mill in the garden, which I had often done as a child and gazed out over the countryside, easily identifying the patches of woodland I knew every inch of, the *tambas* all in their right place, the dusty road winding away to La Esperanza. Marta took us to Napaleofú for shopping. The *boliche* where Guillermo and I watched the fight was exactly the same, even the rail where we tied our horses was still there, the station unchanged, a few extra houses perhaps, on the far side of the railway.

Marta took us to the gate where Guillermo's land begins, she and Wendy went back leaving me alone to walk to the house, over a low hill. It was a simple place, a few sheds behind, a cool verandah, some trees, grass round the door, a yard behind with old carts, bits of farm machinery. There was no one to be seen, only a small boy playing in the dust. 'Is Guillermo at home?' He looked up at me with round eyes, disappeared behind the house, 'Abuelo,' I heard him call and then, more urgently, 'Abuelo – un señor – ven rapido' – Grandfather – a gentleman – come quickly. Guillermo came round the corner of the house, the boy holding his hand. He stopped and looked at me and I at him. He was shorter than I now, a stocky figure, only slightly lined forehead, his hair receding, a moustache, the same black beret. I watched as slow recognition spread over his intelligent features, at first puzzled, then unbelieving, then a flash of pleasure. 'Guillermo – hombre – qué tal?' He looked at me in astonishment. 'Carajo – el niño Ponky – no puede ser' – it can't be. We embraced, thumping each other on the back in disbelief.

Wendy and I forgot about the sea for ten days. Wendy rides well, with a good seat although it took her a few days to get used to her horse's *criollo* gait. She could not be described as a forceful horsewoman; Strogonov, who was allocated to her,

... thumping each other on the back in disbelief

199

was a large, amiable creature with a penchant for the tall Scottish thistles with big blue flowers which inhabit the verges of the camp roads. He would browse among them while Wendy remonstrated, 'Strogonov, really, you must come, really,' pressing her heels to his flank gently, so as not to cause him any distress. We rode over the whole *estancia*, to the top of the hill at the southern end of the camp, a small undulation but remarkable in this flat land. We found a clump of delicate orchid-like flowers growing wild. The view from the top was as I remembered it. I had described it exactly to Wendy during our voyage; the camp all dotted with *montes*, the pale blue patches of alfalfa, the green hillside, the *tambas* and the big herds that Julian was grazing.

There were no longer twenty horses in the home paddock, Clive had his work cut out to find us two and one for his daughter Sally, who came with us. There was no *recado*, no big round stirrups, no silver-studded bridle; we used English saddles. The *palenque* Uncle Billy built had long since fallen down; now there were so few horses that there was no need for another. Montenegro was forgotten, I could find no one except Guillermo who had ever heard of him. But the gaucho pony Clive gave me to ride knew how to open the wire gates, nor had I forgotten the trick. Julian's *tamberos* still drank *mate amarga*; it was too bitter for Wendy. Even Eva's old flame Millie, in his 80s, was still alive and well. He came over to the *estancia* for tea and talked about the camp as it used to be. The motor car and the tractor have imposed their authority over Argentina as they have over every corner of the world but perhaps not with such exclusive efficiency. *Estancias* still have horses around, the tethering bar outside the *boliche* in Napaleofú is still used, the odd horseman can still be seen covering the ground with that slow, distinctive *criollo* canter.

Clive organised all manner of festivities for us; dinner parties, a trip to Mar del Plata, visits to nearby *estancias*. One of his guests, an Argentine Air Force admiral, Rivera-Kelly, had come through the Falklands War without opprobrium, his force having covered itself with glory, although largely unrecognised among Argentine people. He was a pleasant man, with a boat on a mooring near *Iskra* at the Argentine yacht club.

Another *estancia* about twenty miles distant was owned by Guillermo Moore, a cousin of the Cuban hero Che Guevara, who was born and brought up and qualified as a doctor in Argentina. El Che, as he was nicknamed in Cuba, was already a legend by the time I went there in *Iskra* in 1970. Guillermo's *estancia* is one of the oldest in Argentina. The house was still as it had been in the 1880s with the same furniture, the same ornate Edwardian bedsteads, the cool, traditional layout still seen in Spain. The house is built round a shady, tiled patio, one room leading into another like the *estancia* house I had stayed in with Uncle Billy as a child. Perhaps it was the same one; it was on the old road between Napaleofú and Mar del Plata. We drank *mate* round a fire, the place all dim and cool, redolent of the settled serenity of life in the camp.

Guillermo Moore's sister, Almeira, lived in a tiny house on the banks of the River Napaleofú. It was an ingenious improvisation of a house which she seemed to have expanded to accommodate her increasing library of books and records. She gave us tea in a glass-fronted studio balanced above the river, the thoroughbred horses she was breeding grazing in the paddock behind.

My remembrance of Mar del Plata was accurate enough, the hotel, the crescent beach of pure sand, the smart shops. It is a fishing port as well as a resort. Extraordinarily, our ride to Mar del Plata with Uncle Billy and Eva was remembered and talked of. Clive took us to dinner in a beach club near the resort where we met a spritely lady of eighty-five, Gwenny Cameron, who was conversant with the whole thing and who had known me as a child.

Memories are long in Argentina. When we stayed with Julian and Marilyn, in their newly completed house on the *estancia*, we were always meeting people whom I had known fifty years previously; Marilyn's step-aunt, Penny Moffatt, I had known well, Julian's cook had been a small child when I had been there. Uncle Billy, even CB were known to or remembered by reputation by people too young ever to have met them. It is a characteristic of Argentines of English descent that they always know or at least know of every other one of the clan.

Julian had made himself into a real Argentine, having thrown off many of the trappings of his upbringing. He regards himself as an Argentine, not as an English expatriate. He did his national service in the Argentine Navy, which taught him a great deal about his country. The old *estancia* house where Clive lives was full of English books, English pictures, artefacts Uncle Billy had collected in a lifetime of travel all over the world. In Clive's house you could pick up a volume of Shakespeare or Dickens from any shelf. Wendy wanted to read books and focus her inquiring mind on Argentina. There wasn't a morsel of information to be found on the subject in the *estancia* house.

Julian, on the other hand, has his shelves full of Argentine and Spanish writings, from Garcia Lorca to Martin Fierro. He has immersed himself in the culture of Argentina as well as making himself into a respected agriculturist. He has applied his ideas and his expertise to the camp with spectacular results. His yields are higher, his land more productive and the *estancia* probably more profitable than most. His dairy herds supply milk to Buenos Aires, taken away every day in a refrigerated truck. A casual eye can see that El Choiqué is a model, almost an oasis in the featureless camp.

We rode our horses to the *estancia* next door, a wealthy and gracious place. The *estancia* house was surrounded by extensive, tree-lined gardens but the camp around it lacked the *montes* that are such a feature of El Choiqué. Few trees are indigenous to the *pampa*; they must be planted and cared for but once established they gather moisture, provide shade and add an element of variety to the otherwise bleak plains.

Wendy and I rode over to have lunch with Guillermo and his wife Heide. Strogonov was persuaded to forgo the thistles for long enough for us to gallop the 6 miles to the other side of Napaleofú. We stopped in the *pueblito*, tethered our horses outside the *boliche* and went in among the piles of boxes, the rows of shelves with dusty bottles high up the walls, the long bar counter down two sides where the gauchos and the *carreteros* once drank *caña* and played dice and talked and argued and fought, the clusters of *alpargatas* and bundles of skins hanging from the ceiling. Word of our coming to El Choiqué had spread quickly, the old man who owned the *boliche* remembered Uncle Billy and had heard tell of el niño Ponky. I bought two pairs of jeans and Wendy a skirt.

Guillermo and I launched into reminiscence, launched into the old songs with a bottle of vino inside us. He was astonished that I remembered all the songs, was delighted that we had come on horseback, he thought Wendy must be a most unusual lady to sail in a small boat across that ocean he had seen from the beach at Mar del Plata and then to ride Strogonov 6 miles to have lunch with him. We were back where we had been fifty years before. I felt a flush of affection for this man I had not seen for so long but whom I had visited with my thoughts many times in the interval. He was the most interesting Argentine we met on this voyage. He had a wise understanding of the ills that prevail in his country.

Guillermo had spent most of his life in Napaleofú yet he was at least as well informed and as well founded in his view of the world as I, who have spent my life travelling over it. He had been lucky enough, or shrewd enough to get his land under Perón's reforms, when something of an attempt was made to break up the estates, many of which were keeping tribes of people in idleness who never as much as saw the source of their wealth. To Guillermo and to thousands of Argentines, Perón and Evita Perón were benefactors who at least tried to use some part of Argentina's riches to alleviate poverty. Guillermo had prospered, building his house, raising his family and becoming a person of substance in Napaleofú. He was aware of the underlying cause of Argentina's economic problems; I was beginning to understand it myself. He knew that the wealth of his country was being creamed off and frittered, he had heard tell of the mansions Wendy and I had seen in Uruguay.

Heide gave us lunch without meat. They were amused by our vegetarian habits. 'Un gaucho que no come carne?' Guillermo laughed. 'Qué va?' A gaucho who doesn't eat meat? What next? In fact we found a large number of people in Argentina who ate no meat, much to our surprise. Traditionally, Argentines are the biggest meat-eaters in the world. In some places it was quite difficult for us to get vegetables although in Buenos Aires we found a greengrocer whose produce was all organic, within a bike ride of the boat.

We had a restoring siesta after lunch. 'What of Andrea?' I asked Guillermo, 'Do you know where she is, what happened to her?' He told me she had married Mr Bridger's chauffeur from a neighbouring *estancia*, La Esperanza. They had gone to Buenos Aires, her husband had died, she was living with her son and daughter-in-law; he would find out her address for me. We saddled up the horses, left Guillermo and set off for El Choiqué in the late afternoon, Strogonov now quite keen to get home regardless of thistles.

We moved *Iskra* when we returned to Buenos Aires, to the yacht marina recommended to us by Jorge. Admiral Rivera-Kelly came on board before we left the yacht club, curious to see what kind of boat we had come in, perhaps not quite believing my description of her. 'No instruments? – incredible.' 'There were sailing boats before there were instruments.' I replied. Jorge and his girlfriend, another Marta, came with us up the river to the Barlovento Marina, a pleasant place, not then completed so that we lay with our bowsprit to the bank. 'Shout for the boat when you want to go ashore,' the manager told us, 'there is a boat on duty day and night.' There was some discussion; would we be asked to pay or would they treat us as guests and give us a free berth? It would be better to pay, I decided, the charge was modest and I had no wish to be beholden. I paid two month's charges to get a cheaper rate. It turned out to be a mistake. I might have known that the duty boat took hours to come when we shouted, often not coming at all, especially at night. We used our rubber dinghy or climbed ashore along the bowsprit, a precarious business. The night-watchman was usually cross when we came back late, taking us on board with bad grace.

More disturbingly, when we had been in the marina for a few days, a letter was left for us at the gate. The translation is: 'My name is Carlos Culasso Moore, like you I am of English descent – but I am an Argentine – an Argentine who has sailed to the south and has not been allowed to berth in a part of my own country, Puerto Argentino, Islas Malvinas [Port Stanley]. I consider that you are abusing traditional Argentine hospitality. You are offending me by flying your flag in my club – you should go at once and leave this country immediately.' I wrote to Mr Culasso, telling him that I sympathised with and was inclined to agree with his point of view about the Falklands. I asked him on board so that we could discuss the matter but he declined to come, instead writing me a short note to say that he reiterated his remarks. Culasso was clearly unwilling or unable to make his point face to face.

The letter with its veiled threat upset us; we wondered whether *Iskra*, even we ourselves, were safe in the marina but I wasn't going to be frightened out of the place, particularly as I had paid two months in advance. It appeared that Culasso was on the committee of the club and had made a fuss about *Iskra* being there, causing some dissension. The incident was the exception proving the rule; we found no other hostility in Argentina although we were always on the lookout for it. The man at the gate said to us after we had been there for a week or so and had got to know him, 'Don't worry – he's a nutcase.' I confess I rather respected Mr Culasso and was sorry I never met him. Later we met people from a more modest and more friendly marina next door but we didn't desert the Barlovento, not wishing to add to the existing unpleasantness.

An advantage of the Barlovento was that it was within a pleasant bike ride of Juanita and her husband Rolly. Juanita is my mother's niece, my first cousin. She remembers meeting me when I came to Argentina in the *Celtic Star*. I had a faint recollection of a spotty girl of twelve who became such an attractive person, in looks and in personality. I never really knew her until this voyage. I found her name in the telephone directory when we got to the Barlovento and she and Rolly asked us out to dinner in Recoleta, a smart part of Buenos Aires near the cemetery. From that moment on, Juanita's house was our second home; we used it as a convenience, leaving our bicycles, having baths and showers, listening to Mozart on Rolly's gramophone. In no time Juanita introduced us to cousins I had forgotten about, or had never known, and their friends and relations who all wanted us to visit, have dinner, even stay for a night or a week. They were spread over Argentina from one end to the other. Marta and Clive's house in Buenos Aires was also open to us and Marta's friends wanted us to visit and stay. We had become slightly notorious through an article I wrote in the *Buenos Aires Herald* about our voyage. Carlos Culasso had it right about Argentine hospitality; we tried not to abuse it. Juanita said, 'You must go and stay with my two sons who live in El Bolsón, near Bariloche." We took the bus for some 750 miles, through the *pampa* and to the south of the province of Buenos Aires to Bahia Blanca and then across the width of the country to Neuquen, over hundreds of miles of flat scrub-land, half desert, with no redeeming feature except the steel pylons carrying electricity from the dams of the Andes foothills. We spent the night on the bus, not uncomfortably, waking in the morning to watch the countryside change its character. Now we could see the mountain range in the distance, snow glistening in the morning sun, the endless plain at last giving way to gentle hills and woods and green fields, until we were driving beside the lake to Bariloche. The bus arrived on time, the fare was modest, at least to us with our US dollars. We found a guesthouse in which to spend the night, our room with a picture-window facing Lake Nahuel Huapi.

For three weeks we roamed about this miniature Switzerland around Bariloche; lakes, waterfalls, forest, glaciers, the Andes all around, snow-capped to the west, the frontier with Chile a few miles off. It was a place of unpolluted,

Paul loaned us a log hut by the side of Lake Epuyen

unexploited beauty, the quiet broken only by the music of falling water, birdsong, the hum of bees. Paul loaned us a log hut by the side of Lake Epuyen where we lived for a few days. We took stores, cooking stove, blankets. There was no person within miles except an old lady living in a tumbledown cottage deep in the woods.

We found the old lady's cottage after we had been there for two days. We drank *mate* with her and she gave us fresh baked bread. Her oven was made from an upturned oil-drum, an ancient kettle stood on top. She had one son, a dog, a cat, a horse, some chickens, a pig. They managed to earn a little money for flour and a few stores brought her by a man who sometimes came to the lake to fish. She had lived in the little house for forty years. A few years ago the forest caught fire, the house was almost destroyed. It was saved by a team of volunteer fire-fighters who fought to save the house until the fire subsided. The rest of her family had long since gone, her daughters married and departed, her husband gone one day over the mountains to Chile, never to come back. She wasn't sure how long ago – one year, two years perhaps. They ate fish from the lake, nuts and fruits from the forest. She was happy, but she liked to chat over a gourd of *mate.* She sold us some tomatoes for a very small sum, refusing to accept more on the grounds that she didn't need money. It was a burden she said, she would rather be without it.

We walked in the forest, filled every bag we could muster with sweet wild apples, discovered waterfalls, secret bowers in the woods, swam in the freezing lake. We never saw a soul except the old lady. We cut wood and made a roaring fire against the cold night. Through the unglazed window of the hut there was the lake, haunting shadows sweeping across from the ever-changing clouds and mountains, sudden flashes of bright sunshine. The stream where we filled our water-jar tumbled down outside the door. We got up with the sun, went to bed full of exercise and crisp mountain air, read to each other by the light of an old oil lantern.

We became tourists for a few days, went in a steamer across Lake Mascardi to Puerto Tronador at the head of the lake, walked through the valley beside a stream to the foot of the snow-capped Mount Tronador. The glacier falls down the mountainside, disintegrating in a cliff of rock and earth and blocks of stone still loosely bound together by melting ice. It tumbles down with a roar as the river eats into its base. We sailed across Lago Frias in a small boat, almost to the Chilean border, climbed up beside crystal falls, scaled a modest peak to gain unbroken views of lakes and forests and mountains.

Paul and his brother Alan live near El Bolsón, in a valley 50 miles from Bariloche along a wild mountain road. The *chacra*, a farm smaller than an *estancia*, produces organically grown raspberries for sale in Buenos Aires and the cities of Argentina as well as for export to Europe. Like Clive and Julian the brothers live one at either end of the farm. Paul is keenly concerned with local affairs, goes abroad to conferences and business jamborees on behalf of the province of Chubut, where the *chacra* is situated. It is an idyllic part of the country, far away from the political fights of Buenos Aires, remote from the commercial jungle which Paul and Alan have rejected. As well as the raspberries, Paul runs cattle on the farm, a few fields of corn.

We lived in Alan and Patti's house. There were sheepskins on the floor, the table was two wide boards supported by tree trunks. The most comfortable chair was made from a hollowed-out tree lined with sheepskins, the room made snug with a log fire. Alan had a relaxed attitude to life. The tap in the bathroom came away from the wall when it was turned on. It required a sharp blow with a hammer to put it back, but the hammer was left conveniently to hand. Paul's and Lalli's house had contracted with the expansion of the family by Lalli's twins.

We went riding up a mountain track, the horses sure-footed, intelligent. They took us up and up along winding alleys through the forest, over streams, ducking under low branches, far up where the trees are sparse. We could see Paul's farm laid out in detail below us. Paul's friend, Oreja, had sixteen sons from two wives. He had carved a farm out of the forest on a plateau of high land surrounded by mountains, building himself a log house. Gradually he stocked the farm with animals, cattle, poultry, sheep. He paid nothing for his land which he got as a grant from the government; if he kept it and used it he was entitled to own it. Two of his sons were at home; nice boys of twelve and fourteen, both like men, competent, hard-working, easy to talk to. Oreja was away visiting a herb doctor who lives in the forest nearby. The children all go down to El Bolsón to school during the winter but Oreja stays in the mountains to look after the animals and keep the farm safe. The boys gave us *mate* and showed us a wild boar they had captured with their dogs a week ago. He would be kept and fattened and eaten at Christmas. There are pumas in the forest and foxes, as well as boars.

Oreja came back on his horse in a few minutes and drank *mate* with us, a quiet-spoken man, a smile playing round his lips, a serene view of his life, comparing it favourably with the hubbub raised by clever people who live in cities. He was an organic farmer; there seemed to be very little chemical farming

209

in Argentina. The story of Oreja ended in disaster, as I was told by Juanita two years later when she visited us at home in England. She told us that Oreja was in the habit of beating his wife. One day, after a session of violence, the eldest boy shot him dead.

Paul himself is something of a philosopher, valuing his lot against a life of business which he could have had. Camp people are a different breed from the city-dwellers of Buenos Aires. They will all tell you, with a good deal of reason, that Buenos Aires, with its wheeler-dealing, its political intrigue, its corruption, its flagrant waste of the nation's wealth, is a root cause of Argentina's economic ills. If the power of Buenos Aires could be broken, they believe, the real wealth of the nation, which is in the camp, would soon put the economy back on a proper footing. There is a strong movement afoot to move the capital city to a new site in Patagonia, just to the north of the Rio Negro.

Paul took us on a day's drive in his car. We went down to what are known as the 'English Estancias'. These are in sheep country, still owned by absentee landlords who, it is said, put little back into the land and keep the workers in poverty. Their shares are quoted on the Dutch stock exchange. For a long time it was thought that the English Estancias belonged to the English Royal Family. Certainly the Prince of Wales visited them in 1935 when he came to Argentina. Another school believes they were sold back to Argentine ownership during the Perón era. We drove for miles across open country, away from the Andes and into another range of mountains, a much older geological formation, to the east. It was flat, featureless land with the two ranges of mountains on either side, the Andes snow-capped, hardly a sign of human habitation, a few sheep finding their sustenance.

One *estancia* is so large that no one knows how large it is, except that it is more than a 100,000 hectares, the equivalent of a quarter of a million acres. The *estancia* house is in a well cared for, irrigated garden but the majordomo, who was known to Paul, wasn't there. We were content to wander through the garden and look at the outside of the house, a traditional building not unlike, but bigger than Guillermo Moore's *estancia* near El Choiqué. On our way home we stopped at the *estancia* of an old Scot and his wife. The house might have been in the Highlands, even down to the stag's head above the open fireplace and comfortable, shabby easy chairs. They both spoke English with a strong Scottish accent yet neither of them had ever been to Scotland. They gave us whiskey and soda and fat trout caught in the stream which runs through the garden. 'We don't take a lot of notice of Buenos Aires down here,' the old man said, 'When they have a revolution we usually hear about it in a day or so.' He said, unequivocally, that the English Estancias no longer belonged to the British Crown but to the Pay family in Buenos Aires, one of the richest land-owning families in Argentina.

We took the bus south from El Bolsón, first to Esquel through the foothills of the mountains and along the shores of Lake Menendez. Esquel is a dull place, famous only for 'the family of three' who fled there from America with booty from bank robberies in 1901. Butch Cassidy, the Sundance Kid and the beautiful daughter of an English remittance man, Etta Place, made their way to Argentina hoping to find a safe haven when the Federal lawmen began to get the upper hand and the hold-up business folded. They bought an *estancia*, La Cholila, which means 'the little half-breed girl', in Esquel and at least Butch Cassidy seems to have made a real effort to go straight. Although he had never killed a man, he was the most wanted criminal in the USA. The Sundance Kid, even Etta, who wore a wig as a male disguise, were the killers, Butch the brains. It was he who organised the getaways with teams of thoroughbred horses to outpace the law.

The 'family of three' under assumed names were given 12,000 acres of camp in Esquel by the Argentine land department, just as Paul's friend Oreja was given his virgin land, also in Chubut. Butch stocked the *estancia* with sheep bought from an English neighbour and paid for in cash. He built an attractive *estancia* house, now a store, and they lived

211

there for five years. They were well enough liked by the natives and seemed to jog along quite nicely, although local people said they were not good mixers. It wasn't long before the law caught wind of them, they began to run short of funds and their old habits resurfaced. In 1905 they robbed a bank in Santa Cruz and again, in 1907, the Banco de la Nación in San Luis. They sold La Cholila to a beef syndicate and were never seen in Esquel again. The rest of the gang ended with bullets in their guts in Uruguay but Butch survived – at least there is no record of his death. His friends, particularly among Mormon families in his native Wyoming, never believed he was dead; people saw him frequently from 1915 on and his sister, Mrs Betenson, gave him blueberry pie at a family dinner in 1925. She believes he died of pneumonia in the 1930s.

The road forks at Esquel, one part going south for another 750 miles to Ushuaia, Argentina's southernmost city, in Tierra del Fuego, no more than 50 miles from Cape Horn itself. Our bus took the other fork that crosses the width of Patagonia to the Atlantic peninsular of Valdes, a mere 350 miles. We stayed a night in Esquel, finding ourselves with the following day to waste because the bus across to Rawson and Puerto Madrin was a night bus. Having exhausted the possibilities of Esquel we took the local bus a few miles south to Trevelin. This is country colonised by the Welsh, still speaking the Welsh language, Welsh names to the towns, Welsh tea-rooms open to tourists, witches on broomsticks close round the corner. History is never far behind in Argentina.

There is the grave of a horse in Trevalin, one 'Malacara' or 'ugly face', who died in 1909. John Evans went into the hills behind the town on a prospecting expedition with three companions in 1885. On their way home, on 14 March to be precise, they stumbled on a band of Indians who chased them with murderous intent. It was at the time of the killing expeditions of General Roca, who led the last glorious riot of blood-shedding, hard-riding, boleador-throwing, shooting, throat-cutting gauchos against the remaining Indians of Patagonia. They were exterminated, men, women, children.

The four horses raced for home, pursued by howling Indians until they came to a 40 foot river gorge. Three of the horses stopped in their tracks but Malacara jumped, somehow gaining foothold on the other side, John Evans clinging to his back. When the horse died John Evans inscribed on a rock over his grave, 'Here lie the bones of my horse Malacara who saved my life from Indians in the Valley of the Martyrs'. His companions were found murdered, their genitals in their mouths.

The night bus-ride across the plain was lit by a full moon so that the meagre countryside could be seen for miles around, some scrub, some grass, a few sheep scratching a bare living. The bus stopped in the night at a remote outpost called Paso de los Indios, where another road wandered away to the south for hundreds of miles. By morning we were in another Welsh town, Trelew, and then Rawson on the Atlantic coast at last. The Welsh people have lived happily under Argentine rule for a hundred years, maintaining their own culture, even their own schools, without undue interference.

The Valdez Peninsular is the mating ground for, among other creatures, the extraordinary sea elephant. We hired a taxi with a lady driver who spoke fluent English, with a trace of Welsh singsong in it. She was a qualified naturalist and in

... near El Bolsón, in a valley 50 miles from Bariloche

addition, an international fencer who had been a member of Argentina's Olympic team. She knew a friend of mine in London, Leon Paul, who owns a fencing equipment company. Having established good relations she took us on a day's excursion. On the way out to the end of the peninsular, which is all a strictly protected national park, we saw herds of guanaco, a species of wild llama with gracefully curved neck, slender legs, and long, soft hair. There were ostrich, a type of rabbit called the mara, bigger than an ordinary rabbit and with short ears, foxes and even an armadillo, as well as millions of sheep.

The sea elephants are the spectacular of this southern Galapagos. Thirteen thousand of them swim north to the Valdez Peninsular every year to mate and bear their pups. The females lie stretched out on the gravel beach, for all the world like sunbathing tourists. The males, weighing up to 4 tons, spar with each other in the shallows in preparation for the real fighting at mating time when the victor will become father to the whole herd. He rules for as long as he can stand the pace before he is displaced by the next strongest. The males have long trunks they can extend at will to a length of some three or four feet. They have faces like Spaniel dogs, flippers with five fingers. They seem to have no fear of humans. When we got close to them they would open a lazy eye and let out a low growl.

There were thousands of penguins, quite tame, sitting about outside their sand burrows or strutting importantly, herds of seals lying in the sun on the rocks, all manner of strange birds. At certain times of the year, not when we were there, whales congregate off Valdez. Our charming and erudite taxi-driver took us to the Argentine naval base of Puerto Madrin, where the submarines are berthed and put us on another night bus. We arrived back in Buenos Aires the next evening. The whole excursion had cost us about a hundred pounds.

The buses were very cheap because they are the people's only means of transport; we found that the best buses were the

They seemed to have no fear of humans

worst and the worst the best. The best buses had smart new seats that were difficult to fit to our reclining bodies for a whole night, they had radios that blared out continuously or, worse, film shows and dark blinds closely drawn. The worst buses were old, no film shows, comfortable, warm, soft reclining seats with more room for the legs and broken-down radios so that we could talk to each other and to others in the bus. We met some splendid people in our travels by bus. Wendy always had sandwiches, fruit and a thermos of coffee to sustain us. When we got back to Barlovento *Iskra* was just as we had left her, the same welcome home.

XIV

Old Loves

One day Guillermo said to me as we sat on his shaded verandah looking out over the camp, 'This is a rich country Señor Ponky – you can see it for yourself just by looking around. Yet it is full of poor people. Something is not as it should be.' His dictum carried the strength of truth. Brazil is an even richer country where the people are even poorer, where the rich flaunt their wealth without shame. The dog-guarded, locked and chained mansions have the *favelas* hard against the wall. In Buenos Aires you can still walk along the streets as safely, or perhaps more safely, than you can in London. Like Uruguay, the place has an air of quiet security. This is not to say that you will not be robbed if you do not conduct yourself with propriety. In Buenos Aires the middle class suburbs like Martinez and San Isidro, where Juanita and Clive live, and Belgrano where my cousin Stephen, lives are clean, pleasant, shady places with wide streets, dignified, comfortable houses; schoolchildren in crocodiles, litter bins, the occasional security guard paid by the residents. Argentines are introverts full of sad tango music direct from the culture of Italy and Spain. Brazilians are extroverts, the drums of Africa still close behind them. Uruguayans are somewhere between their big neighbours, more like northern Europeans than either of them.

The poorer suburbs of Buenos Aires, like Banfield, where Andrea lives, are similar to their more prosperous neighbours but with smaller houses, the street doors left open, children playing ball in the road. The very poor suburbs round the Boca and on the outskirts of the city where there are slum tenements, but no worse than parts of Liverpool or Glasgow, are still not 'no go' areas like the *favelas* of Rio de Janeiro. We never saw people sleeping in the streets in Buenos Aires.

A fat slice of the wealth of the country that Guillermo was talking about is exported. The yachts in Punta del Este, the pink-tiled mansions, the houses and farms owned by Argentines in Chile and elsewhere, the yachts in the Caribbean chartered by Argentines, are an export of wealth. Argentina will not be solvent until this plunder is stemmed by an administration powerful enough to raise taxes and enforce its edict. In the meantime the poor suffer. Wealth is exported at all levels of society. Marta's maid in Buenos Aires spent every penny she could lay her hands on buying dollar notes on the black market and tucking them under her mattress. 'I have to,' she told me, 'it's my only insurance against inflation.'

The Generals, when they were in power, created an artificial exchange rate so that they could plunder the money borrowed from the World Bank. The World Bank itself was apparently happy to go along with, even to encourage this act of thievery which has brought Argentina much of the economic distress which now engulfs it. The World Bank pressed the Generals to plunge Argentina into the red, from which there is no escape for as long as the rich world continues to exact its ton of flesh from the poor world. It is usury on the grand scale.

There are still people in Argentina - Julian is one, Paul in El Bolsón is another, Rolly himself is among them, also Guillermo in his small way, who believe their money should be invested in Argentina where it can create more wealth. They plough the profits of their enterprises back where they came from thus giving themselves a real stake in the prosperity of their country. If there were official encouragement of this investment, coupled with a tough exchange control, the people of Argentina would soon be as rich as any. It is estimated that there is enough wealth put by abroad by Argentines to cover the whole of the country's foreign debt.

Marta's brother Roberto is rich by any standards. His wealth comes from buying and selling oil tankers on commission, an occupation which seems to bring in a tidy reward to himself and, indeed, to Argentina herself. He owns a motor yacht with pile carpets, cocktail cabinets, lounges, sun decks and bridges ascending in an ever decreasing pagoda. The wheel, with a little seat, is right at the top. We went for a day on the Tigre River, a labyrinth of creeks and backwaters and shaded cul-de-sacs near the head of the estuary of the River Plate where the great River Paraná meanders into its delta. I believe Marta thinks that to be any good, a boat should be like Roberto's boat. It was a lovely day, only spoilt for me by the knowledge that the big, round muttering exhausts were spilling pollution, that the boat's wash was destroying the habitat of the river bank, that the people rowing boats and sailing frail dinghies were bringing down curses on our heads as we swept by. Roberto and Gloria, the kindest, most considerate of people, were unaware of the mayhem their vessel caused as it surged up the narrow creeks and rivers. Wendy and I had never been at the giving-out end of motor boating. We found the reproach and muttered censure of the recipients of our wash unnerving, hid behind the dodger.

I could see how the ownership of such a vessel, even the manipulating of it, would engender such a sense of power as to encourage the mildest of men to arrogance, though Roberto was not arrogant. Sitting at the controls, high in the sky, it was easy to mistake oneself for God. A mere touch to the chromed levers caused the boat to leap like a startled horse, raising a wave enough to drown a regiment. A flick of the finger on a tiny wheel could bring instant disaster to some phlegmatic fisherman, his worms beside him in a glass jar, or to engrossed lovers lost in the humid bower of a punt. We stopped for lunch at a riverside restaurant that laid out enough food to last us a week.

Roberto came on board *Iskra* to look at her. I don't know what he made of her. Later, we went to a birthday party in his house in Buenos Aires, Clive and Marta and Wendy and I penetrating with some difficulty the encircling fences, with their gates and bells and safety devices. It was a lovely party full of seductive young girls and good-looking young men, the furniture made in Argentina, the books including all the

Argentine authors, the pictures, showing Roberto's keen, aesthetic eye, by Argentine painters. Maruja, Roberto's elderly but vivacious aunt, had cooked a Galician fish stew with octopus and squid and *mejillónes* – mussels – and spices, which reminded me of the north-west of Spain, where she comes from. We had a nice time singing Galician songs.

I went to see Andrea by myself, leaving Wendy on board *Iskra* with washing and domestic chores. I took the train to Buenos Aires, left my bicycle at the station. It was a long way to Banfield, I had to cross Buenos Aires from Retiro station to Constitution station and catch another suburban train. The local trains were as I remembered them as a child; I had been out on the Constitution line because my cousin, the one I fought with at the Scots' School, lived in Quilmes. As my only memory of him is one of unbridled hostility it has never occurred to me to try and make his acquaintance again; I'm sure he is a worthy and likeable fellow. Guillermo had given me Andrea's address as Andrea Baldovino, No. 1798 Almafuerte, Banfield. Almafuerte means 'strong soul'.

I was directed from the station down a street of neat, small houses, Almafuerte crossing it at right angles. The even numbers were on my left, ascending as I walked along until I came to an open door; No. 1798 Almafuerte, marked by a metal plate. There was no bell or knocker. A small child was playing on the floor inside the door. 'Andrea esta en casa?' 'Is Andrea at home?' The child looked at me with the same solemn eyes, just as Guillermo's grandson had looked at me. Then he called out - 'Abuela - abuela!' An overwhelming emotion bubbled up inside me, I felt the blood tingling round me, my hand shaking, my face flushing. She came to the door and opened it wide - stood looking at me. I knew her as if I had seen her the day before, the roman nose, the wide-set eyes, the smile, the clear forehead, the beautiful dark hair all white now but still beautiful. We stood in silence, looking at each other. I watched as her face changed, puzzled at first, then a narrowing of the eyes as she strove to slot my features into the file of memory, then incredulity, then the tears. 'Andrea - Andrea'.

I knew her as if I had seen her the day before

'El niño Ponky,' she said 'Dios Mio - el niño Ponky,' and she collapsed into a chair, rivers running down her cheeks.

We talked all afternoon, my whole experience tumbling out of me, hopes, fears, loves, disasters, fulfilments, failures, all in a torrent, the amalgam of a lifetime. Andrea had conducted her life with faultless decorum, as I would have expected. Her husband had died twelve years ago, leaving her a tiny pension, decimated by inflation, and the house. Her son and her daughter-in-law lived with her. They were poor, I dragged out of her, just as all the people who lived around her were poor, struggling to make ends meet, struggling to bring up children, struggling to live some kind of a decent life against the ruthless erosion of inflation. She showed me where the roof needed mending, where the bedroom ceiling and the wall in the child's room were stained and peeling with damp. A few days later I went again with Wendy and we met her daughter-in-law, a well-informed, perceptive girl who told us that she was caught in a poverty trap from which there was no escape. Her husband worked in a government office and his periodic increases in salary never quite matched inflation, so that they became progressively poorer.

Andrea had left El Choiqué to get married before Freda died. When Freda was in Buenos Aires in hospital and after she died, Andrea had been a mother to Clive and Julian just as she had been to me. She had visited Freda daily in the British Hospital, had formed a tight bond of affection with her. After Freda's death Andrea had been forgotten, no one in the family had thought to discover how she was, where she was, anything about her. She had been discarded, but she bore no trace of resentment. I took Clive and Julian to see her, I gave Clive a sum of money for her which he and Julian promised to match so that the roof could be repaired at least. We went to see her again before we left Buenos Aires for a heart-wrenching goodbye. Later Wendy wrote in her log, 'I realise that Frank learned about love from Andrea.'

Iskra was beginning to look run down, her gear was getting worn, she needed refitting. We never quite got over the feeling that we were not welcome in the marina because of Culasso, but as the weeks turned into months the place became more friendly. Juanita and Rolly came to tea with us on their bicycles and we called in on them every time we went shopping in San Isidro. We got on with the work slowly, painting the decks and topsides, sandpapering and varnishing, overhauling the gear. We were frequently interrupted by people who asked us to their houses or took us off to the theatre or to a concert. We went to a performance of the Mozart *Coronation Mass* in San Isidro Cathedral and to the camp for a day's riding. We were asked to a chain of dinner-parties. *Iskra*'s refit progressed in spurts of activity, she wouldn't be smart but she would be in a proper state when we left.

Juanita is librarian at the same Scots' School that had a hand in my education. It was a very different Scots' School from the one I had known, moved far up market now from the run-down part of the city round Constitution where it had been. The new premises and grounds were between Barlovento and Juanita's house so that we passed it every day on our bicycles. Tea-parties on board *Iskra* became a feature, droves of people we had met, or who had heard of *Iskra* and were curious to see her, or my relations, near and distant, came to see us. They climbed along the bowsprit to get on board or came in the launch if they were lucky enough to find it. We formed close friendships with my cousin Stephen and his wife Mary, with Juanita's brother Peter, with Jorge whom we had met in Punta del Este and his girlfriend Marta. With her perfect English she translated articles I wrote for a local magazine. Clive and his Marta brought the children to Barlovento and they played in *Iskra*'s rubber dinghy and crawled about the new paint leaving their indelible fingermarks.

Hundreds of people passed through *Iskra*'s magnetic circle of attraction. One day as we were painting, a man called at us from across the marina, from the far side of the fence separating Barlovento from the marina next door, 'We would like you to come and have dinner with us,' he shouted. Guillermo, or Muni as he is known, with Suzannah were about to embark on a voyage, possibly to England; they wanted advice. Muni is a naturopathic doctor in Buenos Aires. The club in the next marina was informal, friendly; if we go back to Buenos Aires again that is where we will berth. We got to know them all, including Don Alberto. He told us he had always dreamed of making a voyage in his little boat, charged our batteries, gave us bits for the engine, thought *Iskra* was the finest boat he had ever seen. Muni and Suzannah drove us all round the foreshore of Buenos Aires, introducing us to all manner of intrepid sailors. The place is full of them, some with great sailing experience.

I was persuaded to give a talk in Spanish at the club, a frightening prospect. Hearing about it on the grapevine, first Juanita and then Marta, who teaches at a different school, conscripted me to give talks. Wendy and I did it together, the children came on board at Barlovento and we showed them over *Iskra* in turns, Wendy talking to them on the quay, in English, which they understood perfectly, and me showing them the mysteries of *Iskra*. A few days later we did the whole thing again for Marta. The children gave us a book they prepared entitled '*Iskra*'s visit to Argentina' with their drawings and wry comments - a treasured document.

We went on another bus excursion, this time to the north to the Iguazu Falls and on to Salta and Jujui in the very north of Argentina on the Paraguayan border. I have never seen Niagara Falls, some say they are the finest, others that they are tame beside the 2-mile escarpment the River Iguazú plunges over before it joins the River Paraná in the north of Argentina. The flow of water has increased in recent years, the wholesale destruction of rain forests in the far north of the continent allowing new torrents to sweep south. The Iguazú falls are higher and twice as wide as Niagara; Eleanor Roosevelt thought they made Niagara look like 'a kitchen faucet'. They are magnificent.

Wendy wrote in her log: 'The falls are unforgettable. We wandered around them, underneath them, on top of them. We explored them on foot, by rowing boat and motor-boat. Butterflies flitted everywhere, some as big as dinner plates - orange, red, bright blue, black and white, striped, spotted. They even settled on us but never for long enough to photograph them. Thousands of swifts swooped in and out of the falling curtains, always the roar and mist of rushing water enveloped us. The river was calm, even placid as it approached the precipice, then it became a torrent, spitting fury as it thundered down. Fleeting rainbows appeared and disappeared and then came back." I remember the 'Boca del Diablo' - the Devil's mouth. We went in an outboard dinghy to within feet of its base, looking up at a 200 foot cliff of falling water. It was overpowering so that our senses were crushed to humility, some 450,000 cubic feet of water per second sliding over the edge, the mist of spray suspended over it to a height of 50 feet. Half a mile down stream the river is as placid as it is above the falls.

The falls were 'discovered', as Europeans describe things they have not seen before, in 1541 by Alva Nuñez on an incredible cross-country journey from Santa Catarina in Brazil to Asunción in Paraguay. He called them the Santa Maria falls, with a certain lack of originality, but the name didn't take and the old Guarnaí Indian word *i* for water and *guazu* for great, prevailed. The Guarnaí Indian civilisation was eventually crushed by the Spanish invaders of the fifteenth and sixteenth century, but not before a most extraordinary phase of enlightened administration by Jesuit priests. They founded missions over a tract of country the size of modern France, including the Iguazú falls, with a population of 150,000 in thirty mission towns.

The experiment was inspired by Sir Thomas More's *Utopia*, first published in Latin in 1516, whose influence spread quickly over Europe. There have been a collection of Utopias, Sir Thomas More's predated by Plato's *Republic* and post-dated by the Communist manifesto. At the beginning of the seventeenth century a group of visionary Jesuit priests set out to establish a new, pure society, far away from Europe with its unending strife and its subjugation of the human spirit. They came to South America to create a higher civilisation. The first mission was set up among the Guaraní Indians in 1609 and their idea spread quickly. The people lived in communal villages, farmed together and shared what they had. There was a high level of what we would describe now as democracy, the villages were self-governing with their own mayors, their own councils. They administered their own justice, meted out their own punishments. The Indians joined the Jesuit fathers, taking on board Christianity which they laced with their own gods and beliefs. The missions were successful because they offered a fuller and better life and a lead into the more sophisticated European agriculture. The Guaraní stayed in the missions because they were offered protection against wealth-seeking Spanish *encomendoros*, landholders by courtesy of the Spanish crown, and because the missions offered a higher standard of life than they had ever aspired to.

The Indians created works of the graphic arts and works of literature. The remains of San Ignacio Mini, where Wendy and I went on the bus from Iguazú, date from 1632. The ruins are extensive and on a noble scale, the outline of the ancient town still to be seen as are the remains of the church of San Ignacio, with decorated stonework gates, exquisite statuary and the splendid Trinidad pulpit. There was a feeling of space and infinite peace about these ruins, all order and a grace quite alien to the modern world. Once San Ignacio was a humming, thriving place full of activity and emotion, the centre of a whole civilisation that came and went in 150 years. The missions upset the get-rich-quick *encomenderos* who wanted slaves or at least cheap labour. The Guaraní, in fact, never made good slaves; they refused to work in slavery, preferring simply to die and no brutality the Spanish brought to bear would make them change. Groups of armed Spanish settlers began to attack the missions. In return the Jesuits armed the Guaraní and organised them into a defence force. The settlers responded politically, persuading Charles III of Spain to expel all Jesuits from the continent, which he did in 1767. The missions collapsed within five years of the Jesuits' removal, the settlers systematically destroying the mission buildings. San Ignacio, once the focus of a settlement of 4,356 citizens, was so vast that the task of destruction had to be left to the jungle which enveloped it, until its rediscovery at the turn of the century. It is now an Argentine national park.

Our bus ride lasted for two nights and two days, first to Iguazu and then to the province of Salta where we stayed with Marta's friend Sheila, who had heard of us and asked Marta to make sure we came to stay with her and her husband Andrew. They had a sailing boat on the lake; they had read about our voyage in the American magazine *Cruising World.* The bus took us for hundreds of miles through the sprawling, lush delta of the Paraná, across the river and up beside the Uruguay River on Argentina's eastern border. The country became more and more desolate, the people who got on and off the bus more and more Indian. We went through a plain of scrub and marsh-land with few signs of habitation, sleeping fitfully as the bus made its way over a pitted and potholed road, the radio blaring out a mixture of pop music and a boxing match. At one tiny halt we stretched our cramped legs and were surprised to find an excellent vegetarian meal. As it got light we moved into the province of Misiónes, named after the missions, an area of tea and *mate* plantations.

The bus passed through rain forest so dense that it looked impenetrable, covered with creeper as if someone had poured a green sauce over the whole landscape. On another day's trip back from Iguazú, we passed through Posadas and then for a hundred miles beside the Parana again, to Corrientes. The next bus took us across a 3-mile bridge over the great river, so wide it was hard to distinguish the low, forested bank on the other side, the rich brown water well on its 2,500-mile journey to the sea. Resistencia is a town on the west side of the river again. We treated ourselves to a meal in a good restaurant and were given a fish from the river, a freshwater fish tasting like a mixture of plaice and fresh tuna, in steaks some six inches across, washed down with a bottle of the local white wine. Yet another bus took us across the Gran Chaco, 250 miles dead straight. Travelling by bus we usually had a few hours to pass in a new town between connections, giving us time to see places and allowing us to buy our picnic for the next part of the journey. It was, to us, preferable to an aeroplane and gave us nights of free accommodation. I confess I don't like aeroplanes, they frighten me.

The bus stopped at small places in the Gran Chaco where Indians in flowing ponchos, often delicately embroidered and round black hats like bowler hats, came and went about their business. Most of them were speaking the Guaraní language, I thought, or possibly a bastardised Spanish which I couldn't understand, but we did manage a conversation with one of them in understandable Spanish. He had lived in the Chaco all his life, earned his living extracting tannin from quebracho wood, *lignum vitae*, the hardest wood known. Juan Perón came from the Chaco, he said with pride. He had never been to Buenos Aires, had never seen the sea. He was wrong about Perón, who was born in Lobos, a small town near Buenos Aires.

The Chaco was like a sandy ocean, flat with occasional clumps of thorny scrub, sometimes a lone gaucho on some unimaginable errand, sometimes little enclaves of cultivated land. It is fertile, water is close underground, there is abundant rainfall which regularly causes flooding. The government will give you a parcel of land if you are prepared to work it. An infusion of capital and a sustained agricultural effort would bring a good return in the Gran Chaco.

We were tired when we arrived in Salta early in the morning, the poorest city we had seen in Argentina. There were Indians and peasants sleeping in the bus station, on window-sills, concrete benches, the ground, with no bedding. We found a taxi and gave the driver the address we had; he put us off at a pleasant house in a pleasant suburban street and disappeared. At first we thought no one was home, but after some discreet knocking a small boy called Carl opened the door. Andrew appeared in a few minutes and then Sheila with Frans, a larger boy. We had disturbed their Sunday morning.

... a lone gaucho on some unimaginable errand...

Andrew had been a planter in Rhodesia (now Zimbabwe). He had suffered a leg injury in a motor accident, leaving him with a wooden stump which he manipulated with such dexterity that no one would guess it. One night during the rebellion, he was alone in the house; Sheila and the children had gone to Salisbury (now Harare) the day before. Suddenly bullets rained through the window, peppering the walls of the bedroom, thudding into the pillow where Sheila's head would have been, splintering Andrew's wooden leg. He rolled over on to the floor, lay quiet until the terrorists went away. The family decided to leave Rhodesia. They wanted to go to England (Sheila is English) but were refused entry because of Andrew's leg. This effectively barred them from every European country, none would accept Andrew's stump. Argentina offered them a home; farmers were wanted, they were offered land in the Gran Chaco. They left Rhodesia with their furniture, including the bullet-scarred bed and came to Argentina on an assisted passage. They were allowed to take no money out of Rhodesia. Because they had a bed, they were denied refugee status and could get no help from any refugee organisation. In the end, Andrew got work with the British American Tobacco Company in Salta. Sheila went to work as a teacher and started writing articles about Argentina for an American chain of trade magazines. The children went to local schools from where they both won scholarships to schools in Buenos Aires.

After a chilly start at 7 o'clock on a Sunday morning we got to know our new friends quickly. Sheila is a bundle of energy, physical and intellectual, she loves this remote part of Argentina and has immersed herself in its life. She soon had Wendy and me giving a television interview about our voyage, writing a piece in the local newspaper about the Falklands War and talking to her students in the university. Everyone we spoke to in Argentina, including Anglo-Argentines, all believe that the Malvinas should be a part of Argentina. On the other hand they feel nothing but revulsion for the Generals and their odious regime. Most people believe the islands should be negotiated over to Argentina through the United Nations. They were amazed to hear that there are those in England who agree.

Straight after breakfast and a bath we set off by car for the town of Cachi high in the Andes. It was raining and misty when we left the city of Salta but the car soon climbed out of the gloom into bright sun shining from a sky of eggshell blue, said to be peculiar to the high Andes. We climbed through lush vegetation into the thin, clear mountain air. The mountains were at first soft and green, sweeping up to 10,000 feet in great swathes. Soon we came to sudden steep escarpments, the rock wrinkled like the face of an old woman. We came to a plain of desert scrub, giant cacti 15 feet high. A finely grained wood comes from the cactus plant, used to make furniture. In Cachi the ceiling of the sixteenth century colonnade round the square is made from cactus wood. There were a few sheep who

We came to a plain of desert scrub,
giant cacti 15 feet high

scuttled away when they heard the car, wild donkeys observed us from a distance – dignified, free creatures, quite unlike their cousins in captivity made obstinate and stubborn by slavery. These donkeys held their heads high, sniffed the faint aroma of humans, kicked their feet in the air and made off across their wilderness.

Cachi has an austere church, also from the sixteenth century, a shaded square with elegant colonnades all around, dusky alleys of adobe brick houses, a river with a thin stream of crystal Andean water, fresh and cold from the snowy peaks. We had our lunch on a cool verandah overlooking the town, splashes of colour from a million red peppers spread out to dry on roofs, in yards and any flat space. The heady Andean wine assisted our siesta, a dreamy mountain pipe played from somewhere across the sun-baked square. We drove back to Salta a different way, through a yet more lonely road. We saw Arctic foxes, vultures devouring a dead sheep, the shy guanaco slipping away across the mountains. Salta was on the southern borders of the Inca empire; their terraced hillsides can still be seen.

Salta was important to the Spanish colonists because it was on the main export and import route to Spain. By Spanish decree all goods to and from South America had to pass through Lima and Panama. The River Plate was specifically excluded as an exporting port so that gold and silver, the Spaniards' perennial preoccupation, could travel to Spain only in protected convoys from the Caribbean. There was much sense in this decree because the journey by sailing ship from the River Plate to Spain is a hard one, as we discovered on our way home. The Spanish galleons would have found it dangerous and slow, if not impossible. Salta grew rich because the mules and donkeys needed to transport goods to the north through the length of the continent were bred on the plains around the city. There were once donkey farms where dealers congregated and where the creatures were bought and sold. Salta's cathedral, its plaza and the fine colonial buildings date from the sixteenth and early seventeenth centuries and are the inheritance of its 250 years as a centre of culture and trade. There are old stone courtyards, tall palms giving shade and adding to the city's dignity.

Salta was the scene of fierce fighting during the liberation of South America from the Spaniards by the Argentine national hero General San Martin. His gaucho army, highly disciplined and trained by him in the arts of guerrilla warfare, formed the nucleus of the force which threw the Spaniards out of Argentina, Chile and Peru, putting an end to Spanish rule on the continent. San Martin came within a whisker of being killed in a guerrilla skirmish near Rosario on the River Paraná in 1813. His horse was shot and fell on him, pinning him to the ground. A Spanish soldier was about to run his lance through him when he in turn was lanced and killed by Sergeant Juan Cabral, who then protected San Martin with his own body. Cabral died exclaiming, 'I die content we have won'. Cabral saved the life of a military genius.

San Martin's victorious expedition against the Spaniards, the organisation of his gaucho army and the civilian population, his twin crossings of the Andes in a movement that brought chaos to the surprised Spanish defence, is recognised as one of the military feats of history. It is comparable with, some say more brilliant than, Napoleon's crossing of the Alps. It is studied in military colleges on both sides of the Atlantic. As a soldier and as a human being San Martin is one of the great men of South America; there is hardly a town in Argentina without its Plaza San Martin with a statue of the liberator. He was born in Yapeyu, a village on Argentina's border with Brazil, son of a wealthy and autocratic Spanish family. He was taken back to Spain when he was seven, grew up to serve in the Spanish army up to the rank of Lieutenant-Colonel, and returned to Argentina to fight for its independence from Spanish rule.

San Martin knew, as did the other great liberator, Simón Bolívar, that if Argentina was to be free of Spain, Chile and Peru would also have to be liberated. Unlike his kind, having gained his great military victories, he retired at the height of his success, declining to be drawn into the politics of victory and peace. He tried to retire gracefully to his favourite Mendoza, but finding it impossible to live apart from political intrigue, he disappeared to France where he lived alone and in poverty for twenty-five years. He died in Boulogne-sur-Mer in 1850. Thirty years on his ashes were brought back to Buenos Aires to a marble tomb in the cathedral.

Before we left Salta we went on another bus ride into Argentina's most northern province, Jujuy, to the Indian village of Pumamarca, a scorched, dry place surrounded by mountains scarred with blazes of bright red and purple strata. The Indians sold us leather belts and llama-wool sweaters at a fraction of their value in a shop in Buenos Aires, let alone London. Wendy felt that we were exploiting their poverty and gave them more than they asked. The trail goes on through

The Indians sold us leather belts

Tilcara where there is an Inca fort high on the mountainside and an ancient shrine by the road, a stone tower with a cracked bell. The Indians chew coca leaves; they mix the leaves with wood ash and soda bicarbonate to help salivation, a habit originally encouraged by the Incas because the drug made the Indians docile and obedient. We bought a supply for Wendy's seasickness in the market in Humahuaca and she tried it on the passage north from Punta del Este to Florinopolis, when we ran before a southerly gale. It worked.

We left Sheila and Andrew with great regret, wondering how we would ever see them again. We took the bus from Salta down beside the Andes through a sculptured gorge of red sandstone, its mountain walls wrought into strange shapes and configurations by the wind; a display of surrealist statuary on an enormous scale. The bus, loaded with silent passengers, seemed like some minute animal crawling across its floor. Occasionally the bus stopped and one or two people, on one occasion two children, got out. They disappeared into a wilderness so remote that we wondered where they could live and what could sustain them. We stopped at a shack by the road, an Indian girl gave us coffee to sustain us until we arrived at Cafáyate. This town was another delight; hardly any cars, a sunny square, a small hotel with a cool, tiled patio, the whole place straight from northern Spain. It cost £3 for both of us to sleep between spotless sheets, with breakfast. We found a vineyard on the outskirts of the town where we bought a case of wine; the vintner told us it would keep well on board *Iskra* until we got home. He was right; we brought it back to England and when Juanita and Rolly visited us a year later we gave them the wine of La Banda for lunch.

The bus for Tucumán went climbing up and up into the snow the next morning, to 10,000 feet, over a dizzy pass and down into the valley of Tafi. In a few miles everything changed from brown and red to lush green. We followed a dancing river through thick forest, here and there a clearing, the mountains high up on either side. It was like yesterday's gorge in its topography, but wet, fertile and forested. The people on the bus, going about their daily business, were indifferent to it. 'It's very beautiful.' I said to the man next to me. He looked surprised. 'Yes,' he said, glancing at the staggering panorama of mountain and forest opening out round a corner, 'I suppose it is.' At last we came down to the bottom, across the little river for the last time and away towards the plain to Tucumán, through miles of green sugar cane that reminded me of Cuba.

My mother was born in Tucumán; my grandfather was an importer of sugar machinery. There is an old photograph of my mother and Juanita's father and half a dozen others of a large family standing round in a Victorian group. Juanita had given us the address of her uncle who still lives in the city and we set out to find him. The city seemed poor and run down, a bit like Salta but without Salta's superb architecture. The economy of Argentina's provincial cities staggers from crisis to crisis as the effect of a corrupt and mismanaged economy spreads out from the centre. Sheila in Salta was paid for her labours as a teacher in local bonds instead of in the country's currency. They could not be spent outside the province. The bonds were printed because the local authority had no money to pay teachers' wages. Even so, Sheila's salary was invariably paid weeks, sometimes months late, in notes of such small denomination that it took bundles of them to make up the amount. Not every shop in Salta would accept them. It was hardly worth Sheila's while to work at all; she continued out of loyalty to her students and out of an optimistic persuasion that if she ploughed on times would get better. There was no question of changing money into dollars and salting them away in foreign banks for Sheila or for anyone working on a salary in the provinces.

The mismanagement is sad to behold. In Salta a very expensive travel lift had been built to take tourists to see the view from the top of a mountain on the outskirts of the city. It cost millions of dollars in hard currency. It just happened that the main contractor was a close relative of the Mayor. Corruption spread like fire at the time of the now discredited and in some cases imprisoned Generals. The aftermath of the

234

Falklands War had been a golden chance to break the power of the military once and for all. For a time it looked as if President Alfonsin might do it but he was defeated by the twin destroyers of good government, apathy and corruption. There is a sizeable minority which, in spite of the havoc they brought, would welcome a return to military dictatorship. In fact the military spent a year lying low after the war, on the defensive. The Generals were tried and some of them put in prison, in part for their disgraceful handling of the war and in part for the crimes committed against the civilian population at the height of their power. Slowly they have rehabilitated themselves, asserting their power once again. Now they have been released from punishment, the army standing in the background ready to act again in defence of their interests. Democracy is a frail flower.

Toto and his wife were not at home when we arrived at their flat in the afternoon. We rang the bell and knocked and waited. Soon one of Toto's granddaughters, aged fifteen, came and let us in, reluctantly at first until we explained that we were from England and that I was Juanita's cousin. I produced a letter of introduction Juanita had given us for just such an eventuality. Soon her elder sister arrived and they entertained us until Toto and his wife came home. The girls were full of information, full of curiosity about England. They both spoke good English, and we gathered their father, Toto's son, was well enough off to be able to cushion himself against the economic decline. But not Toto himself. He had seen his life's savings whittled away so that he had been forced back to work as a town planner long after normal retirement age. He was remarkably young for his age, vitriolic about the mismanagement of affairs, determined to resist another slide into dictatorship.

They gave us English tea; buttered toast, sandwiches, thin slices of cake. We had the feeling that cake was a rare treat in this lovable household. Toto took us in his car to the house he thought my mother was born in on the city's outskirts, a square building with an imposing wrought iron gate, a tiled, oval entrance, a patio within. Whether it was or was not the house, it fitted the picture I had in my mind of my mother's childhood. The house had a sweeping staircase, dark, cool rooms upstairs, one leading to the next, a rambling garden. It is now a French institute, the old lady who ran it showed us round. We caught the night bus, speeding through the hundreds of miles of plain across the marshland of the Rio Saladillo. It is a river that never gets to the sea, dissipating itself in the marshes and the lakes of Mar Chiquita. Soon we were back to the beginning of the pampa and finally back to Buenos Aires and our boat, always the same, always warm and snug, my dolphin, I believe, pleased to see us.

XV

Farewell

It was time for us to go home; more dinner parties in Buenos Aires were only a repeat of other dinner parties, we were satiated by impressions crushing in on our addled minds one on top of the next. We needed to sieve through it all, to discover some sediment of permanent value. We had made new friends and I had renewed old friendships, stirred up old memories. I had the great trees of El Choiqué to keep with me for the rest of my life. The Falls of Iguazú, the staggering spectacle of the Argentine countryside were fixed firmly in my mind. My awareness of the people's humanity, their capacity for refined cruelty, their cowardice and their bravery, which I had absorbed as a child, was reinforced. Wendy had achieved a remarkable victory over fear, had widened her horizons to embrace the culture of the ocean which before, she had only been vicariously aware of. She had become so used to living on board *Iskra*, so inured to life without refrigerators and freezers, mixers and microwaves and the catalogue of gadgets that engulfs life ashore, that now she no longer wants these things. She came out of the voyage with the sure conviction not only that she can do without them but that the quality of her life is enhanced if she does not have them.

There was much in Argentina we had not seen. We had not been to Tierra del Fuego or to the glaciers of Lake Argentina. Perito Moreno is the only growing glacier on earth. It moves five yards a day and dams the lake, causing its level to rise 100 feet until the glacier collapses, punctually in late March every three years, letting loose a mighty flood of free water. We had not been to Mendoza in the shadow of the 22,834 foot Mount Aconcagua with its vineyards and gardens in the irrigated plain which surrounds the city. San Martin lived in and loved Mendoza. He led the southern prong of his double invasion of Chile in 1817, across the Cuyo Pass of the Incas, from Mendoza. The city was destroyed in an earthquake in 1861 and rebuilt by the great architect and planner Mendocinos with no building over three storeys, sycamore trees along the sidewalks, wide streets so that people could run for safety and a park every four blocks.

On our last night in Buenos Aires Juanita and Rolly took us out to dinner. 'Where shall we meet?' Rolly asked, 'Outside the Casa Rosada,' I suggested, 'just across the road in the Plaza Mayo, we'll watch the guard changing.' They looked at each other and then they said, 'All right – 7 o'clock.' We were there a few minutes early. The plaza is a gracious place, statues of military and political worthies, gardens, nicely kept paths and lawns, the Casa Rosada itself, the Government House, all pink and floodlit across the end of the square overlooking the river. We watched the guard about their business with plumes and swords and silver helmets and polished boots. They were as colourful and as well drilled as those outside Buckingham Palace though there were few bystanders. When Rolly and Juanita came to meet us, Rolly said, 'You know a few years ago under the Generals, if you two stood here and we had come here to meet you, we would all have found ourselves in jail – and we would have been lucky ever to get out.'

The terror was a shameful episode in Argentine history, its effects still there, its wrongs still not righted. The army took control of the country, not for the first time, in 1976 when they removed Juan Perón's widow Isabel from the Presidency and installed General Videla. The country had fallen into civil disorder with guerrilla fighters of left and right battling for political advantage, a runaway inflation. Nowhere was safe, rival gangs terrorising the cities and the countryside, political kidnappings a daily occurrence. When the army came to power they imposed another terror more terrible than the one they took power to defeat, fighting terrorism with terror. On the slightest suspicion of political radicalism people were picked up in the street by police, bundled into cars and often never seen again. There were reports of couples being dropped in the river from helicopters. In the seven years the army ruled, until their humiliation in the Malvinas, 10,000, perhaps 15,000, people disappeared, all of them innocent of any proven crime.

No person was safe who expressed a liberal view, in conversation in a bar or a café, even in the privacy of a friend's house. They would be picked up on the street and would disappear, enquiries by wives, relations, friends meeting a blank wall of silence. There were no Members of Parliament to write to, no human rights groups, the Supreme Court had been disbanded, the Attorney-General sacked. Some liberals survived and got away to tell the tale, some escaped the country, many more were never seen again.

There was a theory among the higher echelons of the army and the navy, along Nazi lines, that if small children of intellectual parents could be taken and brought up by 'safe' people, a new super-race of intelligent citizens with the 'right' outlook would be born. Children were kidnapped wholesale, sometimes pregnant mothers. The parents sometimes found their way back to society but the children were farmed out, most to army and police officers to be brought up as their children. Sometimes the children were given to the very people who had tortured and murdered their parents. These children are now grown up, many of them still with their unnatural parents.

It was incredible to us that such things could have happened in a country which we found to be a peaceable, friendly place where we felt safe and at home. Now the grandmothers of '*Los desaparecidos*' the disappeared ones, still demonstrate every Thursday at 5 pm in the Plaza Mayo each wearing a white headscarf with the names of the lost children embroidered round the edge, along with the dates they disappeared. In some cases the kidnappers are known, the real identity of the children proved beyond doubt by DNA testing, but the false parents are protected by money and the corruption of the legal system. Alfonsin, the first elected president after the terror, did his best. The Generals, or some of them, were sent to prison, some children were traced and reunited with their families. As the army began to recover its strength, in large measure thanks to the apathy of the people, Alfonsin's efforts were whittled down. In the face of military threat he backtracked on the undertaking to prosecute all military people accused of human rights violations, bringing in the Final Stop Bill and the law of Due Obedience which effectively put an end to the trials. Under the new presidency of Menem, another Perónista, things have gone back further. The Generals are released, Galtieri saying that given the chance he would act again as he acted over the Malvinas. The corruption of the judiciary is once more a recognised scandal.

Before we left Argentina we moved *Iskra* back to the mooring we had first picked up in the Argentine Yacht Club, in the Puerto Nuevo. A lovely ketch, the *Don Quixote*, was berthed alongside the quay outside the club; we heard that she was bound for the South of France. The ketch had classic lines, slim and fast with a pretty lift to her bow, a look almost of delicacy about her with a graceful counter, low teak deckhouses. She was the creation of a famous Argentine yacht designer, German Frers. We came to know Pedro and his crew Daniel well on our homeward way through Brazil and the Caribbean as far as Horta in the Azores, where our paths diverged. Sergio was with them at the beginning of their voyage. He took the yacht, as Master, from Buenos Aires to Florianopolis in Brazil, where he left to go back to Argentina and finish a steel yacht he was building for himself. He planned to set out on his own voyage when she was finished.

Sergio had been an officer in the Argentine Navy, in the submarine service. He had been through the Malvinas War, had seen terrible things, had scraped through with his life, disillusioned with the concept of war, disillusioned to the point of revulsion with Argentina's generals and admirals who had so nearly cost him his life, disillusioned with the unconcern of the people in the face of military disaster. He had loved the submarine service, had risen in it quickly to become first

240

lieutenant at a young age. I suppose he was in his early 30s when we met him.

Sergio's submarine was based at Puerto Madryn and was sent out on patrol when the British convoys set sail from Ascension Island. It was not difficult to find them. The convoys were spread out in a more or less straight line between Ascension and the Malvinas, a distance of over 3,000 miles, there was no place for them to hide. The ships' margin of fuel was so small, that the convoy could not deviate from the line. Sergio's submarine was subjected to intensive attack by depth charges from the British destroyer escort. The charges detonated all around the boat as she lay on the bottom at extreme depth with all engines stopped. They stood to their stations, motionless and expressionless as the explosions ringed them, frightened, trembling, expecting the frail steel walls between them and certain death to collapse second by second. The dull, terrifying thump of the detonations moved closer.

The submarine was lying on an uneven bottom so that her bow was high, her stern low. The Chief Engineer was Sergio's close friend – they had joined the service on the same day and had been together in ships for nearly five years. After some minutes his friend came to the control centre where Sergio and the Captain were standing. He reported that there was a leak – the submarine would have to be brought level so that the pumps could be started or they would all be dead in minutes. They would have to start the engines. The Captain looked at Sergio, nodded his head, 'Start the engines,' he ordered. The engines were started, the boat rose off the sea-bed and levelled. Sergio's friend came back to the control tower to report.

They stood round the base of the periscope in a tense group, their faces white, lips blue and trembling. There was an overwhelming thunder of devastating force, the boat seemed to shake, stagger. Sergio stood by the housed periscope, his friend beside him. The explosion threw him to one side, the bottom of the periscope shattered into a hundred pieces, his friend caught the flying metal in his face, obliterating it, taking away half his head. The submarine took a lurch but recovered.

The destroyers went on their way, Sergio's boat, with his dead friend, limped back to Puerto Madryn. Sergio got himself out of the navy as soon as the Malvinas War was ended. 'I am finished with it,' he said to me, 'it is a travesty of common sense, a travesty of decency. It is a stupidity, committed by people who do not have the wit to resolve differences without it, who do not themselves stand to be killed or maimed. War counts its friends as human beings, mourns their suffering, counts its enemies as less than human, rejoices in their misery. But we are all human beings, one no more precious in the eyes of God than another.'

Before we left Argentina we went back to El Choiqué, this time to stay with Julian in the house he and Marilyn have built at the southern end of the *estancia.* It is on a rise, giving a view out of his picture-window of the whole camp, the little woods, or *montes,* the grazing herds, the *tambos,* the *pampa* rolling to the horizon. Julian is steeped in the unfolding drama of Argentina, his preoccupation the improvement of his land. We took a last wander up the avenue of trees. To me they are a symbol of sense and compassion in a world hell-bent for

. . . the rolling pampa to the horizon . . .

disaster. Uncle Billy left his mark on the Argentine camp, CB left his in the city of Buenos Aires; Inginiero Mulville's name can still be seen in the entrance to the Shell-Mex building. One wonders which will endure the longest, the trees or the concrete.

Guillermo and Heide gave us a last dinner party. Guillermo was quite clear about his political allegiance. It may be true, he said, that Perón was the man who started Argentina's economic rot and squandered Argentina's riches, a path so ably continued by the Generals and politicians who followed him. But Perón and the charismatic Evita were the only leaders he knew of, in all Argentina's history, who made any real attempt to bridge the economic gulf between rich and poor. Guillermo, and many like him who benefited from the land reform, will never forget Perón.

We went to see Andrea again, who sobbed over us, promised to pray for us and told us that God would protect us. Don Alberto, from the next marina, sailed with us down the River Plate to the Puerto Nuevo. It was a lovely, hazy day, *Iskra* going like a greyhound, eager to be away and on her travels. Don Alberto steered her all the way down river. 'Como navega este barco,' he said in his slow, precise Spanish. 'Como navega – es una maravilla.' How this boat sails! – it's a wonder. Don Alberto is a philosopher, devoted to the simple life, impatient of what he calls 'progress that takes us backwards.'

Marta and Clive made a fuss of us before we left, showering us with kindnesses; Juanita and Rolly gave us a party with almost everyone we had met in Argentina to wish us Godspeed. Stephen and Mary gave Wendy a rare copy of a book about Argentina we had not been able to find. The day of leaving inexorably arrived. The old *sereno* at the yacht club rowed us on board, offered us his hand, "'Come back again,' he said, 'we like you.' Wendy dropped the mooring, *Iskra* moved slowly out of the harbour, her sails filling to a fair wind. We stood in the cockpit looking back at Argentina. Wendy said in her newfound Spanish, 'Paiz tan lindo – jente tan sinpatico.' – What a lovely country, what lovely people.

The journey home to England was much longer than the outward passage. We sailed up the coast of Brazil to the north-east corner of the continent, a distance of 2,580 miles against the current and often against the wind, then another 2,000 miles along to Grenada in the Caribbean. A further 600 miles took us to Tortola in the Virgin Islands and then a hop of 850 miles brought us to the island of Bermuda, where we were welcomed by Wendy's old nursing friend Iris. The voyage from Bermuda to Horta in the Azores clocked us another 1,850 miles and that from Horta to Kinsale in the south of Ireland 1,285. From there to home in Maldon, Essex, was a mere 560 miles, making the total from Buenos Aires to Maldon 9,125 miles. The actual distance sailed, according to the ship's log, was 10,495 miles. If this is added to the outward voyage it makes a total of 17,485 miles.

It took us from 3 August 1987 to 10 August 1989. I never kept a record of how much it cost but I know we spent less than it would have cost us to have lived at home. *Iskra* was probably in better order when we came back than when we left. She broke no ropes, chafed no sails and wore out no gear that could not be replaced from our own resources. Things went wrong with the engine but we were able to repair them ourselves or with the help of friends. The engine ran for 282 hours, we took on board 93 gallons of diesel; consumption was just better than 3 hours per gallon. We usually ran the engine slowly. On the other hand, we lost many nice, and, to us, valuable things when our house was robbed by our tenants, largely through our own fault for taking people at face value. The house, although intact, was in a huge mess when we came home. It took us months to clean it. We made hundreds of friends on the voyage, we have hundreds of memories. Of all the voyages I have ever made this one was the happiest and the most successful.

We sailed out of the great, wide River Plate, its brown waters lightening in colour as we gained the Atlantic Ocean. *Iskra*'s dolphin dipped to the ocean swells once again, his face at last towards home, the Southern Cross on his starboard beam. As we turned to the north the constellation swung over his tail so that he never saw it again. A strong southerly gale took us helter-skelter up the interminable coast of South America, giving us a mighty send-off for home. We sailed through headwinds and fair winds, under blue skies and under racing cloud, through biting cold and burning sun until we reached the corner of the great continent and turned to port with our old friend the south-east trade wind behind us. Slowly the Southern Cross fell away, melting into the insubstantial horizon astern, sinking below the rim of our world. We passed across the mouth of another great river, this one the greatest of all, its muddy blaze against the ocean's blue clearly to be seen a hundred miles out from the shore. The Amazon and the Paraná Rivers wander for thousands of miles through the centre of the continent, gouging out and spewing forth its soft belly into separate oceans. As we gained latitude to the north, over the Equator and into the Caribbean Sea, another old friend came out to greet us as it has done for me so many times over the years. I found it one clear moonless night, brought Wendy out into the cool air to glimpse it low over *Iskra*'s bowsprit. 'Look Wendy — the North Star — there, ahead — faint, faint, faint . . . .' She saw it and her eyes were damp. 'We'll soon be home . . . .' It gained in height and grew brighter and stronger as we sailed north. The North Star — the Pole — friend and guide to all northern navigators since time began. We carried it with us all the way home; a fixed, secure beacon in a moving universe. It was still with us when we picked up our mooring in Bradwell Creek. I believe it is still there.

Iskra is back in her winter quarters in the mud in Maldon. She looks nothing much, shrouded in her winter cover with the gear all stripped off her mast, the dolphin figurehead tucked into the garden shed for the winter, her bowsprit in the store. She's not very big, not very grand, not smart, not much like a pacer of oceans, but somewhere inside her oak frames she keeps a great big heart.

Spanish and other words used in the text

Adobe	Sun dried brick clay used for building
Alpargatas	Rope soled canvas shoes
Asado	Barbecue
Ayuntamiento	Town Hall
Bastos	Part of an Argentine saddle
Bienvenido	Welcome
Bife de lomo	Sirloin steak
Boca	Mouth - the Buenos Aires dockland where the Riachuelo runs into the River Plate
Boleadoras, or *Bolas*	Three lead or stone weights bound with leather, or a lariat with balls on one end, thrown so as to twist round an animal's legs
Boliche	A small shop, usually with a bar, something like a local pub in England
Bombachas	Gaucho trousers, wide and drawn together at the ankles with two buttons
Bombilla	Perforated silver tube for drinking *mate* from a *mate* gourd, the latter being the fruit of the *mate* tree
Café con leche	Coffee with hot milk
Calador	A long, hollowed-out steel spike, with a hollow handle, for taking samples from grain sacks
Camp	An English corruption of the Spanish word *campo*, meaning countryside
Caña	A type of rum, distilled from cane sugar
Capataz	Foreman
Carreta	Big and heavy ox- or horse-drawn cart, usually drawn by six oxen or up to twenty horses
Carretero	The driver or the maker of the *carreta*
Chacra	Small farm or ranch
Che	Term of familiarity, used in Argentina when addressing a friend
Ciudad de cristal	City of Glass – name given to La Coruña (Spain) because of its frontage to the harbour
Dulce de leche	A sweet conserve made with milk and sugar, used as a spread or a topping
Dulce de membrillo	Quince jelly
Encomendero	A person granted an *encomienda*
Encomienda	A parcel of land together with its Indian population, given to Spanish settlers by the Spanish Crown
Esperanza	Hope

Estancia	A big farm
Fag	A new boy in an English boarding school was made to fag, or do menial tasks, for prefects
Facón	Long, double-edged knife, carried by the gaucho in his belt
Favela	Shanty-town slum area in Brazilian cities
Frigorífico	Meat processing and packing plant
Gaucho	The name given to the inhabitants of the pampa who came from Spanish-Indian stock
Gofio	A gruel made with roasted maize meal – considered an aphrodisiac in Galicia and the Canaries
Gracias	Thanks – thank you
Gringo	A derogatory term usually applied to Englishmen or Americans in Hispanoamerica
Hierba	Herb, grass
Hombre	Man – often used as an expletive
Hornero	Oven-bird. It makes a round, mud hut for a nest
Hórreo	Grain store (Galicia) built of stone, and set on stone pillars as protection against rats
Martín Fierro	Mythica gaucho hero whose story was published in verse in 1873. It is considered the *gauchesco* poetry masterpiece
Mejillónes	Mussels
Mate	Plant similar to the holly tree. Its leaves are used to make an infusion. *Mate* is the tree, the drink and the gourd it is drunk out of
Mayordomo	The manager of an *estancia*
Monte	Wood or thicket
Niño	Boy
Nochero	A horse kept tied up for the night and used for round-up in the morning
Novio	Sweetheart, betrothed
Palabra Inglés	'An Englishman's word is his bond' – an expression once in common use in Argentina
Palenque	Wooden stockade or bar used to tie up horses
Pampa	The plain of Argentina – also a province to the south-west of Buenos Aires
Pampero	A strong, cold wind that blows from the south west of Buenos Aires, suddenly and strongly
Pantano	A bog – a flooded road
Parador	Government owned hostel in Spain
Patrón	Boss, owner
Pegotes	Layabouts, spongers

Percebes	Goose barnacles – a delicacy in Galicia
Peronismo	According to the political philosophy of General Juan D. Perón (1895-1974), President of Argentina 1946-55 and 1973-4
Pirogue	Long canoe used in West Africa
Poncho	Cloak with a hole for the head. Used in the army in the war of independence against Spain
Puchara	Stew – meat, vegetables, sweet corn etc.
Pueblito	A small town
Pueblo	A town
'Que tal?'	How are you? – familiar greeting
Rebenque	Leather whip, with handle, used by gauchos
Recado	The gaucho saddle
Ría	An estuary, akin to a Scottish sea loch, found in north-west Spain. The *Rías altas* are to the north of Cape Finisterre and the *Rías bajas* to the south
Segundo	The second in charge of an *estancia*
Sereno	Night watchman
Siesta	An afternoon sleep – through the heat of the day
Suco	The delectable Brazilian fruit juice
Sulky	A light, two-wheeled horse cart without a top
Tabas	Anklebones of a steer
Tambero	The man in charge of a *tambo*
Tambo	Milking shed – the *tambero* usually lives nearby
Tapa	A snack in a bar (Spain)
Tigre	Part of the delta of the Paraná River. The Paraná and the Uruguay Rivers form the River Plate
Tortilla	An omelette. In the camp it is a kind of biscuit made with flour, salt and grease
Tupamaros	Guerrilla fighters in Uruguay
Vaca	Cow – sometimes applied to a fat person

Nautical terms

Bitts	Two stout pieces of timber holding the inner end of the bowsprit and used for making fast warps or rope
Boom	Spar along the bottom of the mains'l
Beaufort scale	Measures wind strength from calm (Force 0) to hurricane (Force 12)
Bowsprit	Stout spar protruding from the bow from which the jib is set
Bulkhead	A partition between two compartments
Bunk board	A wooden board (in *Iskra* it is of canvas) to stop the occupant rolling out of his bunk
Burgee	A small flag at the top of the mast showing wind direction
Cabin sole	The floor or deck in the cabin
Chain plates	Iron straps bolted to the hull to which the shrouds are attached
Counter	Overhanging stern of a yacht
Cutter	A sailing yacht with two heads'ls – often with bowsprit
Dead reckoning	Charting the position of a vessel without astro-navigation
Dodger	A canvas screen as protection against wind and sea
Fo'c'sle	The for'ard part of a yacht or ship
Fo'c'sle head	The deck over the fo'c'sle
Forestay	Stay from the mast to the bow
Gallows	A raised wooden rest to keep the boom off the deck when the mains'l is down
Gaff	Spar holding the head of the mains'l
Gypsy	Shaped wheel to take the anchor chain over the windlass
Halyards	Ropes used to hoist and lower sails
Hand-bearing compass	Small, hand-held compass, used to take bearings of objects on shore
Heads	Ship's lavatory
Heave-to	Take the way off a vessel, by backing the sails or slowing the engines
Irish pennant	Slang for a loose line or an unwhipped rope's end
Jib	The for'ard sail of a cutter – often on a roller
Leeward	The lee'ard side is the downwind side

Lignum vitae	An exceptionally hard, smooth, wood once used as a bush in the stern tubes of steam ships
Mains'l guy	Rope from the end of the boom to the bow to control the sail when running
Make the bells	To strike the bell which times the watches
Mizzen	The mast furthest aft
Lead line	Weighted line for measuring depth of water
Peak halyard	Rope used to raise and lower the gaff
Pin rail	Low rail near the deck or in the shrouds to which halyards etc. are fastened
Pipe cot	A simple bunk made of canvas stretched on a frame which folds up against a bulkhead
Poop	Raised deck at the stern of a ship
Port	The left-hand side of a ship
Pratique	Certificate of health given to a vessel on arrival in a foreign port
Reef cringle	Eye worked into the for'ard and after edges of a sail, used when a reef is taken in
Reef pennant	Short rope passing through the cringle and used for reefing
Reef points	Ends of small rope worked into the sail and used for tying in reefs
Running free	Sailing with the wind behind and the sail fully out
Safety harness	Used to fasten a man into the boat
Scandalise	Method of reducing sail by lowering the peak
Scuttle	Porthole or deadlight in the side of a ship
Sextant	Instrument for taking the altitude of a heavenly body
Sheer	Upwards curve of the deck of a yacht from bow to stern
Sheets	Ropes for pulling sails in and out
Starboard	The right-hand side of a ship
Stays'l	Inner heads'l hauled up on forestay
Strake	A line of planking in a wooden vessel
Swatchway	A narrow passage between sandbanks
Throat halyard	Raises and lowers the mains'l at the bottom of the gaff – the throat of the sail
Topping lift	Raises and lowers the end of the boom
Tops'l	Small sail set at the top of the mast, above the gaff
Tripping line	Small line used to furl the roller jib – used with Wyckham-Martin gear
Twin stays'ls	Stays'ls used for running – boomed out on either side of the yacht with running poles
Vangs	Ropes from the end of the gaff to the deck, on either side of the sail, to control it when hoisting

	and lowering
Windward	The windward side is the upwind side
Wing of the bridge	The extreme ends of the bridge from which a view is commanded of the whole length of the ship
Wyckham-Martin gear	A roller mechanism used for furling a jib, developed in the 1920s

Frank Mulville made his first voyage to Argentina when he was eight years old, in an old tramp steamer, the *Marcella*. It was the beginning of his long love affair with the sea. In 1940, at the height of submarine and surface raider attacks on British shipping, he lied a year on to his age and joined the Merchant Navy as a cadet. For nearly three years the *Celtic Star* ploughed her slow, painful way through the horrors of the war at sea. Convoys were decimated, ships were sunk all around her – at times the sea was thick with the bobbing faces of drowning sailors. Somehow the old ship came through voyage after voyage from England to Argentina, somehow she evaded the fate they all knew must come to her. Then, one moonless night as the ship toiled on her course, Frank saw the phospherescent track of the torpedo that put an end to the *Celtic Star*. He gained his first experience of ocean sailing from a lifeboat in mid Atlantic. It was enough to set him dreaming – one day he would sail to Argentina.

His first childhood voyage to Argentina in the *Marcella* took Frank to El Choiqué, an *estancia* in the *pampas* where he spent two formative years of his young life. His memory of that period is vivid. He describes the gaucho life, the camp before the internal combustion engine changed its character forever. He evokes a way of life that disappeared soon after he left. Nearly fifty years later he and Wendy sailed back to Argentina in their old gaff cutter *Iskra*, already the heroine of many adventures. It was Wendy's first ocean voyage – a fight against bad weather, crippling sea-sickness and her deeply felt fear of the sea. They returned to El Choiqué together, renewing together the links and bonds with the camp that the intervening years had not weakened. The young trees that Frank and his friend Guillermo nurtured as children had become a magnificent avenue, the loves and friendships of youth had withstood the passing years. Frank and Wendy left Argentina to sail home with the beauty of the Argentine landscape fresh in their minds, the warmth and sincerity of the people in their hearts.